Reproducing Refugees

CHALLENGING MIGRATION STUDIES

Series Editors

Alana Lentin and Gavan Titley

This provocative new series challenges the established field of migration studies to think beyond its policy-oriented frameworks and to engage with the complex and myriad forms in which the global migration regime is changing in the twenty-first century. It proposes to draw together studies that engage with the current transformation of the politics of migration, and the meaning of 'migrant', from the below of grassroots, local, transnational and multi-sited coalitions, projects and activisms. Attuned to the contemporary resurgence of migrant-led and migration-related movements, and anti-racist activism, the series builds on work carried out at the critical margins of migration studies to evaluate the 'border industrial complex' and its fall-outs, build a decolonial perspective on global migration flows, and critically reassess the link between (im)migration, citizenship and belonging in the cross-border future.

Editorial Review Board

Marta Araújo, Senior Researcher at the Centre for Social Studies, University of Coimbra, Portugal

Nicholas De Genova, Reader in Urban Geography, King's College London, UK

Ghassan Hage, Future Generation Professor of Anthropology and Social Theory at the University of Melbourne, Australia

Miriam Ticktin, Associate Professor of Anthropology and Co-Director of Zolberg Center on Global Migration, the New School for Social Research, New York, USA

Series Titles

Race in Post-racial Europe, by Stefanie C. Boulila

The Undeported, by Carolina Sanchez Boe

Radical Skin, Moderate Masks, by Yassir Morsi

Contemporary Boat Migration, edited by Elaine Burroughs and Kira Williams

Reproducing Refugees

Photographìa of a Crisis

Anna Carastathis and Myrto Tsilimpounidi

ROWMAN &
LITTLEFIELD
INTERNATIONAL

London • New York

Published by Rowman & Littlefield International Ltd
6 Tinworth Street, London SE11 5AL, United Kingdom
www.rowmaninternational.com

Rowman & Littlefield International Ltd, is an affiliate of Rowman & Littlefield
4501 Forbes Boulevard, Suite 200, Lanham, Maryland 20706, USA
With additional offices in Boulder, New York, Toronto (Canada), and Plymouth (UK)
www.rowman.com

British Library Cataloguing in Publication Data

A catalogue record for this book is available from the British Library

ISBN: HB 978-1-78661-023-2

Library of Congress Cataloging-in-Publication Data Available

ISBN: 978-1-78661-023-2 (cloth : alk. paper)
ISBN: 978-1-5381-4816-7 (pbk : alk. paper)
ISBN: 978-1-78661-024-9 (electronic)

Contents

Arrivals and Departures

Since 2015, the "refugee crisis" has been characterized as the most photographed humanitarian crisis in history.[1] Photographs taken, for instance, in Lesvos, Greece (the scene of arrival) and Bodrum, Turkey, (the scene of—tragically aborted—departure), were instrumental in generating waves of public support for, and populist opposition to, welcoming refugees in Europe. But photographs do not circulate in a vacuum; this book explores the visual economy of the refugee crisis, showing how the reproduction of images is structured by, and secures hierarchies of, gender, sexuality, and "race," essential to the functioning of bordered nation-states. Taking photography not only as the object of research but also innovating the method of *photographia*—the material trace of writing/*graf* with light/*phos*—this book urges us to view images and their reproduction critically. Watching these images, we confront how institutional violence underpins both the spectacularity and the banality of crisis.

Exploiting the polysemy of crisis both as state of exception and as state of emergence,[2] we intervene at the level of visual discourse to enable critical reflection on how framings, constructions, and circulations of representations of "refugees" shape public feelings and public policies in the society in which we live. By tracing how photographic representations of "refugees" are produced and circulate in a visual economy, we not only examine visual representations of state categories (for

---

1. Jerome Phelps, "Why Is So Much Art about the 'Refugee Crisis' So Bad?" Open Democracy, May 11, 2017, www.opendemocracy.net/en/5050/refugee-crisis-art-weiwei/. We take such claims—of the "most" or the "first"—with a grain of salt. We place the term "refugee crisis" in quotation marks here to indicate that this hegemonic discursive construct is problematic from our point of view. The term appears "under erasure" throughout the book, in Stuart Hall's sense. Staff, "A Conversation with Stuart Hall," *The Journal of the International Institute* 7, no. 1 (1999): http://hdl.handle.net/2027/spo.4750978.0007.107.

2. Homi Bhabha, "Foreword to the 1986 Edition: Remembering Fanon: Self, Psyche and the Colonial Condition," in *Black Skins, White Masks*, Frantz Fanon, trans. Charles Lam Markmann (London: Pluto, [1967] 1986), XXIV.

instance, that of the "refugee" versus the "migrant") but we also theorize the categories *as* representations that congeal around habituated ways of seeing, feeling, and thinking—in the constitution of which images are of central importance. To thematize the perceptual-cognitive underpinnings of hegemonic/institutional and resistant/oppositional epistemologies, we aim to show how certain images not only construct but also grip our imaginations. Juxtaposing visual discourses and visual narratives across divides of power, our aim is to reveal their common and divergent epistemic investments.

This is not a book about problems and solutions; rather, the book asks how people become viewed as problems, by examining an economy of representations that renders in aggressively spectacular ways dehumanization, survival, and death. Refusing to naturalize the hegemonic categories that structure this economy (e.g., "asylum seeker," "refugee," "economic migrant," "unaccompanied minor," "unaccompanied woman"), we synthesize our deliberately "policy irrelevant research"[3] based on four years of ethnographic participant observation in Lesvos and Athens (2014–2019), with critical intervention into the field of (forced) migration studies. The analysis in this book begins with a theoretical framing of crisis and reproduction (chapter 1); it then establishes its methodological trajectory through a discussion of *photographia* (chapter 2). Chapters 3 and 4 examine two visual shortcuts into the refugee crisis and its attendant economies: namely, the life jacket and the container. Chapter 5 delves into ethical and political questions surrounding the photographic (self-)representation of refugees; and, finally, chapter 6 examines the constitution of refugees as subjects of solidarity and political representation in what came to be known as the Refugees Welcome movement.

In this book, we have sought not to expose to the ethnographic gaze our own involvement in activism, following methodologies of refusal.[4] We very reluctantly came to write a book about the representations of phenomena thematized, reified, distorted, and occluded by the refugee crisis. As émigrés from neoliberal academic institutions, we had little interest in valorizing our knowledge production in the "emerging economy"[5] of research on refugees in Greece. We might say the decision to write this book stemmed from our own experiences of being queer bodies in solidarity movements we saw as increasingly "straightening out," and falling into traps of raising borders against those constructed as outsiders to ever more naturalized communities modelled on families. As exiles from families ourselves, and—at best— interlopers in communities of struggle constituted along lines of "race" and nation,

---

3. Oliver Bakewell, "Research Beyond the Categories: The Importance of Policy Irrelevant Research into Forced Migration," *Journal of Refugee Studies* 21, no. 4 (2008): 432–53.

4. See Audra Simpson, "On Ethnographic Refusal: Indigeneity, 'Voice' and Colonial Citizenship," *Junctures* 9 (2007): 67–80; Eve Tuck and K. Wayne Yang, "Unbecoming Claims: Pedagogies of Refusal in Qualitative Research," *Qualitative Inquiry* 20, no. 6 (2014): 811–18. We have elsewhere reflected on how we met and began our collaboration at the Crossing Borders conference in Lesvos in July 2016: Anna Carastathis and Myrto Tsilimpounidi, "Experts, Refugees, and Radicals: Borders and Orders in the Hotspot of Crisis," *Theory in Action* 11, no. 4 (2018): 1–21.

5. Depression Era Collective, *The Tourists*, 2015; see chapter 2.

with multiple/divided identifications and confusing trajectories, we were disturbed by how solidarity solidified around uninterrogated exclusions, dominations, and violences that reproduced heteropatriarchy and racism. As immigrants to global North countries—the colonial metropole and its settler states—and as people whose own embodied subjectivities have been forged by the postcolonial reshaping of borders in the Mediterranean, the facile cuts between "locals" and "refugees," "citizens" and "migrants," "international volunteers" and "solidarians," seemed to us untenable. But all this is the subject of another book, one we're never going to write.

The analysis in the pages that follow points to new departures rather than predetermined arrivals. What might it mean to refuse to accept the arrival of people on the shore of Lesvos (and elsewhere) as the predetermined starting point of what has been called Europe's refugee crisis? The response we offer departs from the premise that these arrivals are not harbingers of crisis; rather, they open up terrains for collectively charting pathways out of fixed territories and fatalistic myths that prop up and naturalize the bordered nation-state, the supranational union, and transnational capital that, together, wage an undeclared war on migration. These departures point towards a *photographìa* of a future yet to come, grounded in shared imaginaries and shaping transformative visions.

1

Crisis and Reproduction

As we are writing this book, crisis is celebrating its tenth birthday.[1] The hegemonic narrative of the Decade of Crisis begins in 2008, after the collapse of the Lehman Brothers investment bank, preceded by the subprime mortgage bubble bursting in the United States. The headlines soon informed us that we were going through a period of global financial crisis, the worst to hit since the Great Depression of the 1930s.[2] Governments made massive transfers of public funds to bail out banks and, we were told, to prevent the collapse of the world financial system. In the European Monetary Union (EMU), the after-effects of this crisis were strongly felt, especially in the countries of the European periphery—the over-indebted economies of Portugal, Italy, Greece, and Spain, or PIGS—where it was transformed into a sovereign debt crisis, albeit of high risk of "contagion" to the entire EMU. Bitter pills were quickly prescribed.[3]

Greece, in particular, became the veritable laboratory of austerity politics, as the troika of its institutional lenders—the European Commission, the International Monetary Fund (IMF), and the European Central Bank (ECB)—took charge of the country's financial and political stewardship.[4] The crisis of global capitalism morphed into a bordered crisis of national scale. After three rounds of bailouts (the

1. Jerome Ross, "Ten Years On: The Crisis of Global Capitalism Never Really Ended," *ROAR Magazine*, September 14, 2018, roarmag.org/essays/lehman-brothers-fallout-financial-crisis/; Jeff Spross, "The Greek Crisis Is Dead. Long Live the Greek Crisis," *The Week*, June 25, 2018, theweek.com/articles/780671/greek-crisis-dead-long-live-greek-crisis.

2. Paul Krugman, *The Return of Depression Economics and the Crisis of 2008* (London: Penguin, 2008).

3. Dominique Strauss-Kahn, quoted in Prime Minister Press Office, "Meeting with Dominique Strauss-Kahn, statements," December 7, 2010, www.primeminister.gov.gr/english/2010/12/07/meeting-with-dominique-strauss-kahn-statements/.

4. Costas Douzinas, *Philosophy and Resistance in the Crisis: Greece and the Future of the Eurozone* (Cambridge: Polity, 2013).

largest loan disbursed to a country in history); an aggressive and deadly[5] structural adjustment programme; the election to parliament of a neo-Nazi party; routinized state and parastate violence against racialized migrants, sex workers, intravenous drug users, LGBTQI+ people, and homeless people; the capitulation of the first elected leftist government to TINA[6] logic on the heels of an anti-austerity referendum; and countless constitutional violations, in the summer of 2018 the Greek financial crisis was declared, somehow, over. Things were getting back to normal. The Greek prime minister, Alexis Tsipras, at once celebrated and disputed the declared end of the crisis with a speech recorded on the island of Ithaca, the home of Odysseus, chosen for symbolic reasons:[7] "I am glad that today's picture will travel all over the world. It will mark the end of a modern Odyssey in order to remember that arriving in Ithaca is not the end of the adventure."[8]

As the financial crisis came under institutional management, then still in its infancy, we were introduced to the idea of political crisis.[9] The constructions "sovereign debt," "underdevelopment," and "representative democracy" were cruel oxymorons for people. People were finally reacting against poverty, precarity, austerity, debt colonialism, food scarcity, and democratic deficits—they were asserting their demands for "*aish, hurriya, adala igtimaiyya*": bread/life, freedom, social justice.[10] All states tried to represent these struggles against their order as political crisis for everyone, culminating in some cases in outright civil war. The Arab Spring uprisings that started in 2010 against dictatorships and absolute monarchies in Tunisia, Libya, Yemen, Egypt, Syria, and Bahrain (and beyond in North Africa, the Levant, and the Arabian Peninsula) inspired the *Indignados* in Spain, the *Aganaktismenoi* in Greece, the Occupy movement—which began as Occupy Wall Street in New York in September 2011, and spread all over the world[11]—the Gezi park protests in Istanbul in the spring of 2013, and the uprisings in Ferguson, Missouri, August 2014 which launched the Black Lives Matter movement. In the early years of the second decade of the millennium, a politicized public seemed to be resisting on the streets and in

---

5. David Stuckler and Sanjay Basu, *The Body Economic: Why Austerity Kills* (New York: Penguin, 2013).

6. "There Is No Alternative," the famous dictum of former British Prime Minister Margaret Thatcher.

7. The prime minister was referring to Homer's *Odyssey*, an epic poem that focuses on Odysseus and his journey back home to Ithaca after the Trojan War. It took Odysseus ten years to reach Ithaca, and in his journey he lost all his allies.

8. Efsyn, "Ithaca Is Only the Beginning," August 21, 2018, www.efsyn.gr/arthro/i-ithaki-einai-mono-i-arhi.

9. Paul Belkin, "Crisis in Greece: Political Implications," CRS report IN10303, July 7, 2015, digital. library.unt.edu/ark:/67531/metadc743369/m1/1/high_res_d/IN10303_2015Jul07.pdf; Michal Rozworski, "The Political Crisis in Greece," *Jacobin*, May 7, 2015, www.jacobinmag.com/2015/07/oxi-tsipras-syriza-euro-default-referendum.

10. Slogan of the uprisings in Tahrir Square, Cairo, which spread throughout Arabic-speaking revolts. They were also united around "*Ash-shab yurid isqat an-nizam*"/"the people want to bring down the regime," first uttered in Tunisia, in protests sparked by the self-immolation of Mohamed Bouazizi in Sidi Bouzid on 17 December 2010, which succeeded in bringing about the resignation of President Zine El Abidine Ben Ali twenty-eight days later on 14 January 2011, who, fleeing to Saudi Arabia, ended his twenty-three-year reign.

11. The Occupy Directory lists 1,518 occupations, in over seventy countries, and on every continent (directory.occupy.net).

squares, in movements that were often consciously multivariant and coalitional. "We may be witnessing a global 'revolt of the masses' against the dominant neoliberal economic order," wrote two academic observers of the Arab Spring, hopefully.[12] Yet, despite the profound hope it manifested and generated, among observers and participants alike, this global revolt was not long-lived: violently crushed by police repression everywhere, and in some places with the restoration of tyranny and the outbreak of war. The deeper entrenchment of fascism—in its multiple forms—and its bubbling to the surface in the consciousness of ever more people, whether because the backlash was so violent or because these movements changed how people perceived fascism, gave way to several electoral victories and coups of far-right, neo-Nazi, and theocratic forces. These political developments removed any illusions: we are, globally, living under fascism.

In the midst of all this, and in the intersection, in the summer of 2015 in Europe, a new chapter of crisis began, a time periodized as the refugee crisis. This crisis could be described as the intersection of the other declared crises because human mobility articulates each of them. In fact, each other crisis, declared and undeclared, discursively creates sociolegal categories to manage the mobility of people. If exiles are created through sociopolitical upheavals, so-called economic migrants flee debt colonialism. While the emigration of citizens due to austerity and resulting unemployment from the European periphery to northern Europe is bemoaned as "brain drain," the loss of precarious legal status, sometimes resulting in return migration for noncitizens due to these same causes, creates new criminalized undocumented migrants. Fleeing parastate and socially distributed violence are asylum seekers, while those fleeing recognized wars and granted international protection are refugees. By mentioning these categories, our aim is not to reify them but to show, as Bridget Anderson, Nandita Sharma, and Cynthia Wright argue, that migration always constitutes a crisis for the nation-state.[13] From the perspective of the EU, the crisis was one of "mixed flows," requiring new infrastructures of "migration management" but also foreign policy that recognizes that "civil war, persecution, poverty, and climate change all feed directly and immediately into migration, so the prevention and mitigation of these threats is of primary importance for the migration debate."[14] Stemming the flows at their roots is "in the interest of all," we are told in the relevant policy document, in a section titled "Reducing the Incentives for Irregular Migration."[15] In May 2015, the European

---

12. Anna M. Agathangelou and Nevzat Soguk, "Rocking the Kasbah: Insurrectional Politics, the 'Arab Streets,' and Global Revolution in the 21st Century," *Globalizations* 8, no. 5 (2011): 551–58.

13. Bridget Anderson, Nandita Sharma, and Cynthia Wright, "Editorial: Why No Borders?" *Refuge* 26, no. 2 (2009): 5–18.

14. European Commission, "A European Agenda on Migration," *Brussels*, May 13, 2015, 7, ec.europa .eu/anti-trafficking/sites/antitrafficking/files/communication_on_the_european_agenda_on_migration _en.pdf.

15. "There are many different motivations behind irregular migration. But often, it ends in deep disappointment. The journey is often far more dangerous than expected, often at the mercy of criminal networks who put profit before human life. Those who fail the test of asylum face the prospect of return. Those who live a clandestine life inside Europe have a precarious existence and can easily fall prey to exploitation. It is in the interests of all to address the root causes which cause people to seek a life elsewhere,

Commission introduced its "hotspot approach";[16] since then, hotspots were instituted on five Aegean islands under Greek jurisdiction and in several ports in coastal Italy.[17] By 2018, the hotspots had become island prisons.

Our Decade of Crisis had turned seven years old; we might say that crisis discourse reached its age of reason with this crisis.[18] The refugee crisis was represented as a humanitarian crisis, and, at a biopolitical-necropolitical intersection, was "managed" by nation-states' military, police, and bureaucracy in collaboration with the United Nations High Commission on Refugees (UNHCR), international NGOs, private detention and deportation contractors, EU agencies (European Asylum Support Office, Europol, Eurojust, and the Fundamental Rights Agency, Frontex), and NATO. But it was also, in a broader sense, "managed" by solidarians, activists, and international volunteers, who took on a conflictual and conflicted role of practical solidarity that, despite its good intentions, has sometimes fallen into, or may be structurally susceptible to, common pitfalls of *"efforts to do good"* in a terrain regulated by state power, civilizational discourses of Europe, and their entanglements with white supremacy and heteropatriarchy.[19] Finally, and perhaps most imperceptibly, even if most spectacularly, photographers "managed" the refugee crisis. They managed how we came to view it and how we came to feel about it. Often the same photograph rouses precisely opposite reactions in different viewers: if some of us were moved by a photograph of refugees walking through the Balkans to reach Germany, to march in our own cities in solidarity with their demands for open borders, that same photograph became the centerpiece in the xenophobic campaign for Brexit and in the elections that cemented Viktor Orbán's authoritarian rule in Hungary. Put to different uses, placed in different frames, circulated in a transnational economy, the photograph gains a different power over us, and we gain a different power through it. Even a single word can be a frame: "Stop" or "Welcome."

In Europe it is difficult to think of a political debate or an election campaign since the summer of 2015 that did not involve an exploitation of the refugee crisis. In this book we discuss the Hungarian example (in chapter 7), but the examples are, unfortunately, many. We say "unfortunately" because, by and large, the tendency is

---

to crack down on smugglers and traffickers, and to provide clarity and predictability in return policies." European Commission, 2015, 7.

16. European Commission, "A European Agenda on Migration," *Brussels*, May 13, 2015, 6, ec.europa .eu/anti-trafficking/sites/antitrafficking/files/communication_on_the_european_agenda_on_migration _en.pdf; European Commission, "Explanatory Note on the Hotspot Approach," 2015, www.statewatch .org/news/2015/jul/eu-com-hotsposts.pdf.

17. See European Commission, "Migration and Home Affairs, 'Hotspot Approach,'" 2018, ec.europa .eu/home-affairs/content/hotspot-approach_en.

18. According to the Canon Law of the Catholic Church, at seven years old, a minor is presumed to have the use of reason and, therefore, moral responsibility.

19. Gada Mahrouse, *Conflicted Commitments: Race, Privilege, and Power in Transnational Solidarity Activism* (Montreal: McGill-Queen's University Press, 2014). Although Mahrouse focuses on different forms of activism than were prominent on the shores, cities, and borders of Europe during the refugee crisis, such as human shield, witnessing, election monitoring activism, and so on, that aims to put human rights abuses in the international spotlight, her insights about the structural relationship between racialized privilege of whiteness, citizenship, and representational power are relevant in this context as well.

that the refugee crisis is used as a political mechanism to promote consensus around conservative, xenophobic, and explicitly racist ideologies. In 2017, in Austria, not only did a nationalist-fascist coalition win by a landslide that had not been seen since the 1930s, but all elected political parties also expressed hatred of Muslim populations and advocated the closure of borders at any cost. In 2018, after Italy's elections, a coalition government formed between the populist Five Star Movement and the separatist, nationalist Northern League party, which ran a campaign solely focused on the refugee crisis.[20] In 2017, Marine Le Pen, France's empowered far-right leader of the National Front, who came second in elections, urged nationalist parties to unite against the "liberal establishment" in the upcoming European Parliament elections and to create a common front against the "invasion of immigrants in Europe."[21]

We reject the linear explanation that the refugee crisis brought nationalist and racist coalitions to power in European countries. In fact, we might reverse this linear thinking and consider how the militarization of borders in the management of humanitarian crisis renewed the hard lines between "us" and "them" through which the global fascist agenda is thriving. Indeed, the transnational empowerment of nationalists made possible the proliferation of xenophobic discourses and practices under the technocratic guise of managing the refugee crisis in an increasingly hostile, fortressed Europe.

In the summer and autumn of 2018, an alarming debate about a different category of global crisis was reawakened. It was by no means the first time that scientific opinion entered the mainstream media to announce environmental disaster and that imperative measures needed to be implemented. But this time, the accelerated signs of a climate crisis were explicitly translated into a threat of unprecedented human mobility, as a difference of a half-degree rise in temperature could mean the loss of their current home for 143 million people over the next twenty years.[22] A recent report by the World Bank indicates that we would not have to wait for the climate crisis to unfold sporadically over the next twenty years; the crisis is already here and "will drive human migration more than any other event in human history."[23] It is not incidental that the discourse of climate crisis has been inflected by the global North's racial anxieties about immigration; already in the refugee crisis, these anxieties were expressed in representations of refugees themselves as pollution, natural disaster, disease, vermin, or garbage (as we discuss in chapter 3).[24]

20. Natasha Turak, "The Future of Europe's Elections Will Be All about Immigration, Foreign Minister Says," *CNBC*, June 1, 2018, www.cnbc.com/2018/06/01/the-future-of-europes-elections-will-be-all-about-migration.html.

21. "France's Le Pen Urges Show of Nationalist Force in European Elections," EURACTIV.com with Reuters, September 17, 2018, www.euractiv.com/section/eu-elections-2019/news/frances-le-pen-urges-show-of-nationalist-force-in-european-elections/.

22. Jonathan Watts, "A Crisis in the Natural World," *Guardian Weekly*, March 30, 2018, www.pressreader.com/uk/the-guardian-weekly/20180330/281505046767694.

23. Kanta Kumari Rigaud, et al., eds., *Groundswell: Preparing for Internal Climate Migration* (Washington, DC: World Bank, 2018), openknowledge.worldbank.org/handle/10986/29461.

24. Stelios Katsanevakis, "Illegal Immigration in the Eastern Aegean Sea: A New Source of Marine Litter," *Mediterranean Marine Science* 16, no. 3 (2015): 605–8; Emily Creighton, "Environmental Im-

Of course, the above Decade of Crisis narrative has two major flaws: it does not question the starting point of crisis, nor does it contest the boundaries of the hegemonic categories of crisis—financial, political, refugee, climate. The financial crisis, the political crisis, the refugee crisis, and the climate crisis overlap, and experts in each crisis have drawn on their disciplinary perspective to argue against thinking of them in time-space-limited ways. But disciplinary perspective also limits the multi-dimensionality of phenomena named and segregated as distinct crises. That means it is inept at seeing the whole picture, as light through a prism. Its geography is also very determinate, which is related to the historical delimitation of the era of crisis.

In the visual discourse of crisis, it's not just that certain antecedents are removed from the picture; it's that war is kept outside the frame or is naturalized as the background.[25] Spaces that have suffered war are not in focus, even when refugees who have survived it seem to be in the foreground. The background condition is more like an unquestioned assumption than the landscape behind the subject, something that happens when the subject is ossified as a category, when a human being is objectified.

Crisis of capitalism changes shape—but war is its constant background. We are no longer in a position not to understand what is happening as war. The war on refugees is not a territorially bounded war but one waged against people on the move. That we live together and struggle together should not deceive us; the scarcity of citizenship drives a dividing line between our experiences, our positionalities, but not always down the predictable lines in the dominant frame. For instance, there is an intersectional, coalitional identity[26] between people on the move and people sleeping rough that cuts across and through the state categories of "refugees" and "homeless."[27] But this collective subject of struggle interpellates any of us who are

---

pact of the Refugee Crisis," *Planet Forward*, March 2, 2017, www.planetforward.org/idea/environmental -impact-of-the-refugee-crisis; Constantina Skanavis and Aristea Kounani, "The Environmental Impacts of the Refugees' Settlements at Lesvos Island," Conference Presentation at 13th International Conference on Protection and Restoration of the Environment; Jennifer Wagner-Lawlor, "Refugee Crisis Creates Ghostly Ocean Debris," *Plastic Pollution Coalition*, June 25, 2016, www.plasticpollutioncoalition.org/ pft/2016/6/24/refugee-crisis-creates-ghostly-ocean-debris.

25. The discursive focus in the "refugee crisis" on people who cross international borders, erasing those who are "internally displaced," yet, who are two-thirds of the sixty-five million reported to be displaced by the UNHCR in 2016, within the territorial borders of their "own" nation-state.

26. In the sense developed by Kimberlé Williams Crenshaw, "Mapping the Margins: Intersectionality, Identity Politics, and Violence against Women of Color," *Stanford Law Review* 43, no. 6 (1991): 1241–99; Cathy J. Cohen, "Punks, Bulldaggers, and Welfare Queens: The Radical Potential of Queer Politics?" *GLQ* 3, no. 4 (1997): 437–65; Elizabeth R. Cole, "Coalitions as a Model for Intersectionality: From Practice to Theory," *Sex Roles* 59, no. 5–6 (2008): 443–53; Anna Carastathis, "Identity Categories as Potential Coalitions," *Signs: Journal of Women in Culture and Society* 3, no. 4 (2013): 941–96.

27. In the absence of systematic studies, in 2011, the NGO Klimaka estimated that homelessness in Athens had increased by 25 percent since 2009. Klimaka, "The Configuration of Homelessness in Greece During the Financial Crisis," European Research Conference: Homelessness, Migration and Demographic Change in Europe, Pisa, September 16, 2011. "From 2009 to 2018 homeless people have doubled or even quadrupled," according to Symeon Mavridis and Savvoula Mouratidou, who cite the (divergent) figures forty thousand homeless in all of Greece (according to the political party DiEM25) and twenty-five thousand people in Athens alone (according to Migreurope) in 2018 and 2017, respectively. Symeon Mavridis and Savvoula Mouratidou, "The Phenomenon of Homelessness During the Greek Economic

out of place or displaced by violent state, parastate, and capitalist aggression. Some of us may not be living literal war (yet), but, we hear often, we are living war by other means. Living on the cusp of a bordered war has far-reaching implications even for those privileged and empowered by citizenship. At the same time, violence is socially distributed so that anyone who looks or is deemed to be out of place is constantly reminded of their social estrangement. Estrangement becomes reified and inscribed on their body.[28] For the state, the crisis is one of others not having stayed put in their natural place. The hardening of these homeplaces is achieved by expelling those deemed politically undesirable and demographically unnecessary[29] as much as it is by pushbacks[30] and gunboats driving bullets into rubber dinghies.[31]

Mobility is the constant mode of appearance of crisis, but it is inverted in representations (like a negative). Climate crisis is said to result in conflict and therefore in mass movement, but war is literally the antecedent of ecocide. The racialized categorical divisions that imperil or facilitate our crossing of borders have gained hypervisibility on human bodies; these borders harden not only through the building of fences, walls, and prisons but also by sedimenting and cementing our perceptions. Objects are represented as subjects, and subjects as objects. Soon we acquire the frames to make the crisis habitual, even banal. Our gaze hardens, or averts itself, as our feelings and perceptions are guided toward objectification and categorial perception.

Crisis 2009–2018," *Humanities and Social Science Research* 1, no. 2 (2018): 23–42. A survey conducted in 2013–2014 by Vassilis Arapoglou and Kostas Gounis using the European Typology on Homelessness and Housing Exclusion (ETHOS) in the Attica region (including Athens) found 2,360 people to be "roofless" (sleeping rough), 15,436 to be "houseless" (living in shelter accommodation), 25,700 to have "insecure" housing, and 514,000 to have "inadequate" housing (including temporary or nonstandard structures). Vassilis Arapoglou and Kostas Gounis, "Poverty and Homelessness in Athens: Governance and the Rise of an Emergency Model of Social Crisis Management," *Hellenic Observatory Papers on Greece and Southeast Europe*, GreeSE Paper No. 90, 2015, 25–27, www.lse.ac.uk/europeanInstitute/research/hellenicObservatory/CMS%20pdf/Publications/GreeSE/GreeSE_No90.pdf. Significantly, they point out that in 2012, for the first time, an operational definition of the homeless appeared in a Greek legislative document, so that the homeless could be categorized as a "vulnerable" group and the government could access EU funding earmarked to relieve homelessness. Law 4052 effectively ties homelessness to legal status, defining homeless persons as "persons legally residing in the country" (as cited in Arapoglou and Gounis, 2015, 13). Yet, as the authors report in their more recent work, the numbers of "visible homeless" "have risen steeply since 2015 with the arrival of people looking for protection in Europe," and in 2016 were estimated at 21,500 people in Athens's metropolitan area, of whom 75 percent were estimated to be non-nationals waiting for asylum decisions or relocation. Vassilis Arapoglou and Kostas Gounis, *Contested Landscapes of Poverty and Homelessness in Southern Europe: Reflections from Athens* (London: Palgrave Macmillan, 2017), 65. Those people who are confined to the more than fifty refugee camps are likely not counted in these statistics.

28. Sara Ahmed, *Strange Encounters: Embodied Others In Postcoloniality* (London: Routledge, 2000).

29. The fascist slogan of the neo-Nazi party of Greece, demonstrating outside the jewellery shop where Zak Kostopoulos was killed: "junkies and gays, you're not necessary."

30. "Greece: Farmakonisi Migrant Tragedy—One Year On and Still No Justice for Victims," Amnesty International, January 20, 2015, www.amnesty.org/en/latest/news/2015/01/greece-farmakonisi-migrant-tragedy-one-year-and-still-no-justice-victims/; Agence France-Presse, "Refugee Boat Sinking: Dozens Including Children Drown off Greek Island," *The Guardian*, September 14, 2015, www.theguardian.com/world/2015/sep/14/babies-and-children-among-34-dead-in-aegean-migrant-boat-sinking.

31. Zach Campbell, "Shoot First: Coast Guard Fired at Migrant Boats, European Border Agency Documents Show," *Intercept*, August 22, 2016, theintercept.com/2016/08/22/coast-guard-fired-at-migrant-boats-european-border-agency-documents-show/.

A central argument of this book is that the banalized invocation of crisis is invested with urgency primarily through the visual. That is, the exigent temporality of crisis is reproduced through a visual economy, in which categories of meaning become perceptually habitual without even requiring our cognitive assent. So, we come to perceive the social world through state-devised categories that shape our subjective and collective experiences of time and space, of our own and other people's bodies, of the real and the possible. A central premise of our methodology of *photographìa*, described in the next chapter, is that photography can communicate what is registered in action (including intentional acts that constitute phenomenal life) but is left unsaid, or is unsayable in language. By examining how visual and textual discourses interact, we can trace the ways in which putatively nonracist and ungendered figures such as that of the refugee are animated in political discourses by representations of their racialized and gendered embodiment, revealing how European and global citizenship regimes and capitalist formations are, in fact, deeply structured by "race" and gender.

In a time of multiple declared, overlapping, and, indeed, *intersecting* crises, crisis discourse seems to be about setting conceptual borders to separate out manifestations of violence, precarity, and suffering.[32] To paraphrase Michel de Certeau, what the map cuts up, the crisis cuts across.[33]

We take a critical approach to the proliferation and deployment of crisis discourse in Europe. That is, rather than taking for granted that crisis refers to an objectively knowable, measurable reality with an uncontroversial causality, we approach crisis as a discursive condition that normalizes extreme state and parastate violence, the establishment of a state of exception,[34] but also—perhaps unforeseen by the hegemony of this discourse—the emergence and mobilization of new commons, solidarity movements, and political subjectivities. Thus, crisis does not only function as a "'screen term' that facilitates slipping under the rug . . . situations that are difficult to interpret," as Stathis Gourgouris argues;[35] it also (re)produces subjects whose perceptual, cognitive, and affective lives are formed by the temporalities and spatialities that crisis materializes in the social world. Thinking of crisis not only as a screen dissimulating the political but as a *frame* through which the political is made visible enables us not only to ask about what becomes known and apprehensible as crisis but also what is rendered unknowable and is misapprehended through this frame. In other words,

---

32. Anna Carastathis, Aila Spathopoulou, and Myrto Tsilimpounidi, "Crisis, What Crisis? Immigrants, Refugees, and Invisible Struggles," *Refuge: Canada's Journal on Refugees/revue canadienne sur les réfugiés* 34, no. 1 (2018): 29–38; Anna Carastathis, "Nesting Crises," *Women's Studies International Forum* 68 (2017): 142–48; Myrto Tsilimpounidi, *Sociology of Crisis: Visualizing Urban Austerity* (London: Routledge, 2017).

33. Michel de Certeau, *The Practice of Everyday Life* (Berkeley: University of California Press, 1984).

34. Athena Athanasiou, *Crisis as a "State of Emergency": Critiques and Resistances* (Athens: Savvalas, 2012) (in Greek).

35. Stathis Gourgouris, "Crisis and the Ill Logic of Fortress Europe," in *Can a Person Be Illegal? Refugees, Migrants, and Citizenship in Europe*, ed. Alexander Stagnell, Louise Schou Therkildsen, and Mats Rosengren (Uppsala: Uppsala Rhetorical Studies, 2017), 33, www.engagingvulnerability.se/wp-content/uploads/2017/10/SRU_can_a_person_be_illegal_WEBPRINT_anthology_1002b.pdf.

how are "epistemologies of ignorance"[36] about crisis produced, and how do these generate consent for its technocratic, biopolitical, and necropolitical management?

In this theoretical chapter, we situate our argument vis-à-vis two central concepts: crisis and reproduction. In the first two sections, we stage an encounter between the concept of social reproduction and the refugee crisis. Although, on the one hand, migration—specifically labor migration, including migrant women's paid reproductive labor—has been integrated into analyses of social reproduction, and, on the other, financial crisis has been theorized as a "crisis of social reproduction" or a "crisis of care," the declared refugee crisis has not been addressed in relation to social reproduction. Our aim is not to show that the refugee crisis is a crisis of care—that would seem to presuppose that we ontologize the refugee crisis, which is something we refuse to do. Rather, our aim is to bring crisis and reproduction into conversation, first through the framework of social reproduction theory (SRT). Then we problematize that framework through a queer feminist perspective that deconstructs reproductive heteronormativity, both as a premise of SRT and as a methodological assumption of scholarship and representations concerning the refugee crisis.

CRISIS OF SOCIAL REPRODUCTION

Against views of class struggle that privilege an implicitly masculine worker as the normative subject of exploitation and transformation, Marxist feminists have long argued that the struggle "at point zero" over reproduction is simultaneously an antiracist and feminist struggle against accumulation by dispossession and an anticapitalist one against patriarchy and white supremacy.[37] Moreover, debt colonialism[38] and structural adjustment policies that have globalized the neoliberal, austere form of capitalism have arguably brought about "a qualitative change in the nature of labor: the characteristics historically present in female work—precariousness, flexibility, mobility, fragmentary nature, low status, and low pay—have increasingly come to characterize most of the work in global capitalism."[39] In other words, the "proletarianization" of labor is coterminous with its feminization, a process inextricable from the "permeation" of capitalist social structures by "racialism," or what Cedric Robinson defines as racial capitalism.[40] Systemic violence is needed to reproduce and normalize social relations under capitalism; these relations are regulated by gender

---

36. Charles Mills, *The Racial Contract* (New York: Cornell University Press, 1997), 93, 96–97.

37. Silvia Federici, *Revolution at Point Zero: Housework, Reproduction, and Feminist Struggle* (Oakland: PM Press, 2012); Mariarosa Dalla Costa and Selma James, *The Power of Women and the Subversion of the Community* (Bristol: Falling Wall Press, 1972).

38. See Silvia Federici, "Women, Reproduction and Globalization," in *Économie mondialisée et identités de genre*, ed. Fenneke Reysoo (Geneva: Graduate Institute Publications, 2002), 60, books.openedition.org/iheid/6171.

39. Johanna Oksala, "Affective Labor and Feminist Politics," *Signs: Journal of Women in Culture and Society* 41, no. 2 (2015): 281–303.

40. Cedric Robinson, *Black Marxism: The Making of the Black Radical Tradition* (London: Zone Books, 1983), 2.

normativities and racialized hegemonies that are not exogenous but inherent to an ongoing process of accumulation by dispossession.[41]

One way the relation between these two terms, crisis and reproduction, has been parsed is through an "unhappy marriage"[42] or even "dangerous liaisons"[43] of Marxist, feminist, and (to a lesser degree) race-critical analytic frames. A second approach takes an intersectional perspective that reveals how crisis differentially affects those who are socially burdened with reproductive labor.[44] Yet, empirical claims of the differential impact of economic crisis on "women" risk naturalizing the distribution of reproductive labor and in that way dehistoricizing reproduction, including the social reproduction of gendered and racialized relations of domination. In accounts of the "international division of reproductive labor," the "international transfer of caretaking,"[45] or of "global chains of care,"[46] "race" and gender are sometimes reified as natural properties of the body. Yet, bodies are not only "shaped by the work they do"[47] but are also shaped by the work that others do (for them). Bridget Anderson traces how domestic workers reproduce the embodied status of their female employers: "middle-class, non-laborer, clean [and, we might add, white] in contrast to herself (worker, degraded, dirty)."[48] Analyzing what she terms the "sensorial corporeality of the devaluation of domestic work," Encarnación Gutiérrez-Rodríguez argues that "domestic work . . . reveals the affective dimension of labor by connecting its value production to the circulation of feelings and emotion. Through affects, notions of value, translated into gestures of 'superiority' and 'inferiority' in the households are expressed by women's bodies and impressed on other women's bodies, leaving a corporeal sense of devaluation . . . Paradoxically, while this labor is perceived as nonproductive, it creates value attached to its affective potential, affective value."[49]

Appealing to "race" and gender as self-evident categories of empirical analysis often neglects to historicize how the labor bodies perform results not only in tangible and intangible products but also produces the body itself as a gendered, racialized materiality. This serves to redouble the always already "thereness," the autonomic visibility of the racialized, gendered body. As such, it renders invisible the processes

41. David Harvey, *The New Imperialism* (Oxford: Oxford University Press, 2003), 137–82.

42. Heidi I. Hartmann, "The Unhappy Marriage of Marxism and Feminism: Toward a More Progressive Union," *Capital and Class* 3, no. 2 (1979): 1–33. Lydia Sargent, ed., *Women and Revolution: A Discussion of the Unhappy Marriage of Marxism and Feminism* (Boston: South End Press, 1981).

43. Cinzia Arruzza, *Dangerous Liaisons: The Marriages and Divorces of Marxism and Feminism* (London: Merlin, 2013).

44. Akwugo Emejulu and Leah Bassel, *Minority Women and Austerity: Survival and Resistance in France and Britain* (Bristol: Policy Press, 2017).

45. Rhacel Salazar Parrenas, "Migrant Filipina Domestic Workers and the International Division of Reproductive Labor," *Gender and Society* 14, no. 4 (2000): 560–80.

46. Arlie Hochschild, "Global Care Chains and Emotional Surplus Value," in *On the Edge: Globalization and the New Millennium*, ed. Tony Giddens and Will Hutton (London: SAGE, 2000), 130–46.

47. Sara Ahmed, *Queer Phenomenology: Orientations, Objects, Others* (Durham, NC: Duke University Press, 2006), 59.

48. Bridget Anderson, *Doing the Dirty Work? The Global Politics of Domestic Labor* (New York: Zed Books, 2000), 2.

49. Encarnación Gutiérrez Rodríguez, *Migration, Domestic Work, and Affect: A Decolonial Approach on Value and the Feminization of Labor* (New York: Routledge, 2010), 127.

of long historical duration, enacted relationally in the everyday, that serve to socially, geographically, and phenomenologically differentiate bodies. Processes of gendering and racialization are necessary to capitalism, dividing us into biopolitically and necropolitically managed populations. As Chandra Mohanty writes, "Global assembly lines are as much about the production of people as they are about . . . making profit."[50] Mohanty argues that approaches that take "race" and gender as phenomenological givens, while empirically analyzing the relegation of women of color to paid reproductive labor, "beg . . . the question of whether there is a connection (other than the common history of domination of people of color) between *how* these jobs are defined and *who* is sought after" to fill them[51]—or, we might add, whether care is defined as work and is remunerated at all. Indeed, Mohanty suggests that what makes some forms of work "so fundamentally exploitative as to be invisible as a form of work" are ideologies and systems of gendered and racialized oppression, appropriation, and exploitation.[52]

George Caffentzis argues that social reproduction is a contradictory concept.[53] On the one hand, reproduction—understood as procreation—evokes a natural, biological process; on the other, the qualifier "social" "connotes a set of intentional and voluntary interactions."[54] Yet, "far from being natural, the reproduction of the contradictory, conflictual capitalist relation, is permanently vulnerable to the possibility of crises and catastrophe."[55] The alleged contradictoriness of social reproduction turns on its purported naturalness that its relation to procreation confers. Yet, procreation can only be said to be natural from a point of view that presupposes a heterosexual political economy.[56] The argument in this book is that gendered and racialized affective and visual economies lend assent and legitimacy to the bordered, militarized reality of the international nation-state system—the political form of globalized capitalism—which crisis simultaneously evokes and effaces. Specifically, we address how the domination of heterosexuality shapes our embodiments, affects, and perceptual life; how reproductive heteronormativity inflects the visual, what can be made visible, what is rendered invisible; and our ability to perceive and imagine outside this totalizing form.

---

50. Chandra Talpade Mohanty, "Women Workers and Capitalist Scripts: Ideologies of Domination, Common Interests, and the Politics of Solidarity," in *Feminist Genealogies, Colonial Legacies, Democratic Futures*, ed. C. T. Mohanty and M. J. Alexander (New York: Routledge, 1997), 5. As such, Mohanty challenges us to examine the "racialized sexual politics" of capitalism drawing on and extending Maria Mies's analysis in *Patriarchy and Accumulation on a World Scale: Women in the International Division of Labor*. There, Mies's recurring question as she develops an account of the "social origins" of the international sexual division of labor is "Why women?" See Maria Mies, *Patriarchy and Accumulation on a World Scale: Women in the International Division of Labor* (New York: Zed Books, 1986).

51. Mohanty, "Women Workers and Capitalist Scripts," 11, emphasis in original.

52. Mohanty, "Women Workers and Capitalist Scripts," 21.

53. George Caffentzis, "On the Notion of a Crisis of Social Reproduction: A Theoretical Review," *Commoner*, no. 5 (Autumn 2002): 1–2, www.commoner.org.uk/caffentzis05.pdf.

54. Caffentzis, "On the Notion of a Crisis of Social Reproduction," 4.

55. Caffentzis traces the evolution of notions of capitalist crisis into crises of social reproduction to the early 1990s, in the wake of the famine in Ethiopia (1983–1985), Sudan (late 1980s), and food crises in other parts of Africa and elsewhere in the global South.

56. Monique Wittig, *The Straight Mind and Other Essays* (Boston: Beacon, 1992).

SOCIAL REPRODUCTION THEORY

In the context of financial crisis, neoliberal austerity functions through the devaluation, privatization, and hyperexploitation of reproductive labor, which is both gendered and racialized.[57] Neoliberal austerity, the contraction of the welfare state, and rising unemployment and precarity are not gender- or race-neutral processes. Feminist accounts often focus on the effects of capitalist crisis on (women) workers' ability to reproduce themselves and their families.[58] A decade into the financial crisis, it seems clear just by looking around that austerity, unemployment, and economic migration have especially targeted people already marginalized or precaritized in labor markets: those with undocumented legal statuses, women, young or elderly people, transgender and gender nonconforming people, and those subject to racist exclusion—in other words, those oppressed within or excluded from the institution of the family, or the nation understood as its racialized homologue.

The current era of crisis has regenerated interest in the concept of social reproduction and has led to the re-emergence of a feminist school of social reproduction theory. As Cinzia Arruzza puts it, "During a time of economic and social crisis, we are currently bringing . . . much-needed attention back to the structural relation between gender oppression and capitalism."[59] SRT draws upon a tradition of Marxist feminist scholarship that sought to overcome this dualism by offering a unitary theory of capitalist exploitation and gender oppression—viewing these not as dual systems but as expressions of a unified social formation and, ideally, a singular field of political struggle.[60] SRT is also a Marxist answer to the theoretical and political contestations surrounding intersectionality, a theoretical framework originating in Black feminist thought, which has become the predominant way of theorizing the mutual constitution of systems of oppression that are falsely constructed as mutually exclusive in single-axis analyses and monistic politics.[61]

---

57. Akwugo Emejulu and Leah Bassel, *Minority Women and Austerity: Survival and Resistance in France and Britain* (Bristol: Policy Press, 2017); Angela Dimitrakaki and Kirsten Lloyd, "Social Reproduction Struggles and Art History," *Third Text* 31, no. 1 (2017): 1–14; and Maria Karamesini and Jill Rubery, *Women and Austerity* (Athens: Nisos, 2015) (in Greek).

58. Sara De Jong and Jacquie Gabb, eds., "Focus: Families and Relationships Across Crises," *Discover Society* 44 (2017), discoversociety.org/2017/05/02/focus-families-and-relationships-across-crises/. Vickie Cooper and David White, *The Violence of Austerity* (London: Pluto, 2017).

59. Cinzia Arruzza, "Feminisms of the Left: On Gender, Marxism, Capitalism," April 30, 2014, www.publicseminar.org/2014/04/feminisms-of-the-left-on-gender-marxism-capitalism/.

60. Lise Vogel, *Marxism and the Oppression of Women: Toward a Unitary Theory* (New Brunswick, NJ: Rutgers University Press, 1983).

61. While a full discussion of the relationship of SRT to intersectionality lies beyond this chapter, the objections of SRT might be condensed in the following three propositions: First, SRT rejects the isomorphism of race, class, and gender it imputes to intersectional frameworks. Second, SRT rejects the "equal causal weight" attributed to "categories of difference"; see Lise Vogel, foreword to *Social Reproduction Theory: Remapping Class, Recentring Oppression*, ed. Tithi Bhattacharya (London: Pluto, 2017), xi. Third, SRT rejects the intersectional focus on "social locations" in favor of a focus on "social relations." Sue Ferguson, "Canadian Contributions to Social Reproduction, Feminism, Race, and Embodied Labor," *Race, Gender, Class* 15, no. 1–2 (2008): 42–57; see Sue Ferguson, "Intersectionality and Social Reproduction Feminism: Toward an Integrative Ontology," *Historical Materialism* 24, no. 2 (2016): 38–60. This

Social reproduction theorists dispute whether social reproduction is actually exterior to the market, the limits of which are artificially defined by productive labor and at times even more narrowly by the wage-labor form. One central point of contention in this debate has been whether reproductive labor, too, creates surplus value.[62] The attempt to trace the increasing dependence of the market on social relations exterior to the wage-labor form supposedly definitive of capitalism led scholars to devise a number of concepts to account for the proliferation of unwaged labor in late capitalism: the "unwaged work" sector,[63] the "social factory,"[64] the "shadow economy,"[65] the "general economy,"[66] the "moral economy,"[67] the "informal economy,"[68] and so on.[69] Immanently critical accounts of classical Marxism showed how colonial plunder, slavery,

---

dovetails, to some extent, with the Marxist critique of intersectionality more generally, which charges the latter with lacking a theory of power and flattening or conflating class exploitation (which ought to be given ontological primacy) with oppression (which are seen as more or less "epiphenomenal"). See Johanna Brenner, "Intersections, Locations, and Capitalist Class Relations: Intersectionality from a Marxist Perspective," in *Women and the Politics of Class*, ed. Johanna Brenner (New York: Monthly Review Press, 2000), 293–324; Martha E. Gimenez, "Marxism and Class, Gender, and Race: Rethinking the Trilogy," *Race, Gender, Class* 8, no. 2 (2000): 22–33; Anna Carastathis, *Intersectionality: Origins, Contestations, Horizons* (Lincoln: University of Nebraska Press, 2016), 142–45; David McNally, "Dialectics and Intersectionality: Critical Reconstructions in Social Reproduction Theory," in *Social Reproduction Theory*, ed. Tithi Bhattacharya (London: Pluto, 2017), 94–111; Ashley Bohrer, "Intersectionality and Marxism: A Critical Historiography," *Historical Materialism* 26, no. 2 (2018): 46–74; Hester Eisenstein et al., "Intersectionality: A Symposium," *Science and Society* 82, no. 2 (2018): 248–91.

62. Caffentzis, "On the Notion of a Crisis of Social Reproduction," 3; Amy De'Ath, "Gender and Social Reproduction," in *SAGE Handbook of Frankfurt School Critical Theory*, ed. Beverley Best, Werner Bonefeld, and Chris O'Kane (Thousand Oaks, CA: Sage, 2018), 1534–50.

63. Mariarosa Dalla Costa and Selma James, "The Power of Women and the Subversion of the Community," *Libcom* (1972), libcom.org/library/power-women-subversion-community-della-costa-selma-james.

64. Mario Tronti, "The Social Factory," *Libcom* (1973), libcom.org/library/deleuze-marx-politics/4-social-factory.

65. Ivan Illich, *Shadow Work* (London: Marion Boyars, 1981).

66. Georges Bataille, *The Accursed Share: An Essay on General Economy* (London: Zone Books, 1988).

67. Edward P. Thompson, "The Moral Economy Reviewed," in *Customs in Common*, ed. Edward P. Thompson (London: Merlin, 1991), 259–351.

68. Serge Latouche, *In the Wake of the Affluent Society: An Exploration of Post-development* (London: Zed Books, 1993).

69. Alongside these was a growing theoretical emphasis on so-called primitive accumulation, or "accumulation by dispossession." Classical Marxism lacks a robust account of the relation between capitalism and colonialism, or between capitalism and enslavement; indeed, capitalism is defined by the predominance of "free labor" in contradistinction to slavery, indenture, or unfree labor—that is, as "commodity production at its highest stage of development, when labor-power itself becomes a commodity." Vladimir Ilyich Lenin, *Imperialism, the Highest Stage of Capitalism*, Marxists Internet Archive, [1917] 2005, www.marxists.org/archive/lenin/works/1916/imp-hsc/. This results from Marx's incomplete thinking on the subject, and specifically his "hypothesis" of primitive accumulation, and the underdeveloped concepts of formal and real subsumption. See Karl Marx, *Capital: A Critique of Political Economy Vol. I*, trans. Ben Fowkes (London: Penguin and New Left Review, [1867] 1976), 873–74, 915. As Marx wrote in 1877, "The chapter on primitive accumulation pretends only to trace the path by which, in Western Europe, the capitalist economic system surged from the womb of the feudal system." Marx, *Capital Vol. I*, 873. In 1881, he further stated, "*Capital* will have to be developed, on more concrete levels, not only in the central capitalist countries (England and Western Europe), but also in the peripheral countries (from 19th century Russia, to 20th century Latin America, Africa or Asia)." Quoted in Enrique Dussel, "The Four Drafts of *Capital*: Towards a New Interpretation of the Dialectical Thought of Marx," *Rethinking Marxism* 13, no. 1 (2001): 20. Nevertheless, the Western Marxist tradition, failing to take up the challenge of

but also the heteropatriarchal family, an institution globalized through coloniality in its long duration,[70] did not constitute merely the hypothesis or prehistory of capitalism but were necessary and internal to its historical development.[71] So-called previous modes of production did not, as Marx would have it, diminish in prominence as they were formally subsumed by capitalist social relations. Indeed, as Kamari Clarke and Deborah Thomas have argued, "contemporary processes of globalization and racialization are . . . further exacerbating pre-existing forms of disenfranchisement, thereby generating new forms of dispossession."[72] Yet, to account for the paradox that late capitalism proliferates what were widely understood as non-capitalist or pre-capitalist social relations (e.g., indentured, enslaved, and violently coerced labor), it is insufficient and misleading to proliferate new "social-economic polarities: formal/informal, production/reproduction, market/moral, rational/customary, modern/post-modern."[73] Such binaries fail to tarry with the simultaneity and imbrication of what, at first glance, seem contradictory but are actually interdependent forms of power: what, in a Foucauldian register, are termed biopower and necropower.

In her introduction to a recent collection of essays "mapping social reproduction theory," Tithi Bhattacharya distils SRT to the following "fundamental insight[s]": First, "human labor is at the heart of creating or reproducing society as a whole"— restating Marx's "first premise of all human history" but immanently critiquing his own failure to take its implications to their radical limit.[74] This limitation is overcome by SRT's rejection of classical Marxism's exclusive focus on productive labor, insisting on making visible forms of work "that are analytically hidden by classical economists and politically denied by policy makers" (2). That is, "labor dispensed to produce people," which, together with "labor dispensed to produce commodities," forms "the systemic totality of capitalism" (2). This leads SR theorists to focus not only on exploitation ("normally tethered to class") but also on oppression (primarily understood through the categories of gender and "race"). Moreover, SRT queries whether this distinction and the respective mappings of its terms is analytically legitimate and empirically or historically adequate (3).

---

filling this theoretical gap, consistently viewed colonial relations of production, indentured, coerced, and enslaved labor, as exceptional, external or aberrant, as the prehistory of capitalism.

70. See Oyéronké Oyewùmí, *The Invention of Women: Making an African Sense of Western Gender Discourses* (Minneapolis: University of Minnesota Press, 1997); María Lugones, "Heterosexualism and the Colonial/Modern Gender System," *Hypatia* 22, no. 1 (2007), 186–209.

71. Robinson, *Black Marxism*.

72. Kamari M. Clarke and Deborah A. Thomas, "Introduction: Globalization and the Transformations of Race," *Globalization and Race: Transformations in the Cultural Production of Blackness*, ed. Kamari M. Clarke and Deborah A. Thomas (Durham, NC: Duke University Press, 2008), 32. If Marx relegated these social relations to the prehistory of capitalism, in late capitalism, accumulation by dispossession is now increasingly viewed as an ongoing process and not merely an "originary" premise of capital. In other words, reproduction is no longer seen to begin where dispossession ends. See Marx, *Capital Vol. I*, 873, 915; David Harvey, *The New Imperialism* (Oxford: Oxford University Press, 2003), 143–47.

73. Caffentzis, "On the Notion of a Crisis of Social Reproduction," 3.

74. Tithi Bhattacharya, "Introduction: Mapping Social Reproduction Theory," in *Social Reproduction Theory*, ed. Tithi Bhattacharya (London: Pluto, 2017), 2; see also Isabella Bakker, "Social Reproduction and the Constitution of a Gendered Political Economy," *New Political Economy* 12, no. 4 (2007): 541–56.

On SR theorists' own account, SRT is riding on "a renewed interest in Marx and Marxism" in the wake of the financial crisis declared in 2008 (3–4), possibly also related to an uptick in electoral socialism in the United Kingdom and United States since the unnatural disasters of Brexit and Trump. But the relation of SRT to crisis runs deeper. From this perspective, crises of capitalism are not only shocks in the cyclical process of the reproduction and accumulation of capital; as disciplinary devices, they also constitute threats to social reproduction.[75] They contend that this crisis, and the global wave of austerity that neoliberal capitalism has spawned, appears as a "crisis of care"—that is, "a crisis of the capacities available for birthing and raising children, caring for friends and family members, maintaining households and broader communities, and sustaining connections more generally" (12, citing Nancy Fraser). Yet, as Nancy Fraser has argued, "the crises evidenced in care work . . . have deep systemic roots in the structure of our social order"; hence, the crisis of care is symptomatic of "a generalized crisis of the system's ability to reproduce itself, brought on by the depletion and decimation of social reproductive functions" (12, citing Fraser).

Indeed, Fraser argues that in austere capitalism, the accumulation of capital comes into acute conflict with the processes and activities forming "capitalism's human subjects, sustaining them as embodied natural beings, while also constituting them as social beings, forming their habitus and the cultural ethos in which they move."[76] This contradiction exists throughout all historical forms of capitalism; "it becomes acute, however, when capital's drive to expanded accumulation becomes unmoored from its social bases and turns against them" (24). What we are experiencing as the current financial crisis, according to Fraser, is a moment in which "the logic of economic production overrides that of social reproduction, destabilizing the very social processes on which capital depends—compromising the social capacities, both domestic and public, that are needed to sustain accumulation over the long term. Destroying its own conditions of possibility, capital's accumulation dynamic effectively eats its own tail" (24).

But this analysis assumes capital's limitless drive toward accumulation coincides with processes of enhanced social reproduction—that, under normal conditions, capitalism favors the reproduction of workers, and crisis signals something has gone terribly wrong in capitalism, that may even result in its self-destruction by undermining workers' ability to reproduce themselves. In a sense, this is to buy into the conceit of progressivism that forms capitalism's own self-image, believing that there was a time when capital was not locked in a deadly antagonism to its "social bases." To be fair, SRT theorists are not unanimous on this point. For instance, in her essay "The Reproduction of Labor-Power in the Global Economy," Silvia Federici argues that "the destruction of human life on a large scale has been a structural component of capitalism from its inception, as the necessary counterpart

---

75. See the special issue on "Crises," *Commoner*, no. 5 (Autumn 2012), www.commoner.org.uk/?p=9.

76. Nancy Fraser, "Crisis of Care? On the Social-Reproductive Contradictions of Contemporary Capitalism," in *Social Reproduction Theory*, ed. Tithi Bhattacharya (London: Pluto, 2017), 23.

of the accumulation of labor power, which is inevitably a violent process"; she is clear that "capitalism fosters a permanent reproduction crisis."[77] But if that is the case, SRT's seizing of the present conjuncture would seem opportunistic and not explanatory of the last decade of crisis. In particular, what remains to be explained, and what a focus on the crisis of reproduction likely cannot explain, is how crisis itself is reproduced.

The limitations of SRT reveal themselves in the naturalization of the loci and the activities of social reproduction under capitalism: giving birth to and raising children and caring for family and friends in the household and in the community. On the one hand, then, SRT seeks to politicize reproduction as economic activity, linking class exploitation and survival to gendered and racialized forms of work. On the other hand, though, it seems to stop short of critiquing reproduction itself as an inherently conservative dynamic, even romanticizing it at times as the "human side" of exploitative production—because who could oppose caring for friends, family, and children? Fraser's implicitly procreative "embodied natural beings," who are simultaneously "social beings" participating in culture, bring to mind Caffentzis's "contradictory" coexistence of the natural (procreative) and social (voluntary) in social reproduction. But what also comes to mind is the recognition/redistribution debate of the 1990s in which Fraser was a key exponent of the position that gay and lesbian politics were "merely cultural" struggles over recognition and not material struggles for redistribution.[78] While recent work in SRT, such as the collection edited by Bhattacharya, includes queer perspectives[79] (how could it not, in 2017?), these do not disrupt the heteronormativity of the paradigm. Specifically, they do not displace the equation of "procreation" with other "physical"—opposed to "social"—activities, repeating Marx's litany of "eating, drinking, and procreating."[80] It is not a coincidence that SRT refers to patriarchy and not to heteropatriarchy, to gender and not to sexuality, that the political demand is, variously, women receiving wages for housework or "commoning/collectivizing reproduction"[81] and not abolishing reproduction as such.[82] The materiality of the body, of its sexuality, of the economic

77. Silvia Federici, "The Reproduction of Labor Power in the Global Economy," in *Revolution at Point Zero* (Oakland, CA: PM Press, 2012), 104.

78. Nancy Fraser, *Justice Interruptus: Critical Reflections on the "Postsocialist" Condition* (New York: Routledge, 1997); Judith Butler, "Merely Cultural," *Social Text*, no. 52 (1997): 265.

79. Or, rather, perspective (singular): Alan Sears, "Body Politics: The Social Reproduction of Sexualities," in *Social Reproduction Theory*, ed. Tithi Bhattacharya (London: Pluto, 2017), 171–91.

80. Tithi Bhattacharya, ed., *Social Reproduction Theory: Remapping Class, Recentering Oppression* (London: Pluto, 2017), 11.

81. Silvia Federici, *Caliban and the Witch, Women, the Body and Primitive Accumulation* (New York: Autonomedia, 2004), 147–48.

82. For a critique of heteronormative assumptions in commons literature and an alternative genealogy of commons as a coalitional queer political project, see Nadja Millner-Larsen and Gavin Butt, "Introduction: The Queer Commons," *GLQ: A Journal of Lesbian and Gay Studies* 24, no. 4 (2018): 399–419. For a discussion of Black Women for Wages for Housework (BWfWfH) and Wages Due Lesbians (WDL), two autonomous groups organizing against "heteronormative reproductive imaginaries," see Beth Capper and Arlen Austin, "'Wages for Housework Means Wages *Against* Heterosexuality': On the Archives of Black Women for Wages for Housework and Wages Due Lesbians," *GLQ* 24, no. 4 (2018): 445–66.

(redistributive) field of political struggle, and its naturalized social relations—that is, kinship—is always already heterosexual.[83]

THE ECONOMIC/POLITICAL BORDER

Given the emphasis placed by SRT and other (intersectional) theorists on the empirical relationship between crisis, austerity, and reproduction, it is surprising that the "other" declared crisis—reified through the figure of the refugee—has not been examined through the lens of reproduction. Although migration, and specifically precarious migrant labor—excluded from citizenship and impacted by austerity—is analyzed in SRT,[84] in contrast with the financial crisis, the refugee crisis has not been viewed as a "crisis of social reproduction" or as an opportunity to revisit systemic articulations of capitalism, patriarchy, and the postcolonial inheritances of white supremacy and the international nation-state system. We suggest this lacuna stems primarily from a hegemonic construction of the figure of the refugee and of the phenomena understood as forced displacement as noneconomic. This is evident in the dichotomy between the economic migrant and the asylum seeker fleeing political persecution. This dichotomy is institutionalized in international law: a refugee is defined as "someone who is unable or unwilling to return to their country of origin owing to a well-founded fear of being persecuted for reasons of race, religion, nationality, membership of a particular social group, or political opinion."[85] The refugee is defined not only against the "national," or the citizen, but also vis-à-vis the "alien." The division of people on the move into (economic) migrants and (political) refugees is reflected in the division of labor between the supranational entities charged with regulating human mobility since World War II. On the one hand, the International Labor Organization, a United Nations agency, and the International Organization for Migration (IOM), an intergovernmental organization that since 2016 has become a "related organization" of the United Nations,[86] vying for control over the

---

83. Judith Butler, "Is Kinship Always Already Heterosexual?" *Differences: A Journal of Feminist Cultural Studies* 13, no. 1 (2002): 14–44.

84. Eleonore Kofman and Parvati Raghuram, *Gendered Migrations and Global Social Reproduction* (London: Palgrave Macmillan, 2015); Gwyneth Lonergan, "Migrant Women and Social Reproduction Under Austerity," *Feminist Review*, no. 109 (2015): 124–45; David McNally and Sue Ferguson, "Precarious Migrants: Gender, Race, and the Social Reproduction of a Global Working Class," *Socialist Register* 51 (2015): 1–23; Isabella Bakker and Stephen Gill, eds., *Power, Production, and Social Reproduction: Human In/Security in the Global Political Economy* (London: Palgrave Macmillan, 2003); Helma Lutz, "Care as a Fictitious Commodity: Reflections on the Intersections of Migration, Gender, and Care Regimes," *Migration Studies* 5, no. 3 (2017): 356–68.

85. See Article 1 of the 1951 Geneva Convention, "Convention and Protocol Relating to the Status of Refugees," United Nations High Commission on Refugees, www.unhcr.org/3b66c2aa10.html. Initially the definition applied only to refugees displaced within Europe prior to 1951, but these geographical and historical restrictions were removed in the protocol adopted by the General Assembly of the United Nations in 1967.

86. As Alison Mountz points out, although IOM "presents itself as a UN-like international organization," it is, in fact, "an entrepreneurial company contracted by governments to provide services," such as its Assisted Voluntary Return and Reintegration programme to repatriate asylum seekers, who receive free

field of economic migration. On the other hand is the United Nations High Commission on Refugees, which is the United Nations' refugee agency.

Raia Apostolova traces the economic/political binary as it attaches to and regulates human mobility to the hegemonic ideological construction of the economy as a space of voluntary exchange, unmarked by violence.[87] Production—and, we might add, reproduction—is made to appear as a process of "free" exchange of labor for a wage (or, in the case of reproduction, the free, necessary, and natural expression of biological drives, innermost affects, and innate desires) absent coercion and violence.[88] Thus, while "economic" migrants *choose to* move in order to improve the future prospects of themselves and their families," refugees *have to* move if they are to save their lives or preserve their freedom."[89] It is as forcibly displaced citizens, who "lack the protection of their own country"[90] or who have been made stateless, that refugees are afforded humanitarian protection. What is not contested, even as "failed states" proliferate, is the legitimacy of the nation-state system. In that sense, asylum does not disrupt the isomorphisms between the national, the citizen, the sovereign, and the state. Since by definition "no one chooses to become a refugee," the opposite term, "economic migration," is constructed as an antinomy to the nation-state and its naturalized isomorphisms. Migration is viewed from the hegemonic perspective of stasis (staying put in one's supposedly natural place); so, if refugees are fleeing "failed states," migrants are constructed as "failed citizens."[91] By *choosing* not to stay put, migrants are constructed as self-interested and disloyal to their natural bonds to community, nation, and even family. It is assumed that migrants' "disloyalty" is

---

transportation back to their country of origin or exile and a small amount of money on the condition that they withdraw their asylum application. Alison Mountz, "Where Asylum-Seekers Wait: Feminist Counter-Topographies of Sites Between States," *Gender, Place, and Culture* 18, no. 3 (2011): 381–99, at 396n7. On its website, IOM misleadingly states it is the "UN Migration Agency," whereas it is—and only as of 2016—a "Related Organization of the UN," a classification that is explicitly distinguished from "Specialized Agencies" in the directory of United Nations System Organizations (www.unsystem .org/members/related-organizations). See United Nations General Assembly, "Agreement Concerning the Relationship Between the United Nations and the International Organization for Migration," seventieth session of the General Assembly, July 8, 2016, www.un.org/ga/search/view_doc.asp?symbol=A/70/976; Antoine Pécoud, "What Do We Know About the International Organization for Migration?" *Journal of Ethnic and Migration Studies* 44, no. 10 (2018): 1621–38, DOI: 10.1080/1369183X.2017.1354028, at 1624–25.

87. Raia Apostolova, "The Real Appearance of the Economic/Political Binary: Claiming Asylum in Bulgaria," *Intersections: East European Journal of Society and Politics* 2, no. 4 (2016): 33–50.

88. Apostolova, "Real Appearance," 35.

89. UNHCR website, cited in Apostolova (2016), 36, emphasis added. See UN High Commissioner for Refugees (UNHCR), *"Refugees" and "Migrants": Frequently Asked Questions (FAQs)*, August 31, 2018, www.refworld.org/docid/56e81c0d4.html.

90. UNHCR, 2018.

91. On the perspective of stasis overdetermining constructions of migrancy, see Thomas Nail, *The Figure of the Migrant* (Stanford, CA: Stanford University Press, 2015), 3. Bridget Anderson discusses "failed citizens" in the context of the UK to describe "groups who are imagined as incapable of, or fail to live up to liberal ideals." Bridget Anderson uses this term in a slightly different sense than we mean it here—that is, to mean the construction that migrants have failed to be good citizens by refusing to "stay put" in their "countries of origin" where they are deemed to "belong." See "Introduction: Citizenship and the Community of Value: Exclusion, Failure, Tolerance," in *Us and Them? The Dangerous Politics of Immigration Controls* (Oxford: Oxford University Press, 2013), 4–5, 7.

rewarded by capitalism—although migration also involves downward class mobility, which is usually overlooked in these debates.[92]

In the hegemonic view, the desire to keep the terms of this binary apart defies the necessary acknowledgment that those designated "refugees" and those designated "migrants" may have overlapping experiences, may travel using similar means and routes, and may arrive together, having risked their lives crossing the same borders. They may have shared pain and suffering at the hands of the same torturers, they may have struggled against the same landscapes of cruelty, and their faces may have become emblematic of the same crisis. They may even be brothers.[93] Nevertheless, we are informed by experts, "refugees are not migrants," and "migrants are not refugees."[94]

What divides migrants from refugees, not only sociolegally but also ontologically—that is, in a deep, internal sense—into two distinct kinds, we are told, is the "psychological impetus for the decision" each made to leave "home." As two Oxford professors opine, "migrants are lured by hope; refugees are fleeing fear. Migrants hope for honeypots; refugees need havens."[95] For these academics, Alexander Betts and Paul Collier, "refugees" are "not moving for gain but because they have

---

92. Using data from the New Immigrant Survey Pilot, Ilana Redstone Akresh reports in a 2006 article that 50 percent of immigrants to the United States "experience downgrading" and "among the highest-skilled immigrants from Latin America and the Caribbean, more than three-fourths end up in lower-skilled jobs than what they had abroad." Ilana Redstone Akresh, "Occupational Mobility Among Legal Immigrants to the United States," *International Migration Review* 40, no. 4 (2006): 854–88. Comparing two periods of migration from the former Soviet Union to Israel (1979 and 1990) using data from the Israel Central Bureau of Statistics, Rebeca Raijman and Moshe Semyonov found that despite there being no difference in labor force participation, the latter group, who had migrated en masse, showed higher rates of downward mobility and greater loss of occupational status compared to the former group, four years after arrival. Rebeca Raijman and Moshe Semyonov, "Best of Times, Worst of Times, and Occupational Mobility: The Case of Soviet Immigrants in Israel," *International Migration* 36, no. 3 (1998): 291–312. Downward mobility may be a structural feature of temporary worker programmes that offer a path to permanent residency (albeit a highly difficult one), such as Canada's Live-in Caregiver Program. See Bukola Salami and Sioban Nelson, "The Downward Occupational Mobility of Internationally-Educated Nurses to Domestic Workers," *Nursing Inquiry* 21, no. 2 (2014): 153–61. Shahrzad Mojab has traced the effects of "de-skilling" (nonrecognition of credentials) on immigrant women's downward mobility in Canada, particularly during a period of economic recession and neoliberal restructuring. Shahrzad Mojab, "De-Skilling Immigrant Women," *Canadian Woman Studies/les cahier de la femme* 19, no. 3 (1999): 110–14. For a discussion of the theoretical and methodological issues, see Herbert J. Gans, "Acculturation, Assimilation, and Mobility," *Ethnic and Racial Studies* 30, no. 1 (2006): 152–64; Herbert J. Gans, "First Generation Decline: Downward Mobility Among Refugees and Immigrants," *Ethnic and Racial Studies* 32, no. 9 (2009): 1658–70.

93. The case of Arash Hampay and Amir Hampay is a case in point: the two brothers fled political persecution in Iran and arrived in Lesvos, where one brother (Arash) was granted asylum, while the other (Amir) was refused and detained in Moria, later to be released due to mobilization on his behalf. At the time of writing, Amir, two years later, is still prevented from leaving the island, while Arash says he was forced to leave Lesvos by authorities due to his political activities (www.change.org/p/asylum-for -amir-hampay-now-two-years-waiting-is-a-crime?recruiter=2658267&utm_source=share_petition&utm _medium=facebook_link&utm_campaign=share_petition).

94. Alexander Betts and Paul Collier, *Refuge: Rethinking Refugee Policy in a Changing World* (Oxford: Oxford University Press, 2017), 30. Originally published as *Refuge: Transforming a Broken Refugee System* (London: Penguin, 2017).

95. Betts and Collier, *Refuge*, 30.

no choice."[96] That absolute driving "refugees" distinguishes them from "migrants" whose absolute desperation doesn't qualify. What is that "absolute"?

Betts and Collier could not state it more clearly or deceptively: "People seeking refuge are not fleeing poverty, *they are fleeing danger*" (16, emphasis in original).[97] This danger is defined as "mass violence" (18). If "traditionally" mass violence was waged between states, through "invasions from hostile neighbors," Betts and Collier contend that in our times, interstate violence has receded in prominence. Today, refugees are fleeing "fragility": "a fragile state is a *poor country* marked by weak state capacity and legitimacy" (18, emphasis in original). Identifying forty to sixty "fragile states" around the world, Betts and Collier claim that only three (Syria, Afghanistan, and Somalia) account for 50 percent of all refugees (25). Notwithstanding the circularity of this claim, based on Western states' recognition of asylum claims based on certain national origins and not on others, we read that "fragility is the single most salient cause of displacement around the world today" (18). "Each fragile state is distinctive," they write: "an 'unhappy family' with its own peculiarities" (32). But what they have in common, for these authors, is their potential to devolve into intrastate violence, producing "refugees."

The authors are resolute that forced displacement must be analyzed separately and apart from debates about "the broader, and distracting, right to migrate" (6), which they do not affirm (not even for refugees). Indeed, they warn, "were the international community to be too intellectually lazy to distinguish the quest for refuge from the desire to migrate, a vital need which is manageable [that is, the provision of "havens" to refugees] would get drowned in a tidal wave of would-be migrants" (30). The reference to drowning in tidal waves is as cynical as it is apposite—for drowning, in addition to perishing in deserts,[98] is the leading cause

---

96. Betts and Collier, *Refuge*, 1; hereafter cited in text.

97. In fact, if a refugee who has been living in a "host country" does not leave when it is finally safe to "go back home," the authors claim that "he has transformed himself from a refugee to an economic migrant" (121). Bridget Anderson tells a more plausible story of how one status can transform into another, giving the example of Eritreans in Greece who had been granted refugee status by UNHCR in Greece, which was withdrawn in 1991. "Many yearned to return to the newly independent Eritrea but were unable to go: because they had been confined to extremely low paid, undocumented work, they barely had managed to survive in Greece and did not have money to return to Eritrea, one of the world's poorest countries. So, they had to remain in Greece, thereby running up ever-increasing fines as overstayers, making return to Eritrea even less likely. So, although once 'political refugees,' they are now 'economic migrants,' trapped in Greece because of economic circumstances." Anderson, *Doing the Dirty Work*, 30.

98. In the absence of statistics, UN officials estimate that twice as many people have died in an attempt to cross the Sahara Desert as have died in the Mediterranean crossing from North Africa to Europe. Tom Miles and Stephanie Nebehay, "Migrant Deaths in the Sahara Likely Twice Mediterranean Toll: UN," *Reuters*, October 12, 2017, www.reuters.com/article/us-europe-migrants-sahara/migrant-deaths-in-the-sahara-likely-twice-mediterranean-toll-u-n-idUSKBN1CH21Y. According to IOM statistics, thirteen thousand sub-Saharan African migrants were expelled by Algeria in 2018 alone and were forced to walk, without navigation, through the Sahara to the border with Niger. European Council for Refugees and Exiles, "Algeria: Growing Number of Migrants Expelled into the Sahara Desert to Face Death by Exposure," June 29, 2018, www.ecre.org/algeria-growing-number-of-migrants-expelled-into-the-sahara-desert-to-face-death-by-exposure/. North African states (including Algeria, Libya, Tunisia, and Egypt) refused to sign and ratify the African Union protocol defending the freedom of movement of people and the right of residence attached to the African Continental Free Trade Area Agreement in March 2018. "Libya Rejects

of death of people risking the Mediterranean passage to arrive in Europe.[99] Yet, their deaths are not caused by "would-be migrants"—fellow travellers whose stay will be refused by authorities—but by political will, the weaponization of the sea, the militarization of borders, and the waging of permanent war. Contra Betts and Collier, it is difficult to find a single conflict in our postcolonial world that is not instigated or motivated, armed and supplied, directly fought, or monitored/regulated jointly by multiple state, parastate, and supranational actors. The "refugee-producing" wars the authors cite in Syria, Afghanistan, and Somalia furnish three of the most obvious examples of multilateral—some would say imperialist—war.[100] Yet, abstracting from the transnational economy of war, effacing the globalized military-industrial complex, Betts and Collier attribute "state fragility" to the idiosyncrasies inherent to each bordered nation. The reference to "family"—the most naturalized political institution—to secure this claim is not incidental. Just as "there's no such thing as society," but only "individual men and women" and "families"[101] in neoliberal capitalism, there is no global society, no global economy,

---

AU Free Movement Protocol," *Libya Observer*, March 24, 2018, www.libyaobserver.ly/news/libya-rejects
-au-free-movement-protocol.

99. "It's 34,361 and Rising: How the List Tallies Europe's Migrant Bodycount," *The Guardian*, June 20, 2018, www.theguardian.com/world/2018/jun/20/the-list-europe-migrant-bodycount.

100. In their narrative of what caused the "refugee crisis," Betts and Collier come close to acknowledging this, describing the war in Syria as "an internationalized civil war" (72). Later in the text, they reject "Western" involvement: "A lingering vestige of colonialism is that Western commentators are inclined to explain whatever happens anywhere as being due to Western actions, but Syria was a long-lasting autocracy. It was destabilized by contagion from the Arab Spring, itself an autonomous pro-democracy uprising" (99). They fail to note that the dictators the uprising sought to topple had tacit or explicit support, like Hosni Mubarak, who was a US ally militarily propped up by NATO. See Eitan Y. Alimi and David S. Meyer, "When Repression Fails to Backfire: Movement's Powers, State Power, and Conditions Conducive to International Intervention," in *Popular Contention, Regime, and Transition: Arab Revolts in Comparative Global Perspective*, ed. Eitan Y. Alimi, Avraham Sela, and Mario Sznajder (Oxford: Oxford University Press, 2016), 170. Moreover, renewed diplomatic relations in 2008 between then French president Nicolas Sarkozy and Syrian president Bashar al-Assad paved the way for foreign investment in Syria, including oil and gas (Total) and the Lafarge cement factory in Jalabiya, which, at $680 million, accounted for a tenth of the Syrian state's budget. Aron Lund, "The Factory: A Glimpse into Syria's War Economy," *The Century Foundation*, February 28, 2018, tcf.org/content/report/factory-glimpse-syrias
-war-economy/?agreed=1#easy-footnote-bottom-26. Lafarge has been indicted for complicity in crimes against humanity and financing terrorists for allegedly making payments of €13 million to ISIS and other militants in order to keep the factory open during the war. Agence France-Presse, "Lafarge Charged with Complicity in Syria Crimes Against Humanity," *The Guardian*, June 28, 2018, www.theguardian.com/world/2018/jun/28/lafarge-charged-with-complicity-in-syria-crimes-against-humanity. In characterizing the Syrian war as a "simply local" war absent direct Western state involvement, commentators such as Betts and Collier sidestep the enduring significance of proxy war in the post–Cold War era of the War on Terror and the significance of the military economic sector. See Andrew Mumford, *Proxy Warfare* (Cambridge: Polity, 2013). On peacekeeping in Somalia as an extension of imperialist power and racial symbolism, see Sherene Razack, *Dark Threats and White Knights: The Somalia Affair, Peacekeeping and the New Imperialism* (Toronto: University of Toronto Press, 2004).

101. As Margaret Thatcher (in)famously stated in an interview in 1987: "They are casting their problems at society. And, you know, there's no such thing as society. There are individual men and women and there are families. And no government can do anything except through people, and people must look after themselves first. It is our duty to look after ourselves and then, also, to look after our neighbors." "Margaret Thatcher: A Life in Quotes," *The Guardian*, April 8, 2013, www.theguardian.com/politics/2013/apr/08/margaret-thatcher-quotes.

but only individuals (citizens) and nation-states in late capitalism's political form, the international nation-state system.

In their gloss of the causality behind human mobility, Betts and Collier refute any "economic" motive (or economic rationality) for seeking refuge at the microlevel of the individual, while essentializing underdevelopment (effacing its roots in debt colonialism and extractive capitalism) at the macrolevel of nation-states. It is poor states that are "fragile" and prone to "mass violence," they emphasize, but refugees are not fleeing poverty, they insist—they are fleeing war. But why the restriction to "mass violence"? What about other categories of asylum seekers, who are targets of other forms of persecution, violence, torture, and state impunity (such as, for instance, SOGIE[102] asylum seekers or political dissidents in authoritarian—and not at all "fragile"—states)?

Throughout their book, the authors subtly undermine other protected grounds for asylum by rejecting the legal notion of persecution in favor of the ostensibly "universal" concept of "*force majeure*"—that is, "the absence of a reasonable choice but to leave" (44).[103] More specifically, they propose, "the threshold for refuge" should be "fear of serious physical harm," which would be tested through a logic of substitutionality.

---

102. SOGIE asylum claims are based on persecution on the basis of sexual orientation and gender identity and expression. See UNHCR, "Guidelines on International Protection No. 9: Claims to Refugee Status Based on Sexual Orientation and/or Gender Identity Within the Context of Article 1A(2) of the 1951 Convention and/or Its 1967 Protocol Relating to the Status of Refugees," United Nations High Commission on Refugees, October 23, 2012, www.unhcr.org/50ae466f9.pdf; see Sharalyn Jordan, "Un/Convention(al) Refugees: Contextualizing the Accounts of Refugees Facing Homophobic or Transphobic Persecution," *Refuge* 26, no. 2 (2009): 165–82; Guillain Koko, Surya Monro, and Kate Smith, "Lesbian, Gay, Bisexual and Transgender Asylum Seekers: Multiple Discriminations," in *Queer in Africa: LGBTQI Identities, Citizenship, and Activism*, ed. Zethu Matebeni, Surya Monro, and Vasu Reddy (London: Routledge, 2018). As Elena Fiddian-Qasmiyeh observes, "the challenges experienced by LGBTI asylum seekers and refugees in their countries of origin, asylum and resettlement," including criminalization of their relationships, gendered violence, "corrective rape of lesbian [and transgender] asylum seekers, forced sterilization, forced marriage, and corrective surgery of intersex individuals" constitute a "relatively new area of academic inquiry and policy implementation." Elena Fiddian-Qasmiyeh, "Gender and Forced Migration," in *The Oxford Handbook of Refugee and Forced Migration Studies*, ed. Elena Fiddian-Qasmiyeh, Gil Loescher, Katy Long, and Nando Sigona (Oxford: Oxford University Press, 2014), 400. Indeed, this acknowledgement is the only discussion of LGBTQI+ refugees or SOGIE asylum seekers in *The Oxford Handbook of Refugee and Forced Migration Studies*.

103. Originating in Roman law (*vis major*), "force majeure" means "superior force." In contracts, it usually refers to an unpredictable, unpreventable event or extraordinary circumstances beyond one's control that releases one of the parties from upholding the terms of the contract. In international law, the concept refers to "an unforeseen or foreseen but inevitable or irresistible event external to the obligor which makes it impossible for him to perform the obligation concerned" and is invoked in a state of emergency or exception. International Law Commission, "'Force majeure' and 'Fortuitous event' as Circumstances Precluding Wrongfulness: Survey of State Practice, International Judicial Decisions and Doctrine," *Yearbook of the International Law Commission* 2, no. 1 (June 27, 1977): 68, 66, legal.un.org/ilc/documentation/english/a_cn4_315.pdf. In some jurisdictions (e.g., Greece) the law foresees that force majeure can be invoked in cases of disaster-induced displacement, distinguished from humanitarian grounds. See Michael D. Cooper, "Migration and Disaster-Induced Displacement: European Policy, Practice, and Perspective," Center for Global Development Working Paper No. 308, October 2012, 61–63, www.cgdev.org/sites/default/files/1426605_file_Cooper_disaster_displacement_FINAL.pdf.

When would a reasonable person not see her- or himself as having a choice but to flee? . . . The value of "fear of serious physical harm" is that it is a universal concept. While "persecution" is a historically and culturally contingent idea, "fear from physical harm" is a universal common denominator. Why would someone not see her- or himself as having a choice but to flee? Because she or he is afraid, as you would be. Fear is not country-specific. Unlike migration, which is usually about an upside, refuge is needed when horrible things have happened to you and your family: members of your family have been attacked by militias, your daughters have been raped, or your village has been destroyed by serious flooding and there is nowhere else to go. (45)

The naturalizing reference to family, in combination with the patriarchal overtones in the second-person mode of address (not "you" but "your daughter" has been raped) secures, once again, the appearance of universality. Yet, determinations of fear of physical harm are no less culturally specific or politically constructed than are notions of persecution, and no more universal. The examples chosen are instructive, because they animate a dominant imagination, and a highly mediated one, of fugitivity, centring the implicitly male head of family as the subject of the substitution (and of protection).[104] What if you are raped not by militias but "correctively" by your own father or other members of your family or community?[105] In a heteropatriarchal imaginary, rape as a weapon of war or an instrument of genocide is constructed as a communal injury and as a disruption of reproductive normativity within racialized boundaries.[106] Yet, rape is also used intracommunally to "correct" nonconformity

---

104. "A classic case, cited by international human rights lawyers in their fight to bring about change in the legal recognition of the experience of refugee women illustrates the issue. A man was tied to a chair and forced at gunpoint to watch his common law wife being raped by soldiers. In determining the case for refugee status, he was deemed to have been tortured. His partner was not." Cited in Eileen Pittaway, "Only Rape: An Examination of the Power of Ideology and Discourse in the Policy Process with a Focus on Policy Pertaining to Refugee Women" (PhD diss., Sydney: University of Technology, 2001), 161.

105. The terms "corrective rape," "curative rape," or "hate rape" originate in black lesbian and feminist activism in South Africa: "This form of violation is perpetrated with the explicit intention of 'curing' the lesbian of her love for other women. . . . Although many heterosexual survivors of rape attest to the stated intentions of their assailants as punitive (they have done something wrong, and thus 'deserve' rape) . . . survivors of 'curative rape' make it clear that their attackers were interested both in humiliating and punishing them for their choice of sexual identity and lifestyle and in 'transforming' them—by coercion—into heterosexual women." Nonhlanhla Mkhize et al., *The Country We Want to Live In: Hate Crimes and Homophobia in the Lives of Black Lesbian South Africans* (Cape Town: Human Sciences Research Council, 2010), 26, open.uct.ac.za/bitstream/handle/11427/7660/The_country_we_want_to_live_in_-_Entire_ebook.pdf?sequence=1. Visual activist Zanele Muholi has politicized corrective rape through her photography, writing, and community organizing. See Zanele Muholi, "Thinking Through Lesbian Rape," *Agenda* 18, no. 61 (2004): 116–25; Kylie Thomas, "Zanele Muholi's Intimate Archive: Photography and Post-apartheid Lesbian Lives," *Safundi: The Journal of South African and American Studies* 11, no. 4 (2010): 421–36; Z'étoile Imma, "Zanele Muholi's Intimate Archive: Photography and Post-apartheid Lesbian Lives," *Journal of Lesbian Studies* 21, no. 2 (2017): 219–41. See also Human Rights Watch, *We'll Show You You're a Woman: Violence and Discrimination Against Black Lesbians and Transgender Men in South Africa* (Johannesburg: Human Rights Watch, 2011), www.hrw.org/sites/default/files/reports/southafrica1211.pdf.

106. As Doris Buss argues, "within nationalist ideology, women are, in effect, the 'symbolic representations' of the body politic, to be protected during war as the very nation itself. Women thus become the embodied boundaries of the nation-state, and as such, are targets for violence directed against a national collectivity." Doris Buss, "Rethinking 'Rape as a Weapon of War,'" *Feminist Legal Studies*, no. 17 (2009):

with heteronormativity and reassert heteropatriarchal power. In this context, the dominant view is that rape of women who are nonconforming in terms of sexuality or gender is not injurious but therapeutic.[107] What this example reveals is that substitutionality, the test of "*force majeure*" as the authors present it, often articulates precisely those relations of power expressed in various forms of gendered violence that women and SOGIE asylum seekers, and their feminist advocates, have struggled to have sociolegally recognized (resulting in some transformation within the asylum system, including an expanded conception of persecution and its gendered grounds).

One might think the answer lies in the numbers: Betts and Collier focus on mass violence because it results in mass displacement. In one sense this is true, but it appears that what motivates this narrow emphasis on a numerical majority of refugees turns out to be not a humanitarian concern but an economic one. To understand this, we need to analyze Betts and Collier's normative proposal for "a new institutional architecture" (9) to "fulfill . . . a duty of rescue" (5) for those who "are not moving for gain but because they have no choice" (1).

Their normative proposal is an economic one, premised on the "idea that refuge must be understood as not only a humanitarian issue but also one of development" (10). Indeed, they view "refugees as a development opportunity" for their regions of origin, where refugees should remain to optimize possibilities for their post-conflict repatriation (142). The idea struck them while on a visit to the Za'atari refugee camp in Jordan. A fifteen-minute drive away, a Special Economic Zone (SEZ) was operating below capacity despite a £100 million investment by the Jordanian government (167). The problem is that Jordanian nationals do not want to work there (10).

In part due to the authors' influence,[108] in February 2016, a deal was struck between Jordan, the UK, and the World Bank to build five new SEZs to employ two hundred thousand refugees along with Jordanian nationals in exchange for $2 billion in investment (169).[109] Furthermore, the EU agreed to import products from Jordanian SEZs (such as garments) with favorable trade concessions (170). Span-

148. Buss draws on Floya Anthias and Nira Yuval-Davis, who argue that women are involved in nation-state practices in four primary ways. Crucially, for our purposes, three of them involve reproduction: (1) biological reproduction of members of ethnic collectives; (2) reproduction of the boundaries of ethnic groups; (3) ideological reproduction and transmission of culture; (4) signification of ethno-national difference; participation in economic, political, and military struggles. Floya Anthias and Nira Yuval-Davis, eds., *Women, Nation, State* (London: Palgrave Macmillan, 1989), 7.

107. Helen Moffett, "'These Women, They Force Us to Rape Them': Rape as Narrative of Social Control in Post-Apartheid South Africa," *Journal of Southern African Studies* 32, no. 1 (2006): 129–44.

108. See Alexander Betts and Paul Collier, "Help Refugees Help Themselves: Let Displaced Syrians Join the Labor Market," *Foreign Affairs*, October 20, 2015, www.foreignaffairs.com/articles/levant/2015-10-20/help-refugees-help-themselves; Alexander Betts and Paul Collier, "Jordan's Refugee Experiment," *Foreign Affairs*, April 28, 2016, www.foreignaffairs.com/articles/middle-east/2016-04-28/jordans-refugee-experiment.

109. Government of the United Kingdom, "The Jordan Compact: A New Holistic Approach Between the Hashemite Kingdom of Jordan and the International Community to Deal with the Syrian Refugee Crisis," London, February 4, 2016, assets.publishing.service.gov.uk/government/uploads/system/uploads/attachment_data/file/498021/Supporting_Syria__the_Region_London_2016_-_Jordan_Statement.pdf.

ning ten years, the "Jordan Compact" foresaw 15 percent immediate Syrian refugee employment, rising to one-quarter of the SEZ workforce after three years.[110]

Mass displacement is the focus, then, because for plans like SEZs to work, what is needed is a mass group of people, contained in the same place, with no legal right to live and work elsewhere, disciplined and guarded.[111] Proposals that camps should be transformed into "incubator cities," "charter cities," or "refugee cities"—that is, "special-status settlements in which refugees would be legally allowed to engage in meaningful, dignifying, and rewarding work"[112]—are defended with respect to the right to work established by the Geneva Convention. Yet, despite their ethical preambles, they are reminiscent of the ethos of "Arbeit macht frei" (Work Sets You Free), emblazoned on the gates of the concentration camps in Auschwitz and Dachau, except that now work guarantees "protection," inclusion at the margins of the capitalist economy, and legal status.

Betts and Collier acknowledge that "Special Economic Zones often have a bad reputation because of being associated with exploitative low-wage labor" but insist that "there is no reason why the model could not be adapted to ensure respect for human rights" (168). No reason, except that the suspension of prevailing labor law (along with tax and trade laws) are what define SEZs as such, and the resulting low labor costs and docile, disciplined workers are in large part what makes them attractive to direct foreign investment.

Development discourses of "self-reliance" or "autonomy" are deployed to justify predatory capitalism in Special Economic Zones, in urban centers, and even in separate island-countries like "Refugia."[113] It is unsurprising that such proposals to combine "development" and "migration management" agendas by developing "market

---

110. Bethan Staton, "Jordan Experiment Spurs Jobs for Refugees," *Refugees Deeply*, July 25, 2016, www.newsdeeply.com/refugees/articles/2016/07/25/jordan-experiment-spurs-jobs-for-refugees. For an assessment of the implementation of the Jordan Compact, see Veronique Barbelet, Jessica Hagen-Zanker, and Dina Mansour-Ille, "The Jordan Compact: Lessons Learnt and Implications for Future Refugee Compacts," Overseas Development Institute, February 2018, www.odi.org/sites/odi.org.uk/files/resource-documents/12058.pdf. A compact was also signed between Britain and Ethiopia in 2016 to create one hundred thousand jobs for refugees living in Ethiopia. Department for International Development, "Press Release: Prime Minister Pledges New UK Support to Help Tackle Migration Crisis," September 21, 2016, www.gov.uk/government/news/prime-minister-pledges-new-uk-support-to-help-tackle-migration-crisis.

111. In its definition of SEZs, the World Bank refers to fencing as an optional, but not necessary, feature. While SEZ has traditionally occupied a "geographically delimited area, usually physically secured (fenced-in)," (9) in its more recent incarnations, "the preferred approach is to allow all enterprises to co-locate within the same area, although the development of separately fenced-off areas solely for zone enterprises . . . is [still] an acceptable approach" (51). The World Bank Group, *Special Economic Zones: Performance, Lessons Learned, and Implications for Zone Development* (Washington, DC: World Bank Group, 2008), documents.worldbank.org/curated/en/343901468330977533/pdf/458690WP0Box331s0April200801PUBLIC1.pdf.

112. "Our Response," Refugee Cities website, accessed October 7, 2019, refugeecities.org/about-the-project/our-response/.

113. See Robin Cohen, "Refugia: The Limits and Possibilities of Buzi's Refugee Nation," *Postcards From*, July 30, 2015, nandosigona.wordpress.com/2015/07/30/refugia-the-limits-and-possibilities-of-buzis-refugee-nation/; Refugee Nation, www.refugeenation.org/; Europe in Africa, www.europeinafrica.com.

solutions" to mass displacement[114] have gained widespread audience (but also strong criticism).[115] Rather than simply dismissing them, we stand to understand something deeper from the "migration-development nexus"[116] about the economic/political border that runs through human mobility.

While asserting the dichotomy between economically driven and politically driven migration ("refugees are not migrants"), Betts and Collier undermine it at the macro-level (since, on their own account, refugees are fleeing "poor, fragile states"). Further, their proposed solution seeks to eliminate it at the normative level, transforming "refugees" into self-sustaining workers—that is, effectively, "economic migrants." More specifically, since, in their view, refugees are not owed a duty of rescue for a lifetime but only for a definite period (until conflict in their country of origin ends), they are effectively transformed into migrant workers on temporary permits. While marketed as bringing the benefits of globalization to refugees, the broader aim is to further entrench the geographies of unequal development in spatially segregated, biopolitically and necropolitically managed populations.

Although refugees are sociolegally constructed as noneconomic, precisely by naturalizing the social relations constituting the capitalist economy as apolitical, the infrastructures that have already been devised to control their movement and contain, sort, or further displace refugees as well as other people on the move constitute an economic sector, what Ruben Andersson terms the "illegality industry."[117] Refugees are constructed as "expensive,"[118] but tracing the commodification of the "refugee crisis" as an object of humanitarian-military-state bureaucratic management (and labor market participation of refugees themselves) tells a different story. Despite (or because of) the political discourse of "crisis" in Europe, "the inflow of asylum seekers is likely to have an immediate expansionary effect on the economy," according to the International Monetary Fund.[119]

---

114. Alexander Betts et al., *Refugee Economies: Forced Displacement and Development* (Oxford: Oxford University Press, 2017).

115. See Heaven Crawley, "Migration: Refugee Economics," *Nature: International Journal of Science* 544, no. 26–27 (2017), www.nature.com/articles/544026.

116. Ninna Nyberg–Sørensen, Nick Van Hear, and Poul Engberg–Pedersen, "The Migration-Development Nexus: Evidence and Policy Options," *International Migration* 40, no. 5 (2002), publications.iom.int/system/files/pdf/migration_dev_nexus.pdf.

117. Ruben Andersson, *Illegality Inc. Clandestine Migration and the Business of Bordering Europe* (Oakland: University of California Press, 2014).

118. To cite but one example: Paul Bedard, "Refugee Costs: $8.8 billion, $80,000 per Immigrant, Free Welfare, Medicaid," *Washington Examiner*, February 5, 2018, www.washingtonexaminer.com/refugee-costs-88-billion-80-000-per-immigrant-free-welfare-medicaid.

119. According to a report published by the International Monetary Fund, "In the short term, the macroeconomic effect from the refugee surge is likely to be a modest increase in GDP growth, reflecting the fiscal expansion associated with support to the asylum seekers, as well as the expansion in labor supply as the newcomers begin to enter the labor force. The effect is concentrated in the main destination countries (Austria, Germany, and Sweden). The impact of the refugees on medium and long-term growth depends on how they will be integrated in the labor market" (4). According to the authors' macroeconomic model simulation, as a result of the "refugee crisis," EU GDP is "lifted by about 0.05, 0.09, and 0.13 percent for 2015, 2016, and 2017, respectively. . . . For the first year, the output impact is entirely due to the aggregate demand impact of the additional fiscal spending. Labor supply is increasing as well, but the effect on potential GDP takes time to unfold. The impact is quite different across countries, reflecting the asymmetric

Refugees' presence in a national economy is beneficial not only to that economy but is also commodified, reproduced, circulated, and exchanged in multiple economies—visual, moral, and affective—producing various interrelated forms of value. In this book, we focus on the visual economy, but a story equally needs to be told about how refugees are produced and reproduced in each interrelated economy. Moreover, examining how refugees are reproduced takes us to the heart of what lies behind, beneath, or outside what is narrowly framed as "economy."

REPRODUCTIVE HETERONORMATIVITY

What lies beneath, behind, or outside the economy is reproduction. As we have seen, what is defined and remunerated as work under capitalism is labor productive of surplus value. The labor necessary to reproduce labor power is invisible, relegated conceptually to the exterior of the market. If the welfare state provided for some aspects of social reproduction, neoliberal austerity privatizes that burden, placing it squarely on the shoulders of hyperexploited racialized and gendered subjects. In other words, both empirically and conceptually, the economic is segregated from the reproductive, which is constructed variously as duty, desire, or destiny though the stranglehold of heteronormativity.

All migration politics are reproductive politics. The nation-state project of controlling migration secures the racialized demographics of the nation, understood as a reproducible fact of the social and human body, determining who is differentially included, who is excluded, and who is exalted. Citizenship, illegality, asylum—whether they are affirmed or rejected—are constructed as inheritable, transitive properties that adhere to a person in virtue of heteronormative (or, more rarely, homonormative) configurations of kinship. As Eithne Luibhéid has argued, sexual normativity is crucial to nation-state projects of "biological and social reproduction of the citizenry, but also for the cultivation of particular kinds of social, economic, and affective relationships."[120] Sexual normativity is a key register through which the (in)assimilability of noncitizens is projected in media representations of migrants, which increasingly proliferate in a time of declared crisis: as Radha Sarma Hegde observes, we are "routinely exposed to images of men, women, and children undertaking the harsh journey across Central America . . . [or] perilous sea voyages from North and Sub-Saharan Africa" and the Middle East.[121] In this book, we put forward a provocation about the omnipresence of methodological heteronormativity in the visual discourse surrounding the declared "refugee crisis." We suggest that, through

---

distribution of the asylum seekers relative to countries' own population. By 2017, the largest impact is in Austria, with GDP rising by 0.5 percent, followed by Sweden (0.4 percent) and Germany (0.3 percent)" (14). Shekhar Aiyar et al., *The Refugee Surge in Europe: Economic Challenges*, International Monetary Fund Staff Discussion Notes, January 2016, 4, 16, www.imf.org/external/pubs/ft/sdn/2016/sdn1602.pdf.

120. Eithne Luibhéid, *Pregnant on Arrival: Making the Illegal Immigrant* (Minneapolis: University of Minnesota Press, 2013), 4.

121. Radha S. Hedge, *Mediating Migration* (Cambridge: Polity, 2016), 2.

the heteronormalization of refugees, the survival trajectories of refugees are perceived through framings not only of their own reproductive histories and futures (figurations of family, childhood, maternity, and paternity) but also of their capacity or incapacity to reproduce institutions—family, religion, nation—as a precondition of their social belonging. Survival and fugitivity as such become framed as questions of reproductive justice or reproductive danger, conditioning empathy, hospitality, and social integration on the one hand, and indifference, hostility, and social exclusion on the other. In short, the survival of refugees is framed in reproductive terms—both in fascist discourses, which view them as a demographic threat, and in solidarity discourses urging their integration.

If heteronormalization structures the state of emergency (the humanitarian crisis) to which social movements then seek to respond with socially reproductive and discursive interventions, then part of what such movements are reproducing is heterosexuality. To be clear, heterosexuality in this sense is not a sexual preference but an institution and—in most places in the world—a compulsory form of social life, which is violently enforced: in war zones, on the route of escape,[122] in detention centers and camps,[123] on food lines run by Christian NGOs,[124] and in housing squats occupied by solidarians.[125] With respect to the latter, but also to refugee activism more broadly, as we argue in chapter 6, one cannot, without tragic contradiction, oppose nation-state borders and then erect or defend borders that

---

122. Jane Freedman, "Sexual and Gender-Based Violence Against Refugee Women: A Hidden Aspect of the Refugee 'Crisis,'" *Reproductive Health Matters* 24, no. 47 (2016): 18–26.

123. See Lesvos LGBTIQ+ Refugee Solidarity, "LGBTIQ+ Refugees at Grave Risk of Exposure, Violence, and Death as Conditions Worsen on Lesvos," Press Release, November 4, 2017, tinyurl.com/LesvosLGBTIQ; Matt Broomfield, "Queer Refugees on Lesvos Are Crying Out for Help," *The New Arab*, November 10, 2017, www.alaraby.co.uk/english/indepth/2017/11/10/queer-refugees-on-lesvos-are-crying-out-for-help.

124. Since late 2015, after most NGOs withdrew from the Moria camp in Lesvos in protest, housing and other services have been mainly coordinated by the NGO EuroRelief, the humanitarian arm of Hellenic Ministries, an international evangelical Christian missionary organization incorporated in the United States. In the summer of 2016, the NGO was publicly accused of using its position in the camp to religiously convert refugees. Patrick Kingsley, "Aid Workers Accused of Trying to Convert Refugees," *The Guardian*, August 2, 2016, www.theguardian.com/world/2016/aug/02/aid-workers-accused-of-trying-to-convert-muslim-refugees-greek-camp-detention-centre-lesvos-christianity. According to refugees and frontline volunteers, "EuroRelief allegedly use food, clothes, travel permits, and even access to WiFi, to coerce vulnerable refugees into converting to Christianity." Matt Broomfield, "The Abusive American-Christian NGO with a Stranglehold over Refugees' Lives," *New Arab*, May 1, 2018, www.alaraby.co.uk/english/indepth/2018/5/1/the-abusive-ngo-with-a-stranglehold-on-refugees-lives. Although proselytism is a crime under Greek law (due to the influence of the state religion of Greek Orthodoxy), of which the founder of Hellenic Ministries had been convicted in the 1980s (the conviction was overturned), at the time of writing EuroRelief has not, to our knowledge, been investigated by authorities. EuroRelief workers and volunteers have reportedly referred to LGBTQI+ refugees as "sinners," and the NGO's religious views preclude the provision of condoms or contraceptives. See Broomfield, "Queer Refugees on Lesvos," 2017. See also "EuroRelief: Evangelical Organization Providing More Harm Than Aid to Refugees," *Are You Syrious Daily Digest*, January 11, 2018, medium.com/@AreYouSyrious/ays-daily-digest-11-01-2018-euro relief-u-s-807717ec51f8.

125. Anastasia Vaitsopoulou, "The Smallest Minority in Athens in Search of a Safe Haven," October 18, 2017, medium.com/athenslivegr/there-is-one-group-in-athens-1d2df920efdf, translation of "There Is a Group of People Who Are Not Safe in Greece, and Nobody Cares," *Popaganda*, October 8, 2017, popaganda.gr/lgbtqi-prosfiges-athina/ (in Greek).

constitute nation-states—that is, borders of a gendered order that heteronormativity naturalizes.

It is not just through photographic representations that we are enjoined to view refugees as fathers, mothers, or children; asylum law, detention, deportation, and relocation policies increasingly rely on constructions of "family." For instance, family reunification policies govern the resettlement of refugees who have been separated from members of their family. Family reunification is mandated by UNHCR, based on the right to family enshrined in the UN Declaration of Human Rights: "Family is the natural and fundamental group unit of society and is entitled to protection by society and the State."[126] In principle, UNHRC favors a liberal interpretation of family to include not only husbands, wives, and minor children but also unmarried partners, including same-gender partners, adopted children, siblings, and other relatives between whom exists a relationship of "dependency" (defined as a social, emotional, or economic relationship or bond between family members "which is strong, continuous and of reasonable duration"), regardless of whether this relationship was initiated "pre-" or "post-flight."[127] In practice, in most jurisdictions in Europe, reunification is limited to heterosexual legally married spouses and their dependent minor children, and there is a strong evidentiary burden on applicants for reunification to prove their legal and biological relationships, sometimes through genetic testing (to demonstrate filiality).[128] Yet even if definitions of family were, in practice, more liberal, open, or reflective of actual relationships, this would not displace the nuclear, heteropatriarchal family as its prototypical form and dependency as its normative content. It is not incidental that this normative prototypicality is secured visually through representations of refugees that animate those sociolegally recognized and privileged forms of kinship, leaving other bonds, relationships, separations, longings, and desires outside the frame.[129]

By methodological heteronormativity, we refer to the ways states and supranational organizations construct the figure of the deserving "refugee" but also to the

126. UN High Commissioner for Refugees (UNHCR), *Refugee Family Reunification: UNHCR's Response to the European Commission Green Paper on the Right to Family Reunification of Third Country Nationals Living in the European Union (Directive 2003/86/EC)* (Geneva: United Nations, 2012), 3, www.refworld.org/docid/4f55e1cf2.html.

127. UNHCR, *Refugee Family Reunification*, 7–10.

128. Council of Europe, *Realizing the Right to Family Reunification in Europe* (Strasbourg: Council of Europe Commissioner for Human Rights, 2017), 39–43, rm.coe.int/prems-052917-gbr-1700-realising-refugees-160x240-web/1680724ba0.

129. For instance, in the summer of 2018, the German and Greek governments struck a binational deal (similar to the Greece-Turkey deal and the EU-Turkey deal that replaced it in 2016): Greece would "take back" around 1,500 asylum seekers then currently in Germany (based on the Dublin III Convention) who had entered Europe through Greece; in return, Germany would accept between 950 and 2,900 refugees located in Greece, who had filed pending or successful applications for family reunification with relatives living in Germany. "Reception Crisis in Greece: The Malignancy of Attica's Refugee Camps," *Refugee Support Aegean*, August 13, 2018, rsaegean.org/reception-crisis-in-greece/#_edn5. In this calculus, fulfilling obligations to reunite family members is traded by one state as moral and human currency to deport those not granted stay in that country to another, regardless of the relationships, connections, and desires the latter may have formed there since their arrival. Thus, state recognition of family ties, for some, is used as pretext to deracinate others who cannot legally make the same claim.

ways solidarity movements and critical scholarship on forced migration have adopted the same logic in constructing an ideal subject of solidarity and of research about the "refugee crisis." The "refugee," whether embraced as a victim or reviled as a threat, is constructed as presumptively heterosexual and as (potentially) reproductive—that is, as displaced reproductive citizens (un)deserving of moral concern. On the one hand, they are "welcomed" into the affective economy of the nation by becoming "part of the family" (e.g., in private sponsorship[130] and hosting schemes).[131] On the other hand, they are represented as a demographic or cultural threat according to nationalist and fascist ideologies. For instance, as Jill Walker Rettberg and Radhika Gajjala argue, the "predatory sexuality and undisciplined male aggression" imputed to Syrian refugees in hostile discourses reacting to the Refugees Welcome movement in Europe draws on orientalist tropes eliding Middle Eastern men variously with rapists or terrorists.[132] Sympathetic representations rely on the heterosexualization of refugees: their participation in family and kinship structures makes their loss, grief, or vulnerability legible, as they are gendered variously as courageous but desperate fathers, sacrificing mothers, and innocent children. In hostile representations, refugees may be said to embody "queer" or "monstrous" heterosexualities.[133] Their uncontrolled, undesirable (from the point of view of the state) reproductive agency is constructed as dangerous to the continuity and coherence of a racialized national subject, understood in biological terms of heredity and heritage.

We want to problematize the multiple forms of bordering that make possible the above-mentioned substitution, of a citizen's family for a family of refugees. Meth-

---

130. Private sponsorship of refugees began in Canada in 1979, when the Canadian government promised to sponsor one Vietnamese refugee for every refugee sponsored privately by Canadian citizens. In 2015, the Canadian government introduced the #WelcomeRefugees programme, which has resettled 40,081 Syrian refugees to Canada (as of 29 January 2017), of whom 14,274 were privately sponsored and 3,931 were vetted through the Blended Visa Office-Referred programme, a mixed private-public model where vulnerable individuals are identified by UNHCR, approved and financially supported by the Canadian government, and socially supported in resettlement by private citizens. "#WelcomeRefugees: Key Figures," Immigration and Citizenship Canada, February 27, 2017, www.canada.ca/en/immigration-refugees-citizenship/services/refugees/welcome-syrian-refugees/key-figures.html. Now championed by the Global Refugee Sponsorship Initiative (a partnership between the Government of Canada, UNHCR, Open Society Foundations, Giustra Foundation, and the University of Ottawa, which promotes "community sponsorship"), the private sponsorship model has been exported to other countries, including Britain, Australia, New Zealand, Ireland, Spain, Argentina, and Germany. See refugeesponsorship.org. Also see Jennifer Hyndman, William Payne, and Shauna Jimenez, "The State of Private Refugee Sponsorship in Canada: Trends, Issues, and Impacts," Refugee Research Network/Center for Refugee Studies Policy Brief, Toronto: York University, December 2, 2016, refugeeresearch.net//wp-content/uploads/2017/02/hyndman_feb'17.pdf.

131. Alicia Canter, Kate Lyons, and Matt Fidler, "'It's Like AirBnB for Refugees': UK Hosts and Their Guests: In Pictures," *The Guardian*, May 8, 2017, www.theguardian.com/world/2017/may/08/airbnb-for-refugees-uk-hosts-guests-in-pictures?CMP=Share_iOSApp_Other; Joe McCarthy and Olivia Kestin, "Powerful Photos of Families Welcoming Refugees into Their Homes," *Global Citizen*, February 15, 2018, www.globalcitizen.org/en/content/photos-families-hosting-refugees/; Donato Paolo Mancini, "The Italian Family Hosting Six Refugees in Their Home," *Al Jazeera*, February 25, 2017, www.aljazeera.com/indepth/features/2017/01/italian-family-hosting-refugees-home-170129120252941.html.

132. Jill Walker Rettberg and Radhika Gajjala, "Terrorists or Cowards: Negative Portrayals of Male Syrian Refugees in Social Media," *Feminist Media Studies* 16, no. 1 (2016): 180.

133. Cohen, "Punks, Bulldaggers, and Welfare Queens"; Jasbir Puar, *Terrorist Assemblages: Homonationalism in Queer Times* (Durham, NC: Duke University Press, 2007).

odological heteronormativity is ubiquitous in the move of humanizing refugees (or dehumanizing them) through framings of their own reproductive histories and futures, constructing them as fathers, mothers, families, pregnant women, or, in taken-for-granted binary gender/generational terms, as "men, women-and-children." These figurations affirm their (in)capacity to reproduce institutions—family, religion, nation—as a precondition of their social belonging, conditioning both empathetic and hostile responses. The survival of refugees is framed in reproductive terms—both in fascist discourses, which view them as a demographic threat (as in the discourse of "anchor babies" in jurisdictions that grant citizenship on the basis of *jus soli*) and in solidarity discourses urging their integration. The latter, namely, political ideologies that challenge the legitimacy of nation-state borders yet reproduce one of the nation-state's most important institutional logics: what Gayatri Chakravorty Spivak has termed "reproductive heteronormativity," the "assumption that producing children by male-female coupling gives meaning to any life"; "the oldest, biggest sustaining institution in the world, a tacit globalizer" that reproduces itself through "war and rape."[134]

As Penelope Deutscher has argued, biopower normalizes reproduction as a "fact of life," prompting reflexivity with respect to how we tend to reproduce its facticity even when we contest as feminists the injustices and violences which mark reproduction as a political field.[135] Analyzing the "pseudo-sovereign power" ascribed to women—that is, the attribution to them of "a seeming power of decision over life" (104)—Deutscher deconstructs "modern figurations of women as the agents of reproductive decisions but also as the potential impediments of individual and collective futures," demonstrating how in both constructions women's bodies as reproductive are invested with "a principle of death" (101). If this seems counterintuitive, it should, since, ultimately, "we do not know what procreation is" (72).

Exploring the "contiguity" between reproductive reason and biopolitics—specifically the proximity of reproduction to death, risk, fatality, and threat (63)—its thanatopolitical[136] underbelly—Deutscher reconstructs what she terms the

---

134. Spivak in Nayanika Mookherjee, "Reproductive Heteronormativity and Sexual Violence in the Bangladesh War of 1971: A Discussion with Gayatri Chakravorty Spivak," *Social Text* 30, no. 2 (2012): 125.

135. Penelope Deutscher, *Foucault's Futures: A Critique of Reproductive Reason* (New York: Columbia University Press, 2017); hereafter cited in text.

136. Deutscher argues in favor of a distinction between thanatopolitics and necropolitics, even though the two terms are often used interchangeably (103). Here she discusses the (essentially Marxian) concern in Foucault studies about the historical relationship between "modes of power," variously argued to be supplanting, replacing, absorbing, or surviving each other (88). Taking us beyond the equivalent to the "mode of production" narrative in Marxism, Deutscher argues for sovereign power's "survival" in biopolitical times, wherein it has *both* "dehisced" (burst open) and become absorbed by biopower, akin to a radicalized notion of formal subsumption we encounter in post-Marxist accounts of accumulation by dispossession and in SRT. Deutscher's eight-point definition of thanatopolitics show how it infuses the biopolitical with powers of death, constituting the "underside" (7) and condition of possibility of biopolitics, the "administrative optimization of a population's life" (102). She argues that thanatopolitics should be confused neither with sovereign power nor with necropolitics, a term introduced by Achille Mbembe to refer to the "management in populations of death and dying, of stimulated and proliferating disorder, chaos, insecurity" (102–3). See Achille Mbembe, "Necropolitics," Libby Meintjes, trans., *Public Culture* 15, no. 1 (2003): 11–40. This distinction seems crucial to Deutscher's argument that reproduction is thanatopoliticized the

"procreative/reproductive hypothesis," which reveals as biopower's aim "to ensure population, to reproduce labor capacity, to constitute a sexuality that is economically useful and politically conservative" (76, citing Foucault). Despite its marginal location in Foucault, who makes scant reference to what he terms, at one juncture, the "procreative effects of sexuality" (73, citing Foucault) as an object or a field for biopower, Deutscher argues that procreation is actually the "hinge" between sexuality and biopolitics (72). Procreatively oriented sex and biopolitically oriented reproduction hinge together to form the population (77).

Paradoxically, biopoliticized reproduction functions "as a 'power of death'" (185): through its "very association of reproduction with life and futurity (for nations, populations, peoples)" it becomes "thanatopoliticized"—that is, it becomes irrevocably associated with "risk, threat, decline, and the terminal" (4). The figure of the foetus reveals the thanatopolitical saturation of reproduction as a political field. That is, although the embryo or the foetus is not an independent entity, once it becomes understood as "precarious life," wom(b)en become "a redoubled form of precarious life" (153). This is because despite being invested with a "pseudo-sovereign" power over life, "women do not choose the conditions under which they must choose" (168). Under heteropatriarchal conditions, women become "relays" as opposed to merely "targets" or passive "recipients" of "the norms of choice" normalizing reproductive subjectivity (170). Women are interpellated as pseudo-sovereigns over their reproductive "capacities" or "drives" (or lack thereof); for instance, they are pressed into becoming "deeply reflective" about the "serious choice" with which reproduction confronts them (169). Yet, pronatalist politics do not perform a simple defence of the foetus, or of the child. Since biopoliticized reproduction is always already racialized, always already invested in a demographic politics, "a child might be figured as 'at risk' in the context of trafficking or when accompanying adults on dangerous immigration journeys" (205n27), while the same "figure of the child can also redouble into that which *poses* the risk," as in "anchor baby" discourses (205n27, emphasis in original).[137] Moreover, as we will see in chapter 3, in "zones of suspended rights," women are rendered "vulnerable in a way specifically inflected by the association with actual or potential reproduction" (129). The racialized "differentials of biopolitical citizenship" suggest that "the womb, rather than Agamben's camp, is the most effective example of Foucault's biopolitical space" (105, citing Miller).[138] Reproduction as a category is expansive, totalizing how we perceive survival, futurity, precarity, grievability, legitimacy, and belonging.

Yet, the taken-for-grantedness, the facticity of reproduction, conceals—beneath the obvious and obviating surface of its ubiquity—the operations of thanatopolitical power in "commonsense," "legible," and even "humanizing" representations of

---

moment it becomes biopoliticized, aimed at managing "women's agency as threatening and as capable of impacting peoples in an excess to projects of governmentality" (185).

137. See also Luibhéid, *Pregnant on Arrival*; Eithne Luibhéid, *Entry Denied: Controlling Sexuality at the Border* (Minneapolis: University of Minnesota Press, 2002).

138. Ruth Miller, *The Limits of Bodily Integrity: Abortion, Adultery, and Rape Legislation in Comparative Perspective* (New York: Routledge, 2007), 29.

refugees as "men, women, and children." So much so that this is not even seen as a representation but, rather, "just what refugees are": "People flee mass violence as families, not individuals."[139]

As Rosalba Icaza and Rolando Vázquez have written, the ahistorical assumption, normative projection, and affective structure of "methodological heteronormativity . . . has silenced other forms of embodied and social experience,"[140] but critiquing methodological heteronormativity and how it shapes subjectivities in crisis is not just a question of acknowledging diversity. Rather, it is a question of showing how what exceeds and threatens the hegemonic economy of desire/reproductive violence enforced by the "colonial/modern gender system"[141] is systematically placed out of view. Extending the conceptualizations of "methodological nationalism"[142] and "methodological whiteness,"[143] the concept of methodological heteronormativity allows us to trace how representations of refugees are driven by a reproductive logic or by "reproductive reason," to use Deutscher's term. But, perhaps more importantly, this leads us to bring to light how regimes of power that ossify the figure of the refugee are reproduced.

In their landmark article, Andreas Wimmer and Nina Glick Schiller define methodological nationalism as "the assumption that the nation/state/society is the natural social and political form of the modern world," showing how it shapes research, theory, and perceptions of migration.[144] Urging us to resist the "territorialization of social science imaginary and the reduction of the analytical focus to the boundaries of the nation-state," which naturalizes national society as a "container" (307), they point to an assumed "isomorphism between people, sovereign, and citizenry" that migrants trouble with their presence: "The citizenry is mirrored in the concept of a national legal system, the sovereign in the political system, the nation in the cultural system and the solidary group in the social system, all boundaries being congruent and together defining the skin holding together the body of society" (309). Ironically, "migration studies have faithfully mirrored the nationalist image of normal life," (325) which privileges sedentarism, constructing immigrants as a threat to the nation-building project, and their integration or assimilation into the national community variously as a challenge or an impossibility (310). Still, the authors warn against simply replacing the sedentarism of methodological nationalism with what they view as an equally problematic shift to "methodological 'fluidism,'" privileging movement but ignoring the "continued potency of nationalism" (326) in postmodern times. The tendency is

---

139. Betts and Collier, *Refuge*, 79.

140. Rosalba Icaza and Rolando Vázquez, "The Coloniality of Gender as a Radical Critique of Developmentalism," in *The Palgrave Handbook on Gender and Development: Critical Engagements in Feminist Theory and Practice*, ed. Wendy Harcourt (London: Palgrave Macmillan, 2016), 67.

141. Lugones, "Heterosexualism and the Colonial/Modern Gender System."

142. Andreas Wimmer and Nina Glick Schiller, "Methodological Nationalism and Beyond: Nation-State Building, Migration and the Social Sciences," *Global Networks* 2, no. 4 (2002): 301–34.

143. Gurminder K. Bhambra, "Brexit, Trump, and 'Methodological Whiteness': On the Misrecognition of Race and Class," *British Journal of Sociology* 68, no. 1 (2017): 214–32.

144. Wimmer and Glick Schiller, "Methodological Nationalism and Beyond," 302; hereafter cited in text.

to map homogeneity and stasis onto homeplaces of the past and heterogeneity and mobility onto the globalized present.

Although Wimmer and Glick Schiller gesture at the reproductive heteronormativity implicit in the container model of the nation, since the estrangement of migrants is rendered as "not being a member of the national family" (310), they do not examine how methodological nationalism is upheld by an equally (if not even more) potent assumption: namely, that the family is the container for kinship, intimacy, care, and affective relationships. This unexamined assumption becomes even more prominent in Glick Schiller's work on transmigration, in which transmigrants[145] naturalistically appear as members of nuclear families and households, albeit ones that are geographically distributed across various nationalized spaces. Indeed, both the "uprootedness" of transmigrants and their maintenance of a sense of connection to "home" (both affective and economic, as in sending remittances) are described in reference to their "transnational family relationships . . . offsetting their global vulnerability," and often making possible their return to their country and family of origin (53).

To repurpose Glick Schiller and Wimmer's critical insight, migration studies have faithfully mirrored the heteronormative image of normal life. Indeed, in this respect, they reproduce state logics of grievable and ungrievable lives, of legible and illegible suffering, of visible and invisible desires, of licit and illicit movement. This is not only a matter of which analytic categories we use but of how through knowledge production we are made unaware of how our imaginations are disciplined and contained by a bordered reality (even as we may advocate "open borders" or "free movement").

In this chapter, we explored the implications of relegating refugees to a noneconomic category, while examining how refugees are reproduced on the underside of multiple economies. Taking a detour through social reproduction theory, our aim was not to conclusively show that the refugee crisis consists in a crisis of care or a crisis of social reproduction; rather, we sought to test the limits of thinking "crisis" and "reproduction" together in order to expose the framing of refugees as noneconomic subjects, yet as always already reproductive. Querying how refugees are represented in visual discourses reveals their gender and sexual normativities, heteropatriarchal structures of feeling, and racialized "habits of hostility."[146] The concept of reproduction has a central importance if we are to understand how crisis holds sway over our imaginations and perceptual and affective life—in short, how we are subjectivized in and through crisis.

---

145. The "trans" in "transmigrant" is not the "trans" in "transgender" (as one might have thought) but rather the "trans" in "transnational": "transmigrants are immigrants whose daily lives depend on multiple and constant interconnections across international borders and whose public identities are configured in relationship to more than one nation-state." Nina Glick Schiller, Linda Basch, and Cristina Szanton Blanc, "From Immigrant to Transmigrant: Theorizing Transnational Migration," *Anthropological Quarterly* 68, no. 1 (1995): 48; hereafter cited in text.

146. Linda Martín Alcoff, "Habits of Hostility: On Seeing 'Race,'" *Philosophy Today*, no. 44 (2000): 30–40.

Synthesizing the reproduction of images with a queer view of crisis, we ask, how are refugees visually reproduced? How do representations of refugees reproduce institutions, including reproductive heteronormativity, capitalism, and citizenship as a "scarce good" and as an alibi for "race"?[147] By refugees, here, we do not mean subjects on the move but the sedimented categories, ossified images, and legal instruments through which those subjects are fixed and contained, by laws, borders, or camps, but also by representations. How are refugees reproduced in, and how do they reproduce, economies? The next chapter explores the visual economy of the "refugee crisis," showing how the reproduction of images is structured by and secures hierarchies of gender, sexuality, and "race," essential to the functioning of bordered nation-states.

---

147. As Falguni Sheth argues, a "fear of abandonment lies at the heart of the effectiveness of race as a technology, in that it draws on the fundamental tension of liberalism by engendering a sense of the 'scarcity' of rights (as a kind of resource), and thus helping to induce a fear that facilitates a sense of order and a willingness/complicity to help thrust another population outside the bounds of the law's protection." Falguni Sheth, *Toward a Political Philosophy of Race* (Albany, NY: SUNY Press, 2009), 39.

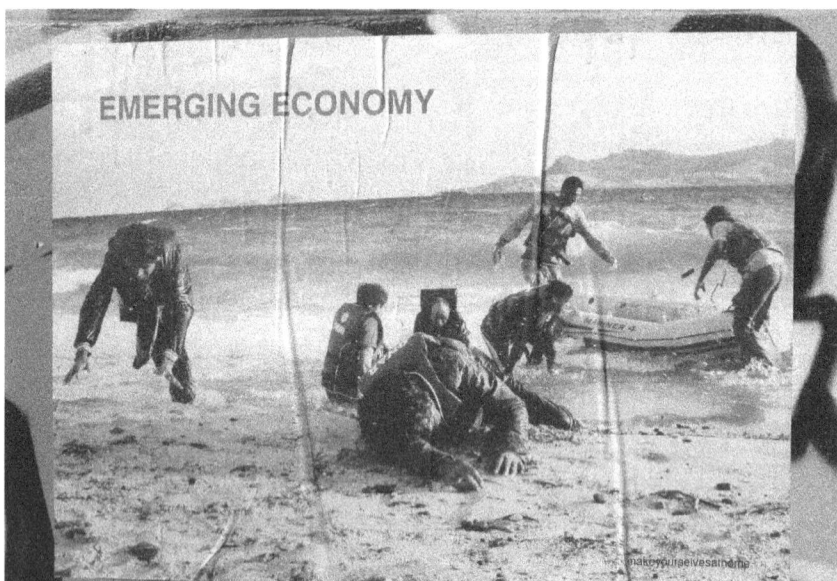

"Emerging Economy," Depression Era Collective
Photograph by Myrto Tsilimpounidi.

"Homeland—Make Yourself at Home," Depression Era Collective
Photograph by Depression Era Collective.

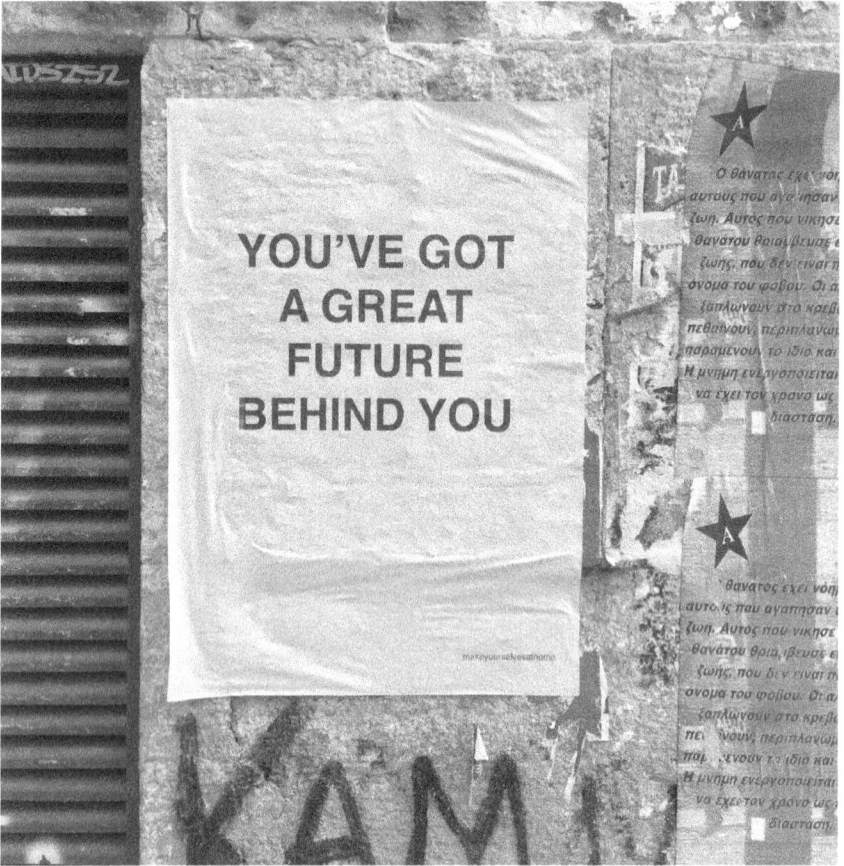

"You've Got a Great Future Behind You," Depression Era Collective
Photograph by Depression Era Collective.

"Emerging Economy, Multiple," Depression Era Collective
Photograph by Depression Era Collective.

These posters are part of Depression Era Collective's campaign "The Tourists."

The Depression Era Collective was founded in 2011 in order to articulate a common discourse and take a stance against the extreme social, economic, and political transformations of the past few years in Greece. Today it brings together thirty-six artists, photographers, writers, curators, designers, and researchers.[148]

"The Tourists" is a collective project for those who cross southern Europe and for those who reach out to or watch them go by. Devised and run by Depression Era, the project operates as a subversive tourism campaign. Starting in 2015 in Athens as a collective research and open discussion platform, "The Tourists" evolved into a public space, poster, and digital campaign in spring 2017 (tag: Make Yourselves at Home[149]); a publication; and a series of exhibitions. "The Tourists" responds to history in the making: the wave of refugee and mass migrations from Asia and Africa to Europe and the simultaneous increase of global tourism in the Mediterranean. These are parallel, converging global events producing states of emergency, distress investment, collateral conflicts, and cultural patronage, at the same place and at the same time. "The tourist" lives in a divided, burned-out, hypermediated public sphere. Her identity and citizenship are in flux; she is lost in transit, perpetually anxious, alienated, resigned, or resisting; he is a simulator of social involvement, impotent to frame history in anything more than a postcard, slogan, or tweet. Among the narratives of power, encounter, arrival, and departure featured in global media and contemporary art, the images and slogans of "The Tourists" expose seemingly idyllic landscapes containing the debris of unspeakable violence; frame portraits of women and men in alien places, strangers in their land, visitors among ruins, stateless, networked, indolent, and conflicted; and document a generation of fearless children. It is not clear whether these belong to tourism ads or disaster news streams.[150]

148. For more details on the Depression Era Collective, please see depressionera.gr/projects.
149. www.facebook.com/Make-Yourselves-at-Home-1735468143342231/.
150. For more details, see depressionera.gr/tourists.

2

Photographìa

As we argued in the previous chapter, the concept of reproduction has a central importance if we are to understand how declared crises construct those seemingly most intimate aspects of our lives: our embodied, perceptual, and affective experience. In this chapter, we are interested in exploring how the reproduction of images through photography results in the reproduction of hegemonic values and institutions, but also resistance to those. Throughout the book, we invoke "reproduction" as a polysemic concept, or maybe less a concept than a broader set of various intertwined senses which can be unravelled with respect to the present argument concerning the visual economy of the refugee crisis. Crisis is reproduced in our phenomenal lives in an economy of representations. Indeed, exploring the contradictory ways images have circulated in Europe's refugee crisis reveals that, despite attempts to naturalize and invert its causes and effects, the crisis did not just occur as a natural disaster. As we have argued, dominant representations of the humanitarian crisis naturalize the political causes of war, displacement, and economic collapse: specifically, their roots in neoliberal capitalism. According to the oft-repeated hegemonic story, the European refugee crisis began in the summer of 2015 with the appearance of refugees on the shores of Europe. Images of the boats arriving at the island of Lesvos have, by now, become iconic of the crisis: they were circulated in mass media and political campaigns as visual shortcuts of the crisis. The crisis thus appears to begin with a cycle of appearances: with the appearance of bodies coming ashore and with the appearance of photographs testifying to refugees' appearance.

In this process of appearances, the European gaze became fixed on the Others. Historically, the Mediterranean Sea has been a space of multidirectional crossings and migrations, defying a Eurocentric, colonial narrative of unilinear movement, civilizational progress, and bordered, autochthonic nationalism.[1] Yet, the declaration of crisis erases this history, fixing the gaze on Others arriving in boats as threats to national and continental sovereignty. Sovereignty is reasserted as a project of capture, containment, expulsion, and elimination: sorting and deporting, pushing back, and letting/making drown people whose attempts to land in safety are constructed, variously, as a civilizational threat, a natural disaster, or as terrorism. The distortive gaze of European supremacy and exceptionalism manifests and sediments what Abdelmalek Sayad terms "state thought": "a form of thought that reflects through its [mental] structures . . . the structure of the state, which thus acquires a body."[2] State thought is "completely inscribed within the line of demarcation that divides 'nationals' from 'non-nationals.' That line, although it is "itself invisible or scarcely perceptible" (279), constructs migrants as a "double absence": they are seen as physically absent from their societies of origin, which are constructed as their natural homeplaces, and they are sociolegally absent from the "host" societies in which they are permanently perceived as strangers, aliens, foreigners—as being out of place (126–27).

State thought is necessary to the functioning of the nation-state, not only in the sense that without the dividing line between nationals and non-nationals "there can be no national state" (279). It is not enough for the state to recognize nationals; nationals "must recognize themselves in it" (279). The nation-state requires this "double mutual recognition effect" (279), and so it cultivates a bordered gaze through its cultural hegemony and its visual economy, which locates the viewer in the corpus of the imagined national community[3] while at the same time positioning the imagined Other as a threat to the continuation and homogeneity of that community—a primary aspiration of the state (280) and our only understanding of community under its logic. The category of the "refugee," then, exists only from the point of view of the national, the "citizen," *who gives state thought a body.* This is a disciplined gaze, but embodying it, we do not reflexively perceive ourselves as engaging in highly regimented and even, to a certain extent, compulsory ways of seeing. Rather, we naturalize this gaze by reifying the relations of domination that we project onto the body of the Other; our perception thus appears autonomic, spontaneous, and natural, yet it actually performs a kind of fetishism, ontologizing the stranger, the refugee, the non-national, by "*cut[ting] 'the stranger' off from its histories of determination.*"[4]

---

1. David Abulafia, *The Great Sea: A Human History of the Mediterranean* (Oxford: Oxford University Press, 2011).

2. Abdelmalek Sayad, *The Suffering of the Immigrant*, ed. Pierre Bourdieu, trans. David Macey (Cambridge: Polity, 2004), 278, see also 281–82; hereafter cited in text. Sayad's work constituted a conscious attempt to historicize an earlier so-called crisis of immigration ostensibly confronting French society in the 1970s, with the arrival of migrants, formerly colonial subjects from North Africa. Sayad identified a "homological" and a "generative" relationship between colonialism and migration: not only do they form part of the same economy, but the former gives rise to the latter. See Emmanuelle Saada, "Abdelmalek Sayad and the Double Absence: Toward a Total Sociology of Immigration," *French Politics, Culture & Society* 18, no. 1 (2000): 28–47.

3. Benedict Anderson, *Imagined Communities: Reflections on the Origin and Spread of Nationalism* (London: Verso, 1983).

4. Sara Ahmed, *Strange Encounters: Embodied Others in Postcoloniality* (London: Routledge, 2000), 5, emphasis in original.

When we embody state thought as a way of seeing, we view the presence of "refugee" bodies on European shores as the source of the "problem": we equate the appearance of the refugees with a crisis, an emergency, a natural disaster. Thus, when we casually engage in talk of waves, flows, influxes, or avalanches, we reify the perception of the stranger overpowering the border[5]—when, in fact, in every aspect of social life, our perception is always already overpowered by the border. We are always ready to encounter the stranger everywhere, since this is the basic structure of our sense of belonging (to the nation). The fact that our perceptions seem immediate and spontaneous does not mean that they are automatic, autonomous, or natural. (Not to mention that people hardly ever "flow": even in the most mainstream representation, they can be seen bumping violently against national borders.)

On one level, photography at the scene of arrival seems to have embodied an empty gaze inasmuch as photojournalists produced images that were transformed into different, even apparently contradictory signifiers with widely divergent affective appeal depending on the viewer's ideological background. For instance, as we discussed in chapter 1, the same image that was used to mobilize feelings of empathy and solidarity with people on the move was also successfully used in the far-right, pro-Brexit campaign.[6] Yet, its divergent uses do not testify to the widespread notion about the neutrality of the image. That is, while we do not believe that images can be read in a singular way, we take issue with an explanation that locates meaning solely in an after-effect of interpretation, the result of the reception of an object (the photograph) by a subject (the viewer). For one, this erases the photographic situation, comprised of other subjects: the photographer, but also the subject of the photograph. The subjects who view a photograph, but also the photographer and the photographed, make up what Ariella Azoulay has called "a virtual political community."[7] We view photographs not as isolated individuals but as members of such communities—and because of the imperceptible hegemony of state thought, we primarily (though not necessarily) view them as nationals. We argue that this is true even as we aim to resist the authority or dominance of the bordered national state, as social movements that "Stand with Refugees" (to quote the social media campaign of UNHCR)[8] have done. Breaking loose from the stranglehold that state thought has over our perception means interrogating ways of seeing that apparently exceed the state, the political, even the historical: this is why, in chapter 1, we introduced the concept of methodological heteronormativity. This concept lays the ground for a deeper critique of the visual life of the refugee crisis, one that goes beneath the dividing line between nationals and non-nationals to show how even empathetic or solidarity responses are implicated in reproducing a naturalized institution that the nation-state requires—namely, reproductive heteronormativity.

---

5. Thus, we agree with Ahmed, who has argued against "reifying borders" by maintaining an "assumption that strangers only populate the borders of a nation" (2000, 101).

6. We are referring here to Nigel Farage's "Breaking Point" poster in the Brexit campaign, which featured a highly circulated photograph depicting "refugees" crossing the Croatian–Slovenian border in 2015.

7. Ariella Azoulay, *The Civil Contract of Photography* (London: Zone Press, 2008), 14, 21.

8. UNHCR, "#WithRefugees," United Nations Refugee Agency, n.d., www.unhcr.org/withrefugees/.

The state tries to control the field of vision, primarily by controlling photography. Photography and state warfare have a long, symbiotic relationship as they share technologies and "ways of seeing."[9] The management of the field of vision becomes a key political component of the geopolitical strategies of managing the crises in our era. The hegemonic visual discourse of the refugee crisis leaves outside the frame EU and European nation-states' complicity in wars and occupations; civil and proxy conflicts; famines, extractivism, and dispossession; and climate change: the main reasons behind people's appearance on the Aegean islands in the summer of 2015—and before/after the so-called Summer of Migration. But, by rendering the scene of arrival spectacular at this moment in time, reifying a process of historical duration in a spectacular, representative event, images of the crisis also dissimulate as to its sudden appearance—as through their absence, some years later, they imply its ostensible conclusion.

Despite appearances, the crisis neither began nor is it over. In refuting this linear narrative, we seek to question the very notion of crisis as appearance. To do so, we discuss the production of the hegemonic gaze, the spectacle of the border, and the border as spectacle,[10] where the figures of the migrant[11] and of the refugee become visible through the administration of the field of vision. To break the vicious cycle of appearances and to reflect on their conditions of visibility, we engage with the methodology of *photographìa,* the material trace of writing/*grafi* with light/*phos.* In photographìa, visual representations, theories—always already indebted to vision—and perceptual habits are revealed as inextricably linked in the process of knowledge production.[12] Photographìa is a way of making photographs speak and thereby assuming our responsibility for caring for their meaning, which is not limited to what they depict or even to what they refer.

In this chapter, we engage with the Benjaminian notion of reproduction, in particular, with Walter Benjamin's thesis on the mechanical reproduction of images. From Benjamin we draw an insight of fundamental importance for our times: that the appearance of fascism is the process of aestheticization of politics. We then discuss two provocative points of view on photography that point to ways we can politicize images in order to intervene in and interrupt their aestheticization, thereby lending an embodied militancy to the contemporary resistance against fascism. Each of these accounts is inspired by Benjamin's theory of photography, yet they translate its normative potential into the apparently opposite registers of citizenship (Azoulay) and refuge (Cadava). If, for Azoulay, resistance to being governed depends on

9. Liam Kennedy and Caitlin Patrick, *The Violence of the Image: Photography and International Conflict* (London: I. B. Tauris, 2014).

10. Nicholas De Genova, "The Border Spectacle of Migrant 'Victimization,'" *Open Democracy,* May 20, 2015, www.opendemocracy.net/beyondslavery/nicholas-de-genova/border-spectacle-of-migrant-'victimisation'.

11. Thomas Nail, *The Figure of the Migrant* (Stanford, CA: Stanford University Press, 2015).

12. The notion of knowledge production is an inherently capitalist notion; we use it deliberately to underline the implication of academic institutions—where knowledge and the labor expended to produce it are commodified—in the capitalist economy.

our signing onto a kind of "civil contract," "rehabilitating citizenship," and indeed becoming/discovering ourselves as citizens of photography, Eduardo Cadava urges us to view all photographs as refugees. Drawing on various theories of representation, finally, we elaborate the methodology of *photographia*.

MECHANICAL REPRODUCTION

Written in 1935, two years after Adolf Hitler was appointed Chancellor of Germany (in 1933), after the Nazi party's electoral victory in 1932, *The Work of Art in the Age of Mechanical Reproduction* represents Walter Benjamin's effort to describe a theory of art that would be "useful for the formulation of revolutionary demands in the politics of art."[13] At the time, Benjamin, a German Jew and a Marxist, was living in exile in Paris. Four years later, in 1940, Benjamin committed suicide in Catalonia, fearing deportation back to Nazi-occupied France by the Spanish authorities. He was en route to Portugal and intended to go from there to the United States, which, exceptionally, had granted Benjamin an entry visa. The United States—like virtually all nation-states—had responded to Nazi Germany's denationalization and forced emigration of its Jewish citizens by closing its borders to refugees.[14]

In *The Work of Art in the Age of Mechanical Reproduction*, Benjamin argues that the reproduction of images, in particular through photography and film, fundamentally alters the structure of representation and the mode of perception prevailing in an age where industrial capitalism had created "masses," which anticapitalist and antifascist movements sought to organize against systems of expropriation.

> Technological reproducibility emancipates the work of art for the first time in world history from its parasitical attachment to ritual. To an ever greater degree the work of art reproduced becomes the reproduction of a work of art designed for reproducibility. From a photographic negative, for example, a multitude of prints is possible; to ask for the authentic print makes no sense. But the instant the criterion of authenticity ceases to be applicable to artistic production, the entire social function of art is reversed. Instead of being founded on ritual, it begins to be founded on another practice—that is, to be founded on politics.[15]

For Benjamin, reproduction is neither imitation, nor merely replication, nor just repetition. Technical reproduction, of which mechanical reproduction is the apex, transforms the ontology of the artwork: Cadava argues it refers "not to the empirical

---

13. Walter Benjamin, *The Work of Art in the Age of Its Technological Reproducibility and Other Writings on Media*, *2nd version* (Cambridge, MA: Harvard University Press, 2008), 20.

14. Nandita Sharma, "From Crisis to Crisis: A History of Immigration Controls" (lecture, Feminist Researchers Against Borders Summer School Taster Workshop, National Technical University of Athens, July 21, 2018).

15. Walter Benjamin, "The Work of Art in the Age of Mechanical Reproduction," in *Illuminations*, ed. Hannah Arendt, trans. Harry Zohn (New York: Schocken Books, 1969), 481–82, emphasis in original; hereafter cited in text.

fact of 'reproduction,' but to the possibility of *being reproduced*, to reproducibility as a mode of being."[16] Indeed, in his essay, Benjamin recognizes the historical development of reproduction, from coin stamping in ancient Greece to the medieval woodcut and nineteenth-century lithography as a technique of graphic art. Yet, mechanical reproduction brings about a world-historical shift through the destruction of authenticity, achieved for the first time through photography. Since "the presence of the original is the prerequisite to the concept of authenticity," mechanical reproduction obviates any notion of an original: artworks are now made to be reproduced (4). The loss of uniqueness of an artwork consists in its detachment from time and space: reproduction "substitutes a plurality of copies for a unique existence," which, moreover, meet the viewer "in his own particular situation" and thereby "reactivate the object reproduced" (4). In so doing, Benjamin argued that mechanical reproduction "lead[s] to a tremendous shattering of tradition which is the obverse of the contemporary crisis" of fascism (4). At once the opposite and the counterpart of fascism's white supremacist cult of racial authenticity, its cult worship of invented tradition and authority embodied in the leader, mechanical reproduction detaches the copy from an authentic origin and defies the authority of a singular author. The liberation of the work of art from its "aura" of uniqueness and authenticity by mechanical reproduction coincides with the liberatory potential of art in his—and, perhaps, even in our—age.

Ultimately, Benjamin is interested in the artwork—invested with authenticity and uniqueness—as a metonym for the racial fantasy of purity and singularity inscribed in the so-called Aryan race by the Nazi ideology of the Third Reich.[17] This is why the mechanical reproduction of the artwork held political potential for Benjamin: reproducibility as a new ontological condition of the work of art was, for him, "intimately connected with the contemporary mass movements" (4) against fascism. Shattering the thrall of tradition, the spell of ritual, and the myth of authenticity that binds the national community, the race, or people (the *Volk*) together, in one realm (*Reich*) under one leader (*Führer*)—as in the Nazi slogan, *Ein Volk, ein Reich, ein Führer*—mechanical reproduction has the potential to mobilize the masses against the social relations of property and "ritual values" of racism that fascism naturalizes.

Here, Benjamin appeals to the distinction between the economic base or "substructure" and the cultural "superstructure": what the phenomenon of proletarianization is to the substructure, the formation of masses is to the superstructure. They are "two aspects of the same process" (19). Fascism appeals to the masses by reifying culture in "race," exploiting the "apparatus" of mechanical reproduction—at the superstructural level—"pressed into the production of ritual values," giving the masses "expression" in the cult of the *Führer*, the lethal fantasy of the pure nation, the imperialist agenda of "*lebensraum*" (living space). But fascism does not allow for a transformation of the basic social relation of property, which the "newly created

---

16. Eduardo Cadava, *Words of Light. Theses on the Photography of History* (Princeton, NJ: Princeton University Press, 1997), 42.

17. See Cadava, *Words of Light*, 3–5.

proletarian masses . . . strive to eliminate" (19). By preserving private property, fascism harnesses the technological potential of mechanical reproduction against the aim of the reproduction of life, directing mass movements to war.

> The logical result of Fascism is the introduction of aesthetics into political life. . . . All efforts to render politics aesthetic culminate in one thing: war. War and war only can set a goal for mass movements on the largest scale while respecting the traditional property system. . . . Only war makes it possible to mobilize all of today's technical resources while maintaining the property system. . . . [War supplies] the artistic gratification of a sense perception that has been changed by technology. This is evidently the consummation of "*l'art pour l'art.*" Self-alienation [of human beings] has reached such a degree that it can experience its own destruction as an aesthetic pleasure of the first order. This is the situation of politics which Fascism is rendering aesthetic. Communism responds by politicizing art. (20)

From this passage, it is clear that mechanical reproduction, for Benjamin, is neither inherently radical nor inherently reactionary. Its negative aspect—realized in fascism—is that it enables the aestheticization of politics: transforming politics into theatre, or war into spectacle. Its utopian aspect—which remains unrealized, in Benjamin's time as in ours, but which he identifies with communism—is the politicization of art.[18] Mechanical reproduction cannot, in itself, disalienate human beings, but, by radically transforming the conditions of perception, reproducible art can make possible a "simultaneous collective experience" (14) that can be harnessed by liberatory mass movements against the domination of capital.

---

18. As Susan Buck-Morss shows, Benjamin was inspired by the "production-art" of the Bolshevik avant-garde, and specifically the Constructivists, as reflected in borrowing their concept of the "artist-engineer" in *The Author as Producer*, which sought to eliminate a separate sphere for art and to reject the notion of the artist as an individual genius and the division between producers (artists) and consumers (audiences) of art. His Marxist aesthetics are informed by the proletarian theatre of Asja Lācis and the dialectical ("epic") theatre of Bertold Brecht. Benjamin remained critical of socialist realism—the official aesthetic theory of Stalinist USSR from 1932 to 1988—which supplanted the Proletkult, the proletarian cultural movement that emerged during and after the October Revolution (1918). Intended to be autonomous nodes of amateur cultural production, Proletkult disputed the division of labor between cultural producers and audiences of consumers; in advocating "creative amateurism," Benjamin rejected the cultural elitism of the party, which eventually predominated in the state ideology of socialist realism. See Susan Buck-Morss, "Anti-Stalinist Art: Benjamin, Shostakovich, and the End of the Story" (keynote lecture, first Congress of the International Walter Benjamin Association, Amsterdam, July 1997). Published as "Revolutionary Time: The Vanguard and the Avant-Garde" in *Benjamin Studies, Studien 1*, ed. Helga Geyer-Ryan (Amsterdam: Rodopi, 2002), susanbuckmorss.info/text/antistalinist-art/. Still, as Leah Dickerman argues, "socialist realism's consecration as an official aesthetics coincides with the birth of historical consciousness of the age of mechanical reproduction" (2000, 150). Socialist realism's appropriation of, and indebtedness to "camera-vision"—the effect of photographic images on popular consciousness and the historically new mode of perception—is marked by a fundamental ambivalence concerning the threat of photography (2000, 148, 150). On the one hand, socialist realist sculpture and painting was often based on photographic representations, while disavowing these origins; on the other hand, socialist realist paintings were often designed and intended specifically for mass reproduction and printed in "staggering quantities" (Dickerman 2000, 148). Moreover, "at times, a borrowed photographic figure even migrates from canvas to canvas, displayed against different painted backdrops . . . their smooth surfaces approximating those of the photograph" (Dickerman 2000, 148). Leah Dickerman, "Camera Obscura: Socialist Realism in the Shadow of Photography," *October* 93 (2000), 139–53.

Mechanical reproduction ensures that the masses are addressed by art, and, more importantly, that they perceive themselves as addressed by it, which changes their reaction toward it: "the reactionary attitude toward a Picasso painting changes into the progressive reaction toward a Chaplin movie" (14). Art is no longer produced exclusively for the enjoyment of elites; it is no longer understood only by experts. Instead, with mechanical reproduction, the masses visually and emotionally enjoy art "with the orientation of the expert" (14). The "fusion" of criticism and enjoyment "is of great social significance": "The greater the decrease in the social significance of an art form, the sharper the distinction between criticism and enjoyment by the public. The conventional is uncritically enjoyed, and the truly new is criticized with aversion. With regard to the screen, the critical and the receptive attitudes of the public coincide. The decisive reason for this is that individual reactions are predetermined by the mass audience response they are about to produce" (14).

In other words, unlike paintings or other artworks produced under the aura of authenticity, film and photography interpellate not an individual but a mass viewer—or, rather, an individual to the extent that they are part of a mass—who is empowered by the technical aspects of these media to criticize and analyze these representations. Our "field of perception" has fundamentally changed with the advent of photography and film, a revolutionary transformation Benjamin compares to the effects of the advent of psychoanalysis on our analytic acuity: "fifty years ago," he writes in 1935, "a slip of the tongue passed more or less unnoticed" (15). Yet, today, "the camera introduces us to unconscious optics as does psychoanalysis to unconscious impulses" revealed in Freudian slips. The ordinary landscapes of our lives, the mundane movements of human bodies, the routine acts that comprise the everyday no longer go unnoticed, as they once did, because of the intervention of the camera: "close-ups of the things around us, by focusing on the hidden details of familiar objects," render them strange (16). The suffocating familiarity of spaces constituting our "prison-world" is transformed into "an immense and unexpected field of action" in which we "go travelling" (15–16). Even our perception of the body shifts: "with the close-up, space expands; with slow motion, movement is extended. The enlargement of a snapshot does not simply render more precise what in any case was visible, though unclear: it reveals entirely new structural formations of the subject" (16). It is not only that by viewing photographs or films we have access to "a different nature [that] opens itself to the camera than opens to the naked eye" but also that, "for the entire spectrum of optical . . . perception, the film has brought about a similar deepening of apperception" (15–16).[19]

Yet, here too, Benjamin's ambivalence toward mechanical reproduction is evident. On the one hand, he is critical of the elitism which derides mass culture (even

---

19. Edmund Husserl defines apperceptions as "intentional lived-experiences that are conscious of something as perceived [but this something as perceived] is not self-given in these lived experiences [not completely]. . . . Apperceptions transcend their immanent content" (624). Apperceptions are regulated by lawful regularities (624) and are thus tied to "reproduction" and "memory," but also to "phantasy" in Husserl's genetic phenomenology (477). Edmund Husserl, *Analyses Concerning Passive and Active Synthesis: Lectures on Transcendental Logic*, trans. Anthony Steinbock (Dordrecht: Kluwer, 2001).

considering it an oxymoron) as "spectacle which requires no concentration and presupposes no intelligence" (18, citing Georges Duhamel). On the other hand, he concedes that in the age of mechanical reproduction, in all fields of art but particularly in film, "reception [occurs] in a state of distraction," so that if the public is simultaneously the critic, it is "an absent-minded one" (19). "Absorbing" the work of art, "the distracted mass" relies on "habits" and "apperception"; that is why, according to Benjamin, if it is "able to mobilize the masses" it will "meet this mode of reception halfway," as do films which shock us to attention (19).

Similarly, discussing the shift from photography at the outset as a medium for portraiture to its development as a means of documentation, Benjamin suggests that the mass viewer needs guidance: when photographs begin to be taken in order to document "historical occurrences" and not to immortalize human faces, they

> acquire a hidden political significance. . . . They stir the viewer; he feels challenged by them in a new way. At the same time, picture magazines begin to put up signposts for him. . . . For the first time, captions have become obligatory. And it is clear that they have an altogether different character than the title of a painting. The directives which the captions give to those looking at pictures in illustrated magazines soon become even more explicit and more imperative in the film where the meaning of each single picture appears to be prescribed by the sequence of all preceding ones. (8)

If the subject of "simultaneous collective experience" is perpetually distracted; needs textual frames to understand documentary photography; perceives in and through habits, sedimented apperceptions, and scripted narratives; and—the most terrifying possibility, but for Benjamin the logical outcome of the foregoing—even experiences the spectacular destruction of war as an aesthetic pleasure, it is clear that, as Benjamin suggests elsewhere, "the illiteracy of the future will be ignorance not of reading or writing, but of photography."[20]

As we have seen, Benjamin was critical of the notion of art for art's sake (*l'art pour l'art*) and also dismissed the—in his time already somewhat stale—debate about whether photography is an art form. As Cadava puts it, what is at stake for Benjamin "is not whether photography is art, but in what way *all* art is photography."[21] To this, we might add, what is at stake is the way all *perception* is photography. This is ever more true in an age when mechanical reproduction has given way to digital reproduction. Perhaps, then, Benjamin was not exaggerating when he described the space of political action as "a sphere reserved one hundred percent for images."[22] If the political can be viewed as the space of the reproduction of images, we cannot ignore the visual in the reproduction of crisis.

---

20. Walter Benjamin, citing Laszlo Moholy-Nagy, *Selected Writings 1927–1934, Vol. 2, Part 2, 1931–1934*, ed. Michael Jennings, Howard Eiland, Gary Smith (Cambridge, MA: Belknap Press, 1999), 527.
21. Cadava, *Words of Light*, 44, emphasis in the original.
22. Walter Benjamin, "Surrealism: The Last Snapshot of the European Intelligentsia," in *Walter Benjamin Selected Writings, Vol. 2, 1927–1934* (Cambridge, MA: Harvard University Press, 2005/1929), 56.

SPECTACLE OF THE CRISIS

Guy Debord famously stated of capitalist society, "all that once was directly lived has become mere representation."[23] The society of the spectacle, for Debord, emerges at the "historical moment at which the commodity completes its colonization of social life": "the becoming-world of the commodity and the becoming-commodity of the world." Extending Marx's argument about commodity fetishism—people appear as things and things as people—under capitalism,[24] Debord defines spectacle not as a collection of images but as "a social relationship between people that is mediated by images" (4). If the society of the spectacle emerges through the colonization of the social by the commodity, capitalism dominates not by economic hegemony alone: it "has already invaded the social surface of each continent by means of the spectacle," offering not only things to be coveted but also "false models of revolution to local revolutionaries" (57).

If crisis is a sudden and spectacular rupture with normality, declared only to be managed, can the result after the transition to a new (or the same yet worse) normativity be still understood as crisis? Can crisis become banal and still be crisis? Is it only by virtue of our desire to believe in a time that will never return and moreover that never was—when "life was normal"—that we have come to experience certain moments or seasons (the Arab Spring, the Summer of Migration) as a rupture in time? This is precisely the state logic, deriving from the "management" of so-called crises, which appropriate and misrepresent human suffering in order to shore up state power. With respect to the construct of the refugee crisis, this imagined, previous time is one in which no one moved, everyone was the same as everyone else, and people shared the same values.[25] This "past" is the imagined community of the nation-state. We do not have images of this time (which never was), but it animates the spectacular representation of our present and is aestheticized as the political imaginary of fascist fantasies of the restoration of purity, authenticity, and heredity.

In the crisis spectacularly staged in the Aegean and Mediterranean Seas, literally washing over the victims of competing and collaborating fascisms, the technocratic

---

23. Guy Debord, *The Society of Spectacle* (London: Rebel Press, 1967).

24. Fetishism is the displacement or transposition of social relations onto an object. See Ahmed, *Strange Encounters*, 5. As a result of this transposition, "*specific social relations of production between people* appear as *relations of things to people*, or else certain social relations appear as the *natural properties of things*." Karl Marx, *Capital, Vol. I*, trans. Ben Fowkes (London: New Left Review/Pelican, [1867] 1976), 1005, emphasis in original. Specifically, fetishism describes the appearance of commodities produced by workers who are alienated from their labor. Under capitalism, "the social characteristics of [human beings'] own labor [appear] as objective characteristics of the products of labor themselves, as the socio-natural properties of these things" (163). To put it another way, our "own relations of production . . . assume a material shape which is independent of [our] control" (187). The commodity, which Marx understands as a "definite social relation" between human beings, thus comes to appear as "a relation between things" (163). See chapter 3 for an elaboration.

25. Encarnación Gutiérrez Rodríguez, "Thinking the Crisis of Capitalism Through Another Grammar: On 'the Refugee Crisis,' Coloniality, and Racism" (lecture, Critical Feminist Research on Migration and Refugee Studies, Convened by the Critical Feminist Network on Migration and Refugees, University of Konstanz, June 22, 2017).

solution is embodied in the infrastructure of the hotspot. This technology of bordering proliferates a logic that we refer to as the logic of the hotspot: the ideology that human lives and bodies can be sorted into populations for simultaneous biopolitical and necropolitical management through the cynical use of geography and sociolegal instruments, such as asylum. By "spectacularity" we mean the ways in which the hotspot is designed ostensibly to "manage the crisis," while accelerating, intensifying, and reproducing human suffering. The hotspot becomes "the scene of inclusion, the obscene of exclusion," to quote Nicholas De Genova's potent formulation of the "Border Spectacle": a spectacle of enforcement at "the" border, whereby migrant "illegality [and, we might add, refugee 'vulnerability'] is rendered spectacularly visible."[26] The pretext of a refugee crisis impelled by the fantasy of autochthony and Otherness has been used to facilitate the militarization of the Mediterranean and Aegean Seas; the institution of the hotspot mechanism ostensibly to hasten asylum decisions but actually to accelerate carceral capacity and mass deportations not only of those deemed ineligible for asylum but also most of those deemed eligible (to so-called safe third countries); the warehousing of those who survive the dangerous sea passage in camps and detention centers, turning national space into a prison, a container (as we discuss in chapter 5).

The continental project of securitization and the transnational politics of migration management that have produced Europe as a fortress are, by now, well documented, as is the death toll of these necropolitical regimes, constituting the Mediterranean Sea passage the deadliest border in the world, while constructing surveillance, detention, and slavery economies. Migration management is therefore a euphemism for the militarization of the borders of Europe but also its interior, since the border is everywhere.[27] If the border is everywhere, and if it is mechanically reproduced, it becomes banal.

More specifically, as we discussed in chapter 1, the spectacle of the crisis erases war, the war on mobility, a mobile war, where the crises that have become normalized as definitive of our age intersect. Mark Neocleous and Maria Kastrinou draw our attention to how the refugee crisis, leading to (or foreseeing) the institution of the hotspot, has changed in dramatic ways the political economy of military EU, its legal and operational parameters, and its political geography.

> Like states themselves, the EU imagines itself as engaged in permanent social wars. In such wars, the police object becomes a target of the war power, while the subject of war becomes the focus of police intervention. The EU hotspot must therefore be seen as by definition a conflict zone saturated with police power, to deal with a growing social enemy. At the same time, the hotspot contributes to the routinization of emergency powers within the EU as a whole and a reassertion of the EU's fundamental message: the situation is under control, police power is in place, the war power is doing its work. That today's European crisis is thought of by the EU as requiring a police war tells us much

---

26. Nicholas De Genova, "Spectacles of Migrant 'Illegality': The Scene of Exclusion, the Obscene of Inclusion," *Ethnic and Racial Studies*, May 24, 2013, 2, dx.doi.org/10.1080/01419870.2013.783710.

27. De Genova, "Spectacles of Migrant 'Illegality.'"

about how the EU perceives the problem. If there has been a "transfer of sovereignty" from nation-states to the EU then the transfer has also involved the way in which the figure of the migrant is imagined and treated. Hotspots *of* what? For the EU, hotspots of crime and conflict. Hotspots *for* what? For the exercise of the new European powers of war and police.[28]

The militarization of crisis has involved the deployment of NATO in the Aegean and across the Mediterranean. It has extended the powers and scope of Frontex, the European Border and Coast Guard Agency, and the institution of a "standing corps" "to ensure a coherent management of the external borders and to be able to respond to situations of crisis a standing corps will be set up, with up to 10,000 operational staff by 2027."[29] It has interpenetrated the national criminal legal systems with EU police and asylum agencies. It has outsourced the functions of the external borders not only through bilateral agreements (for instance, with Libya and Turkey) but also by weaponizing the geography of the desert[30] and of the sea. The militarization of the sea[31] has made the Mediterranean and the Aegean crossings as lethal as possible, turning it into one of the deadliest borders on earth.[32]

The European refugee crisis is based on a spectacular division between refugees, migrants, and citizens, which lies at the heart of the hotspot logic.[33] Here, we make a threefold distinction between the hotspot mechanism, the logic of the hotspot, and the representation of the hotspot. By "hotspot mechanism" we refer to the ap-

---

28. Mark Neocleous and Maria Kastrinou, "The EU Hotspot: Police War against the Migrant," *Radical Philosophy* 200 (2016), emphasis in original. www.radicalphilosophyarchive.com/commentary/the-eu-hotspot.

29. Similarly to the hotspots, the standing corps reflects a carefully choreographed dance of state and EU sovereignties: "member states will retain primary responsibility for the management of their borders, with the agency and its staff providing technical and operational assistance subject to the agreement of the member states concerned. Under the proposed new rules, staff of the standing corps deployed to a member state will be able to exercise some executive powers to carry out border controls or return tasks, always subject to the authorization of the host member state, including the use of force and weapons." Council of the European Union, "Press Release: European Border and Coast Guard: Council Agrees Negotiating Position," February 20, 2019, www.consilium.europa.eu/en/press/press-releases/2019/02/20/european-border-and-coast-guard-council-agrees-negotiating-position/.

30. Patrick Kingsley, "On the Road in Agadez: Desperation and Death Along a Saharan Smuggling Route," *The Guardian*, November 9, 2015, www.theguardian.com/world/2015/nov/09/on-the-road-in-agadez-desperation-and-death-along-a-saharan-smuggling-route; Edward McAlister, "Migrants Who Survive Sahara Face New Torture in Libyan Oasis Town," *Reuters*, May 4, 2017, www.reuters.com/article/us-europe-migrants-africa/migrants-who-survive-sahara-face-new-torture-in-libyan-oasis-town-idUSKBN18021C.

31. "Migrants do not simply die in the sea, but through the strategic use of the sea . . . the Mediterranean has been made to kill through contemporary forms of militarized governmentality of mobility which inflict deaths by first creating dangerous conditions of crossing, and then abstaining from assisting those in peril." Charles Heller and Lorenzo Pezzani, "Liquid Traces: Investigating the Deaths of Migrants at the EU's Maritime Border," in *Drift* (New York: Nightboat, 2014), 658–59.

32. International Organization for Migration, "Four Decades of Cross-Mediterranean Undocumented Migration to Europe: A Review of the Evidence," 2017, publications.iom.int/books/four-decades-cross-mediterranean-undocumented-migration-europe-review-evidence.

33. We develop this argument in Anna Carastathis, Aila Spathopoulou, and Myrto Tsilimpounidi, "Crisis, What Crisis? Immigrants, Refugees, and Invisible Struggles," *Refugee: Canada's Journal on Refugees* 34, no. 1 (2018): 29–38.

proach to migration management outlined in 2015 by the European Commission (see chapter 1). This approach embodies a logic, which nevertheless precedes it, of a state of emergency that can only be managed through the institution of a state of exception. "Hotspot logic" refers to the arrogated right of the state to define and divide people into certain categories, such as the refugee, the grantee of subsidiary protection, the asylum seeker, the vulnerable refugee, the unaccompanied minor, the economic migrant, and so on. It might be understood as a technocratic fine-tuning of what Sayad calls "state thought," with respect to the Other side of the line dividing nationals from non-nationals. Hotspot logic exceeds the sociolegal space of hotspot infrastructure, coming to structure not only the hegemonic discourse of the contemporary "refugee crisis" but also our perceptual and affective experience in spaces apparently far removed from the Aegean islands or the Italian ports where it has been implemented. Indeed, following Aila Spathopoulou's analysis of the "mobile hotspot,"[34] we use the word "hotspot" to refer to a representation generated by the hotspot mechanism which spatially exceeds the actual migration management infrastructure and ends up being ascribed to entire islands, cities, and countries. This spatial slippage is naturalized by the mediatized spectacle of the scene of arrival in Lesvos; the whole island (not only the reception, identification, and detention center in the Moria camp) becomes referred to as a "hotspot." Moreover, after the EU–Turkey deal of 2016, and the closure of borders by Balkan and Central European states, Greece as a country is characterized as the "hotspot of Europe,"[35] becoming, like the hotspot infrastructure itself, at first a space of transit and then a space of containment.

In that sense, Lesvos[36] became a mediatized, spectacular space that came to stand almost as a synonym for what is known as "Europe's refugee crisis." At the advent of the crisis, representational frames, through which the space has been reproduced as

---

34. Aila Spathopoulou, "The Ferry as a Mobile Hotspot: Migrants at the Uneasy Borderlands of Greece," Forum: Governing Mobility through the European Union's "Hotspot" Centers, ed. Lauren Martin and Martina Tazzioli, *Society and Space*, November 8, 2016, societyandspace.org/2016/12/15/the-ferry-as-a-mobile-hotspot-migrants-at-the-uneasy-borderlands-of-greece/. See Aila Spathopoulou, "Migrants' Uneven Geographies Within and Against the Hotspot Regime Governing Greece" (PhD diss., Department of Geography, King's College University of London, 2019).

35. Evthymios Papataxiarchis, "Being 'There': At the Front Line of the 'European Refugee Crisis'—Part One," *Anthropology Today* 32, no. 2 (2016): 5–9; Heath Cabot, "Crisis, Hot Spots, and Paper Pushers: A Reflection on Asylum in Greece," *Cultural Anthropology* 28 (June 2016), culanth.org/fieldsights/898-crisis-hot-spots-and-paper-pushers-a-reflection-on-asylum-in-greece.

36. Lesvos was the birthplace of Sappho (c. 630–c. 570 BCE), a lyric poet who praised female beauty and expressed her sexual desire of women in her poems. Sappho became a symbol of female homoeroticism, which is how the island's place name became the English word "lesbian," which means "of Lesvos" or "inhabitant of Lesvos," in the female gender; it then became a "loan word" back into Greek, now with this dual meaning. In contemporary times, Lesbos (spelled with a b) has been the touristic epicenter for lesbians from all over the world. In 2008, some homophobic locals of the island petitioned the Greek government to bar lesbian and gay organizations from using the word to refer to women who desire other women, saying it was an insult to its inhabitants. It is interesting, given the etymology, that this was reported, then, as an issue of borders: who has the right to call themselves a "native" of a place and who is "out of place." See for example, Julie Bindel, "Sun, Sea and Sappho: Should Only Those Born on the Greek Island of Lesbos Be Allowed to Call Themselves Lesbian?," *The Guardian*, May 8, 2008, www.theguardian.com/world/2008/may/08/gayrights.greece.

the site of a state of emergency, focused on boats packed with people arriving on its shores—a transnationally familiar metonym for displacement and refuge. Four years on, as the crisis has given way to technologies of management, the photographers are no longer there to document what the Greek state and the EU seek to keep beyond view: conditions in the detention center in Moria, dubbed the "Guantánamo Bay of Europe"[37] and "the worst refugee camp on earth,"[38] an illegal de facto regime of indefinite, arbitrary incarceration of people in Moria or on the island. The declaration of emergency and the chaos of management chafes against our awareness that the violent mechanisms repressing people's movement to, on, and onward from Lesvos were carefully studied, detailed, and tested. As one Frontex report put it, in an attempt to justify Frontex officers firing over thirty shots into a vessel transport-

---

37. This characterization draws a parallel to the notorious offshore US military prison in the naval base in Guantánamo, Cuba (captured during the Spanish-American War in 1898 and "leased" to the United States in 1903 with no expiration date, an "agreement" that Cubans regard as an instance of US imperialism). It is based on a statement made by Dimitris Avramopoulos, EU migration commissioner, reacting to the proposal of European Council president Donald Tusk, inspired by an earlier suggestion by Hungarian president Viktor Orbán, that the EU create "regional disembarkation platforms" outside the EU, where agencies collaborating with UNHCR and IOM would sort so-called legitimate asylum seekers from economic migrants before they reach EU borders. Avramopoulos's protestations that such a proposal (supported by numerous other European leaders, including French president Emmanuel Macron and Italian foreign minister Enzo Moavero) goes against "European values" are rather performatively contradicted by the EU's implementation of hotspots on the five Aegean islands, inspired by the so-called Pacific Solution: Australian offshore prisons for asylum seekers arriving by boat to its territory, on the island nations of Nauru, Manus Island, and Christmas Island. The only difference is that Samos, Kos, Lesvos, Chios, and Leros are, legally, within Greek territory and are not separate island nation-states. Yet, up until the hotspots opened, Greece's continued membership in the EU and the EMU was under serious question. See Carastathis, Spathopoulou, and Tsilimpounidi, "Migrants, Refugees, and Invisible Struggles." In fact, evincing the tendentiousness of the offshore/onshore distinction, here, a number of journalistic articles have, before and since Avramopoulos's declarations, referred to Lesvos/Moria as the "Guantánamo Bay of Europe," quoting conservative Lesvos mayor Spyros Gallinos and indicating that the scenario officials variously propose or reject is already a reality under the current European Agenda on Migration. See for instance, Al Jazeera English, "Greece's Lesbos: 'Guantanamo Bay of Europe' for Refugees," November 29, 2017, www.aljazeera.com/news/2017/11/greeces-lesbos-guantanamo-bay -europe-refugees-171129134253661.html.

38. This is the title of a documentary aired on BBC and produced by reporter Catrin Nye, who "went inside" Moria during a media blackout enforced by the Greek military, who have authority over the prison camp. The characterization is based on a statement by Luca Fontana, Médicins Sans Frontiers (MSF) coordinator in Lesvos, who says, "Lesvos is the worst place I've been, in my whole life, and in my whole MSF experience; and I've been working in several countries, war zones; I've been working in refugee camps in Central African Republic, in Congo; in the biggest Ebola outbreaks in West Africa in 2014–2015. But I've never seen—ever—the level of suffering we are witnessing here, everyday." BBC News, "The Worst Refugee Camp on Earth," August 28, 2018, www.youtube.com/watch?v=8v-OHi3iGQI. MSF has operated a clinic just outside the camp since 2016, when along with most INGOs and UNHCR withdrew from Moria and the other hotspot camps in protest, as they were turned into detention centers after the implementation of the EU–Turkey deal. "We took the extremely difficult decision to end our activities in Moria because continuing to work inside would make us complicit in a system we consider to be both unfair and inhumane. . . . We will not allow our assistance to be instrumentalized for a mass expulsion operation and we refuse to be part of a system that has no regard for the humanitarian or protection needs of asylum seekers and migrants," said Marie Elisabeth Ingres, MSF Head of Mission in Greece, cited in The Press Project, "UNHCR and NGO's [sic] Withdraw from Greek Islands, Tension Is Rising in Idomeni," *The Press Project*, March 23, 2016, www.thepressproject.gr/article/91468/UNHCR-and-NGOs-withdraw -from-Greek-islands-tension-is-rising-in-Idomeni.

ing refugees across the Aegean passage, they are simply "following the foreseen rules of engagement."[39]

We can take Lesvos as the prime example of the spectacular spatialization of crisis in nation-states, the EU, and the porous borders between them, as well as the place where European migration and asylum policy is enacted. As the island becomes a space that condenses a logic of concentration, detention, and segregation of so-called migrants from so-called refugees (and, of course, from those recognized as citizens and also visiting as tourists)—in other words, as it becomes transformed into a hotspot—its liminality (that is, its in-betweenness, its spatialization of contradictions shaped by the colonial cut) is reshaped by processes of bordering. In this way, Lesvos becomes a site where the relations between Greece and Europe, native and foreigner, citizen and migrant, recognition and abrogation of rights are spectacularly staged.

The dominant narrative of the "refugee crisis" contributes to the process through which "passive" subjects are made of criminalized border crossers; at the same time, it reinforces particular forms of intervention and management based on the logic of militarized humanitarianism.[40] Dominant perceptions and representations of the Other confirm the logic of the hotspot, a necropolitical logic, which performs a cut between those deemed deserving of "protection"—or, more precisely, between "potential refugees" deserving of an audience to a coerced performance justifying their right to remain—and those slated for deportation, subjected to refoulement, or killed in the course of military "engagements" following "foreseen rules." This links migration management ineluctably and nonmetaphorically to other forms of war. In this sense, the hotspot is represented as an administrative-carceral space of management meant to keep "citizens" safe from "terrorists"; local working classes (already suffering their own economic crisis) safe from "bogus asylum seekers," the "illegal economic migrants" who would compete for scarce jobs; European tourists safe from opportunistic African "tourists" or "asylum shoppers." The hotspot reconfigures asylum as a redistributive mechanism of the "scarce good" of citizenship and European privilege.[41] To achieve this, as we argue in the next chapter, the hotspot becomes a space in which the compulsory, performative enactment of vulnerability[42] is required by biopolitical/necropolitical power.

Long before any crisis was declared, the EU reorganized how capital and goods, including human beings, then trafficked as undocumented migrant workers, flowed across these same borders in containers (see chapter 5). Yet, on the surface, the image of the crisis is a temporary interruption of a condition of normality, after which we

---

39. Quoted in Zach Campbell, "Shoot First: Coast Guard Fired at Migrant Boats, European Border Agency Documents Show," *The Intercept*, August 22, 2016, theintercept.com/2016/08/22/coast-guard-fired-at-migrant-boats-european-border-agency-documents-show/.

40. Jennifer Hyndman, *Managing Displacement: Refugees and the Politics of Humanitarianism* (Minneapolis: University of Minnesota Press, 2000).

41. Falguni Sheth, *Toward a Political Philosophy of "Race"* (Albany: State University of New York Press, 2009).

42. See Judith Butler, Zeynep Gambetti, and Leticia Sabsay, *Vulnerability in Resistance* (Durham, NC: Duke University Press, 2016), 5.

imagine that ultimately normality will return.[43] Following this temporal logic, the last decade should count as a unstable period that will inevitably lead back to normality. But this construction of the crisis as a schism in normality that will eventually be bridged requires a systematic forgetting of what preceded it, but also the lending to the present through the managed image a visceral, eviscerating ipseity,[44] the quality of being itself, a temporality that mimics the structure of authentic subjective experience but which, if we have learned anything from Benjamin, its reproducibility sets up for question. In this way, crisis—a political space constituted by reproducible images—can be lived and relived as a moment of political exception, occluding the permanent conditions that are eroding our grasp on liveable lives.

A RIGHT TO THE IMAGE FOR ALL

Yet, one of the unforeseen results of the explosion of images of emergency, unforeseen from the point of view of the state, was still another appearance in the aforementioned cycle of appearances: the emergence of a mass movement defining the referent of these images not, as state thought would have it, as an "influx" of "foreigners" threatening "our" ways of life or our very lives but, rather, as of now, as members of an emergent community, people whom the violence of war had brought to "our doorstep," with whom we wanted "to live together, to struggle together."[45] This way of seeing arguably activated different relationships, not only to people but also to images, which exceeded the attempts of the state to control both the depictions and the plural referents of the crisis: the *eidôlon* of emergency.

According to Barbara Cassin, the Greek words for "image" distinguish between various "functional characteristics": *eikôn* means "similitude," while *phantasma* means "appearance in light"; *typos* refers to "imprint, impression," while *eidôlon*, "derived from the verb meaning 'to see' denotes the image as something visible by which we can see another thing . . . *eidôlon* is both the Platonic *eidos*, 'idea, essence' and 'image, simulacrum.'"[46] The image is the visible trace of the invisible, mediated through representation in its aesthetic and cognitive senses (479). Inherent in the concept of the image and its diverse etymologies is the "tension between production and reproduction" (479). Cassin explains: The tension between the Greek "*phantasia*" and the Latin "*imaginatio*" is the "difference between the creative force of apparitions . . . and the reproductive faculty of images . . . each of these terms also

---

43. Myrto Tsilimpounidi, *Sociology of Crisis: Visualizing Urban Austerity* (London: Routledge, 2017).

44. "Ipseity refers to the definition, to the essence, to the idea whereby a thing is what it is. Plato links the question of ipseity and intelligibility together with the question of the resemblance to the model and to the idea: the two senses of identity are thus joined dialectically; see eidôlon, mimèsis, species." Barbara Cassin, *Dictionary of Untranslatables: A Philosophical Lexicon*, ed. Emily Apter, Jacques Lezra, and Michael Wood, trans. Steven Randall, Christian Hubert, Jeffrey Mehlman, Nathanael Stein, and Michael Syrotinski (Princeton, NJ: Princeton University Press, 2014), 478.

45. Motto of City Plaza, see chapter 6.

46. Cassin, *Dictionary of Untranslatables*, 478; hereafter cited in text.

itself being internally distressed by this tension. . . . Imitation is understood as resemblance, in terms of a pictorial model (and is in that sense associated with image), and sometimes as representation" in terms of a theatrical model (478–79).

Image as *eidôlon* is something visible by which we can see another thing, which is itself invisible to us in the act of representation. Thus, in being present, images—*eidôla*—are marked by a double absence arguably akin to the "double absence" that, following Sayad, we might say marks migrants who are represented as out of place: as reproductions, images are absent from the site of their creation (when the image was produced, or snatched); as representations, images always signify the absence of that which they represent. And, we might add, as signs in a visual economy, they rely for their meaning on the absence of what images do not show us. Although this has become habitual to us in viewing images, the multiple absences that structure the field of the visible betray the productive agencies of various agents through which meaning is made—perhaps most invisibly, the agency of means of mechanical reproduction: the camera itself.

Azoulay has argued that photographic meaning materializes through a "civil contract," and hence photographers, the subjects of photographs, and those who view or "watch" them constitute a "virtual political community."[47] She

> seeks to develop a concept of citizenship through the study of photographic practices and to analyze photography within the framework of citizenship as a status, an institution, and a set of practices. The widespread use of cameras by people around the world has created more than a mass of images; it has created a new form of encounter, an encounter between people who take, watch, and show other people's photographs, with or without their consent, thus opening new possibilities of political action and forming new conditions for its visibility. The relations between the three parties involved in the photographic act—the photographed person, the photographer, and the spectator—are not mediated through a sovereign power and are not limited to the bounds of a nation-state or an economic contract. The users of photography thus reemerge as people who are not totally identified with the power that governs them and who have new means to look at and show its deeds, as well, and eventually to address this power and negotiate with it—citizen and noncitizen alike. (22)

Thus, through the civil contract of photography, "the governed possess a certain power to suspend the gesture of the sovereign power seeking to totally dominate the relations between us, dividing us as governed into citizens and noncitizens" (21). This is what Azoulay refers to as the "citizenry of photography" that brings together the common ground both in the action of photography and in citizenship: recognition. To restore to the image its democratic potential, as Azoulay argues,

---

47. Azoulay, *The Civil Contract of Photography*, 14, 21; hereafter cited in text. Azoulay has said that her engagement with Walter Benjamin "guided [her] first meeting with photography," referring to "the special way in which [Benjamin] read photographs and the place he allocated to the material aspect of photography—from the camera through the photographer's eye-hand relations." See also Ariella Azoulay, *Once Upon a Time: Photography after Walter Benjamin* (Ramat Gan: Bar Ilan University Press, 2006) [in Hebrew].

we must question the terms of our assent to certain meanings and imperatives in a photograph but also to the web of social relations that governs our gaze. The visual, therefore, is subject not only to hegemonic framings that shape public feelings[48] but can also be and is reclaimed as a territory of resistance.[49]

If the state seeks to exercise sovereignty by establishing citizenship through exclusion, thereby territorializing citizenship, photography deterritorializes citizenship (23). The civil contract of photography constitutes a citizenry without sovereignty, without place or borders, without language or unity, beyond, in excess, and in resistance to the homogenizing fantasy of shared, heritable history and tradition (132). State categories always "threaten to circumscribe one's field of vision and, perhaps worse, the boundaries of one's imagination, as well. They threaten to seal the photographs within a protective shield that will turn the photographed people into evidence that something 'was there'" (16). Against this evidentiary, positivist use of photography in conformity with state categories, Azoulay juxtaposes the democratic potential of the photograph: "in the political sphere that is reconstructed through the civil contract, photographed persons are participant citizens, just the same as I am" (17). This does not eliminate the sociolegal divisions between citizens and noncitizens (131); rather, "the photographed individual . . . can become a citizen of photography and yet remain a noncitizen," turning this conflict, embodied in the photograph, "into a complaint" that exposes the naturalized cuts performed by state thought.

The documentary practice of Abounaddara, "a collective of self-taught and volunteer filmmakers involved in emergency cinema"[50] in Syria, asserts "the right to the image for all"[51] in "a regime of representation that drapes itself in the cloak of the universal, invoking freedom while practicing segregation."[52] Against this regime of representation, the Abounaddara Film Collective "sound [their] rallying cry for the world republic of documentary cinema."[53] From a "fiercely anti-geopolitical position,"[54] the anonymous filmmakers that make up the Abounaddara Film Collective intervene in the "unprecedented spectacle" of war in Syria: "never before in history has a crime against humanity been filmed day by day, turned into a spectacle

48. Judith Butler, *Frames of War: When Is Life Grievable* (London: Verso, 2010); Sarah Ahmed, *The Cultural Politics of Emotion* (New York: Routledge, 2004); Ann Cvetkovitch, *An Archive of Feelings* (Durham, NC: Duke University Press, 2003).

49. Jacques Ranciere, *The Emancipated Spectator* (London: Verso, 2009).

50. www.abounaddara.com. The film collective adopts the Arabic "nickname for a man with glasses," inspired by Dziga Vertov's *Man with a Movie Camera* (1929), see vimeo.com/283595357. Infused by the principles of "life as it is" and "life caught unawares," Vertov's documentary practice was influential of the *cinéma verité* school. Similarly, Abounaddara avows as "its first love . . . short and intimate films . . . more interested in stories of everyday life than in grand narratives."

51. Abounaddara Collective, "A Right to the Image for All: A Concept Paper for the Coming Revolution," n.d., www.veralistcenter.org/media/files/24f5ae024cdca7b1ca9c5c572cd14eb4.pdf.

52. Jason Fox and the Abounaddara Film Collective, "Representational Regimes: A Conversation with the Abounaddara Film Collective," *World Records Journal* 1, no. 10 (The Documentary Camera, 2018): 1–7.

53. www.abounaddara.com.

54. Abounaddara, "The Syrian Who Wanted the Revolution," documenta 14, September 2, 2016, originally published in *Al-Hayat Newspaper*, January 30, 2016, www.documenta14.de/en/notes-and -works/1524/the-syrian-who-wanted-the-revolution.

with the cooperation of both victims and executioners, broadcast by the big television networks and streamed on social media, intercut with ad breaks, consumed by the general public, and commodified by the art market."[55] Abounaddara's politics of representation unfold in a suffocatingly narrow space between state-enforced disappearance and spectacular, dehumanizing hypervisibility reproduced as a commodity: once "the regime rendered his or her body absent through death and indefinite detention. . . . How, then, to resurrect the body of the Syrian who is absent, in order to fight for freedom despite the regime, the opposition, and media power?"[56] The double meaning of "regime" as authoritarian governance and as an order or system—in this case, of visual meanings—seems crucial to understanding this predicament, in which their universalist call for "a right to the image for all" intervenes.

> This is not a problem of "negative representations" but rather a regime of representation that flouts the dignity of the weakest and bolsters the dignity of the strongest. What happened in Syria is that cameras were given to people who demanded dignity, while being told: "If you want a place of your own on the screens of the world, if you want recognition, you have no choice but to film your own indignity. For the more stripped of dignity you are, the more the world will look at you and even help you." . . . Certainly, it is possible to resist by producing dignified images. This is what we've been trying to do ourselves for years. But what chance do films like ours have on the screens of the world governed by today's law of blood ("if it bleeds, it leads") and market algorithms?[57]

It is not merely a question of proliferating images from below but a deeper problem concerning how those images, like all images, circulate in a visual economy structured by a regime of representations. Abounaddara's invocation of a "regime of representations" echoes Stuart Hall's theorization of this concept in "The Spectacle of the 'Other.'"[58] Here, Hall poses the question of resistance to a racialized regime of representations which seeks to totalize our visual and perceptual lives. "Can a dominant regime of representation be challenged, contested or changed? What are the counter-strategies which can begin to subvert the representation process?" (269). He identifies three counterstrategies of "transcoding": reversing stereotypes (270–72), countering negative with positive images (272–74), and contesting the form of representation from within rather than introducing new content (274–76). Yet, Hall and Abounaddara each emphasize that the problem of resistance in the field of the visual is not reducible to supplanting "negative images" with "positive" representations,[59] but,

---

55. Abounaddara, "Regarding the Spectacle: What Happens When a Society No Longer Has the Ability to Defend Itself Against Post-Truth," *The Nation*, December 2, 2016, www.thenation.com/article/regarding-the-spectacle/.

56. Fox and the Abounaddara Film Collective, "Representational Regimes."

57. Fox and the Abounaddara Film Collective, "Representational Regimes."

58. Stuart Hall, "The Spectacle of the 'Other,'" *Representation: Cultural Representations and Signifying Practices*, ed. Stuart Hall (London/Thousand Oaks: Sage/The Open University, 1997).

59. See Abounaddara, collectif de cinéastes syriens, "Ne réduisons pas les Syriens aux images diffusées par la télé: Les médias européens travestissent la réalité syrienne en montrant trop peu les gens ordinaires, pour ne s'intéresser qu'au spectacle de la violence," *Le Monde*, October 21, 2014, www.lemonde.fr/idees/article/2014/10/21/au-dela-de-bachar-et-des-djihadistes-une-autre-syrie-existe_4509917_3232.html;

rather, to expose the rules that regulate the production, reproduction, circulation, and consumption of images as indispensable to, and indeed inseparable from, contemporary forms of rule and power. Or, as Abounaddara more succinctly states: "Images of war are images that wage war."[60]

> The images of the human debris of human madness are too frequently about mutilated and starved bodies, not about persons; they are too frequently images of the dystopian landscapes of wretched camps and the ruins of devastated neighborhoods and not images of the network of social relations and forms of collective cultural and political life that sustains individuals in their struggle for life in dignity and peace. . . . Individuals can "own" their image if they are legally, and by virtue of social conventions, economic power, or political circumstances empowered to speak. But what about those who cannot speak? The persons whose humanity is suppressed in images from wars . . . are not allowed to speak. Their humanity stops at the rights of bystanders to freedom of expression. You can have the dignity of a person or be a victim, but you are not allowed to be both; and, most importantly, you are not legally allowed to choose what you want to be. Your wounds can speak, but you cannot.[61]

The right to the image for all, as Abounaddara parses it, is not merely derived from the right to privacy or the right to freedom of expression but rather constitutes "a bundle of rights," "as much implicit in the right to self-determination [and] . . . political association" as in rights to privacy or speech.[62] With short films, released on its website every Friday, and in longer format, such as their film *Syria: Snapshots of History in the Making* (2014),[63] Abounaddara addresses a virtual political community based on a right to the image for all, reasserting a citizenry of photography and grounding its political claim on the Universal Declaration of Human Rights and other covenants.[64]

ALL PHOTOGRAPHS ARE REFUGEES

But can citizenship be rehabilitated through photography, as Azoulay argues and as Abounaddara's documentary practice attests? And does photography offer a model

---

Collectif Abounaddara, "En Syrie, refusons la fable d'un 'Orient compliqué': À l'heure où les dirigeants peinent à s'entendre sur le dossier syrien, un collectif de cinéastes du pays appelle à une intervention au nom de notre commune humanité," *Le Monde*, September 25, 2013, www.lemonde.fr/proche-orient/article/2013/09/25/en-syrie-refusons-la-fable-d-un-orient-complique_3483268_3218.html.

60. Abounaddara Collective, paraphrasing Serge Daney in Fox and the Abounaddara Film Collective, "Representational Regimes." See Serge Daney, "Before and After the Image," trans. Melissa McMahon, *Discourse* 21, no. 1 (1999): 181–90.

61. Abounaddara Collective, "A Right to the Image for All."

62. Abounaddara Collective, "A Right to the Image for All."

63. vimeo.com/87259134.

64. Including the International Covenant on Civil and Political Rights and the International Covenant of Economic, Social, and Cultural Rights. Abounaddara Collective, "A Right to the Image for All." See also the Abounaddara Collective, ed. *The Question of the Right to the Image*, with Katarina Nitsch, Damascus, 2019 [in Arabic], kkh.diva-portal.org/smash/record.jsf?pid=diva2%3A1301510&dswid=5065.

for a notion and practice of an unbordered citizenship beyond nation-states? By way of answering this question, we juxtapose Cadava's reflection that "every image is a kind of refugee."[65] Contemplating the European refugee crisis, in this provocative statement, he stresses that it is not incidental that photography is one of the most privileged ways of representing the refugee crisis. That is because every photograph, in its own right, is itself a refugee. As he explains, "every photograph turns into a refugee what is photographed": the subject depicted becomes by being photographed the subject of an image circulating in the world of representations, thus leaving its original scene of production. But, as we have seen, photography as a medium that depends ontologically on reproduction renders the notion of an origin suspect. Indeed, as Azoulay argues, the photograph is not "completed the moment one picks up a camera, points the lens toward something, and 'takes a picture.'"[66] If the photograph is, in one sense, the outcome of "focus, excision, and framing" (158) or, more reductively, the opening and closing of the aperture, these do not complete the photographic relation even if they might constitute the bare description of the photographic act.

The photograph has the potential to disrupt the nationalist-cum-fascist imaginary of authentic homelands peopled by autochthonous, pure "races." "What makes a photograph a photograph is its ability to wander, often far from the time and place where it was produced," states Cadava, referring to what he terms "the wandering languages of photography": the diverse routes through which photographs travel through historical periods, national borders, and different means.[67] The mass reproduction of images enunciating crisis requires the development of "a visual and linguistic code to understand their nomadic character and the ability to intervene in their mobility and displacement." Echoing the relationship between reproduction and production in Benjamin, Cadava suggests that recognizing the nomadic character of photographs may also help us in the way we perceive the displacement and migration of people. The displacement inherent in photography reveals something important about the photography of displacement.

All photographs simultaneously capture memory and oblivion, survival and destruction, preservation and loss. A photograph, at one and the same time, reduces and augments the distance between those who view it and what is being held in view. Today, we are overwhelmed by a "flood of photographs," a flood that "betrays indifference to the meaning of things"[68] even as it is taken as the evidence of what was there. This predicament is redoubled in an age when "our political, ethical, and intimate lives are constructed around images, through images, and in

65. Cadava made this comment during the MedPhoto Festival 2018 in Athens, which had as one of its central themes representations of the refugee crisis. His analysis is published in Greek in the newspaper *Efsyn* and is translated here by the authors. For the full interview please see Dimitri Kexri, "'Every Photograph Is a Kind of Refugee': Interview with Eduardo Cadava," *Efsyn*, May 27, 2018 [in Greek], www .efsyn.gr/arthro/kathe-fotografia-einai-ena-eidos-prosfyga.
66. Azoulay, *The Civil Contract of Photography*, 137; hereafter cited in text.
67. Cadava, quoted in Kexhri, "'Every Photograph Is a Kind of Refugee.'"
68. Siegfried Kracauer, cited in Cadava, quoted in Kexhri, "'Every Photograph Is a Kind of Refugee.'"

images"—indeed, around, through, and in "images referring to images."[69] While history is often understood as a series of events "worth photographing,"[70] paradoxically the visual economy of representations may function to dehistoricize our present and indeed compel a kind of collective forgetting. As Siegfried Kracauer, on whom Cadava relies to develop this argument, writes,

> the flood of photos sweeps away the dams of memory. The assault of this mass of images is so powerful that it threatens to destroy the potentially existing awareness of crucial traits. Artworks suffer this fate through their reproductions . . . rather than coming into view through the reproductions, it tends to disappear in its multiplicity and to live on as art photography. In the illustrated magazines people see the very world that the illustrated magazines prevent them from perceiving. The spatial continuum from the camera's perspective predominates the spatial appearance of the perceived object; the likeness that the image bears to it effaces the contours of the object's "history." Never before has a period known so little about itself.[71]

Photography works through this ambivalence: on the one hand, photographs "have a contractual standing that is presumed to ensure a clear, sharp, legible, decipherable, and true image, such that what 'was there' in front of the camera lens, was also really 'there.'"[72] On the other hand, photography "borders on the deceptive": "not because anyone has manipulated it, or allowed the conditions of its production to be sabotaged, but because, despite the fact that it is an énoncé within a discourse, it is only a single component in a sentence . . . that tends to conduct itself in the world on its own, independently, as though it carried its truth on its back" (315).

A photograph, Azoulay and Cadava argue, is never just the image of what we see depicted on its surface—not only because the flat, two-dimensional surface of a photograph carries the traces of an entire network of relations which it nevertheless does not make immediately visible but also because it fails—it cannot but fail, and exists in virtue of its failure—to make what it depicts immediately visible, even if our perception has been trained to trust photographs:

> Under the conditions that subsist on the verge of catastrophe . . . the hit parade of horrors threatens the visibility of any referent. Even under other conditions, however, the referent of photography is not given or self-evident. Photography's appearance on the stage of history, which facilitated the conquest of the world as spectacle, created new conditions for the gaze. Looking at photographs gave rise to the "identificatory gaze" based on the discriminating gesture that determines "this is X" or "this is Y." The identificatory gaze performs a twofold reification—for what is seen in the photograph and for its meaning. . . . This reification is not an essential element of the

---

69. Abounaddara, "A Right to the Image for All."

70. Hani Sayed, "The Right to the Image" (lecture delivered at Abounaddara, Vera List Center for Art and Politics, October 24, 2015), www.veralistcenter.org/engage/events/1977/abounaddara-the-right-to-the-image/.

71. Siegfried Kracauer, "Photography," trans. Thomas Y. Levin, *Critical Inquiry* 19, no. 3 (1993): 432.

72. Azoulay, *The Civil Contract of Photography*, 155; hereafter cited in text.

medium, but a specific dimension of the gaze that came to be dominant with the advent of photography.[73]

In that sense, there is always more to and less in a photograph than what we can see depicted on its surface. "The photograph does not exist in its own right . . . photography is a projective surface that never discloses anything in itself," writes Azoulay (311). Contrary to the presumption of the identificatory gaze, not only what a photograph means (what it signifies) but also what it shows (its referent) is "given for negotiation" (311). Azoulay argues that "the civil contract of photography binds us in a commitment to the referent of photography" (315); she urges us to take responsibility for the projective gaze through which we view photographs, displacing affects onto them and disavowing those affects as our own (309).

Like the photograph, the category of "the refugee" is the product of multiple displacements and disavowals. Displacement does not consist in simply being removed from where one "authentically" or "originally" belongs; it rather consists in never being allowed to find oneself in place, finding "no direction home."[74] Indeed, the anxious assignment of national origin as the turning point of asylum/deportation procedure in the hotspot betrays the disavowal of responsibility for displacement of everyone denied stay under the identificatory gaze of adjudicators. The purported self-evidence of "race," gender, and age on the body—which is also searched and scrutinized for signs of its having undergone torture and its inclinations towards terrorism—is read for the same truth that the photograph is thought to carry on its back. Not only the reification of what is seen but also what it means dominates the spectacle of the crisis.

WRITING WITH LIGHT

Our ability to think about, describe, and study the social world is inextricably linked with the act of looking. As evident in the etymology of the Greek word *theoria*, theory is the establishment of a point of view and analysis within a wider interrelationship of events.[75] This lexical etymology reminds us that "the way that we think about the way that we think in Western culture is guided by a visual paradigm. Looking, seeing and knowing have become perilously intertwined."[76] This brings to mind John Berger's famous comment that "seeing comes before words . . . and establishes our place in the surrounding world."[77] But it also conjures the distinction Serge Daney

---

73. Azoulay, *The Civil Contract of Photography*, 306–7; hereafter cited in text.

74. Electra Alexandropoulou and Erifili Arapoglou, eds., *No Direction Home* (Athens: Rosa Luxemburg Stiftung, 2016).

75. Our approach is closely related with the Writing in Light collective that focuses mainly on photoessays "in the belief that multimodal (visual) forms are not a singular paradigm and that a consideration of a singular research form might help us to rethink a broader array of anthropological questions." For more, see societyforvisualanthropology.org/writing-with-light/.

76. Chris Jenks, *Visual Culture* (London: Routledge, 1995), 1.

77. John Berger, *Ways of Seeing* (London: Penguin, 1977), 7.

makes between the image and the visual, a distinction he states is both "necessary" and "entirely pragmatic": "The visual is both reading and seeing: it is seeing what is given to be read . . . and less and less to see" while the image is "what still relies upon an experience of vision." The visual, according to Daney, is "the optical verification of a procedure of power," while the "condition sine qua non for there to be an image is . . . *alterity*."[78] The illegibility of the image—its radical alterity—contrasts with the "verification of the functioning" of the visual.[79]

There is a fundamental connection between images and our being in the world, our understanding of the Self, the Other, and our surroundings. With the rapid expansion of digital technologies, and the ubiquity of cameras, the omnipresence of mediated experiences is undeniable. In this culture of hypervisualization, almost every part of our daily experiences is always already mediated. Pierre Bourdieu and Loïc Wacquant argue that, observing the social world, we introduce in our description of it a "theoreticist" or "intellectualist" bias.[80] This bias consists in forgetting to inscribe into theories we build of the social world the fact that it is the product of a theoretical gaze, a "contemplative eye."[81] Les Back argues that there is always some kind of relationship between "portrayal and betrayal":[82] the fluidity, complexity, and irreducible alterity of the "real world" cannot easily be captured in a representation. This is not a claim to abandon analysis and the representation of real life but rather to re-examine the limitations of modes of writing as representation. Or, to move away from the scholarly hubris which suggests that research objectively and accurately grasps social realities and offers neat solutions to be implemented as policy. This book, as we state in the introduction, is our deliberate attempt to create policy-irrelevant research.

For us, writing with light is praxis, refusing the division between contemplation and action. The theoretical gaze, with all the betrayals that it entails, is not a mere metaphor. Theory is indebted to vision, to images, and specifically to photography. While the commonplace view of photographs is that they present a true image of what appeared before the lens, what was really there, we are more interested in us-

---

78. Daney, "Before and After the Image," 181–82, emphasis in original.

79. Daney, "Before and After the Image," 185.

80. Pierre Bourdieu and Loïc Wacquant, *An Invitation to Reflexive Sociology* (Oxford: Blackwell, 1992), 69.

81. Bourdieu took many pictures during his fieldwork in the Algerian war of independence from France (1955–1959). Bourdieu served in the French army for a year and then was transferred to clerical work, yet throughout his stay in Algeria he conducted extensive fieldwork. Reflecting on his early field studies in Algeria during the war of liberation at the end of the 1950s, Bourdieu explained: "to see, to record, to photograph: I have never accepted the separation between the theoretical construction of the object of research and the set of practical procedures without which there can be no real knowledge." Bourdieu's early struggle with the position of the academic in times of war and conflict became the central trope of his ethics and attachment to the social world. Bourdieu's photographs from the Algerian war were part of his commitment to the representation of the crimes of colonialism. At the same time, as suggested by his diaries during the period of the Algerian war, the camera was the recording device that could register affects and traces which were difficult to capture otherwise. Interestingly, Bourdieu never really talked about or published his photographs from the Algerian war until late in his life, when he was convinced by Franz Schultheis to publish a book with them. The book was published after his death.

82. Les Back, "Portrayal and Betrayal: Bourdieu, Photography and the Sociological Life," *The Sociological Review* (August 1, 2009), doi.org/10.1111/j.1467-954X.2009.01850.x.

ing *photographia* to interrupt the cycle of appearances that reproduce the notion of events as factically occurring in a determinate space and time. We do not enter, here, into a debate about what comes first, images or words, realities or representations. This is the wrong question, since the binary distinctions on which it rests are barely sustainable. Rather, we seek a space where writing cannot take form without light, and light alone is not enough to guide us in our struggle for words. Writing with light, then, reveals our deep belief that there is space for resistance, a space that urgently needs to be reclaimed through the interwoven layers of the reproduction of words and images.

Perhaps this explains why we feel uneasy with the canonical theoretical attack on photographs. Susan Sontag's *On Photography* has been immensely influential in the ways we think and talk about images and photography. Sontag's fierce and elegant essay, "In Plato's Cave," which opens the book, refers to the Platonic allegory of the cave, in which prisoners confined their entire lives to a cave cannot but mistake shadows cast by objects for the objects themselves. The famous allegory appears in Book VII of *The Republic*, where Plato stages a dialogue between Socrates and Glaucon. Socrates asks Glaucon to "imagine" a cave in which prisoners, "shackled by the legs and neck," have been confined since childhood, unable to move or turn their heads "so that there is only one thing for them to look at: whatever they encounter in front of their faces." A fire burns behind them, obstructed by a wall but casting a glow. A walkway formed by the wall obscures people carrying things, which cast shadows projected on the wall opposite the prisoners by the glow of the fire. The shadows on the wall they face are the only things the prisoners see. Yet, having never seen the people behind them, they believe the shadows to be the things themselves rather than the reflections of things in the light: "those who were chained would consider nothing besides the shadows of the artifacts as the unhidden," concludes Socrates, and Glaucon agrees: "That would absolutely have to be."[83]

In effect, the prisoners in the cave are seeing reflections of reality, mistaking them for reality itself. In her essay, Sontag argues that images are just that: "mere images of the truth."[84] Ironically, though, the device that Plato has Socrates use to convince Glaucon of human beings' ignorance and philosophers' enlightenment, upon breaking the shackles and ultimately exiting the cave (gaining access to the realm of the forms), is allegory—more specifically, a visual metaphor to reveal a hidden meaning about reality. Through the visual metaphor of the cave—an image about images—Glaucon traverses the supposedly impassable terrain separating imagination (images) from truth (reality).

Sontag continues her attack on photography in "In Plato's Cave" by arguing that images of suffering corrupt the human capacity for compassion, since "images anesthetize" (20). Moreover, "to photograph people is to violate them, by seeing them as they never see themselves" (14); "a camera is a sublimation of the gun, to

---

83. Plato, "The Allegory of the Cave." *Republic* VII, 514a2–517a7, trans. Thomas Sheehan. Accessed October 7, 2019, https://web.stanford.edu/class/ihum40/cave.pdf.
84. Susan Sontag, *On Photography* (New York: Picador, 1977), 3; hereafter cited in text.

photograph someone is a subliminal murder—a soft murder, appropriate to a sad, frightened time" (14–15). "When we are afraid, we shoot. But when we are nostalgic, we take pictures" (14). Images are, in her view, an "irresistible form of mental pollution"(18), "imperial" (5), "predatory" (14), "voyeuristic" (7), and "the act of taking pictures is a semblance of appropriation, a semblance of rape" (24). "Never ethical or political," she writes, "the knowledge gained through still photographs will always be some kind of sentimentalism, whether cynical or humanist" (24). "Citizens" under the thrall of photography are transformed into "image-junkies" (24). We are compelled as by an addiction to take photographs: "to turn experience itself into a way of seeing" (24).

Sontag's attack on photography has established a school of critical thinking around the medium which *a priori* examines images with a certain hostility. In *Camera Lucida*, Roland Barthes describes images as "matte and somehow stupid,"[85] "without culture and without future,"[86] as the "agent of Death,"[87] and as "undialectical."[88] Barthes insists that there is nothing he can learn from a photograph, as it "de-realizes the human world of conflicts and desires."[89] What makes two of the most influential thinkers on photography attack photography with such force? Arguably, it is their commitment to a latent realism, "a stable meaning for what is visible" in a photograph, which reduces "the role of the spectator to the act of judgment, eliminating his or her responsibility for what is seen in the photograph."[90] Sontag and Barthes establish a paradigm in which any critical thinking on photography should arise from an *a priori* intellectual hostility to photographic images.[91] Azoulay writes, of postmodern theorists of photography, that bearing "witness to a glut of images [they] fall prey to a kind of 'image fatigue'"; their theoretical accounts urge us to "stop looking."[92] "The world filled up with images of horrors, and they loudly proclaimed that viewers' eyes had grown unseeing," but does that absolve us of "the responsibility to hold onto the elementary gesture of looking at what is presented to one's gaze"?[93]

Abigail Solomon-Godeau, for example, talks about the "double act of subjugation," in which the first act of subjugation takes place in the social world and the conflicts that have produced the "victims," while the second act occurs "in the regime of the image produced within and for the same system that engenders the conditions it then re-presents."[94] Undoubtedly, Solomon-Godeau is raising very important issues

---

85. Roland Barthes, *Camera Lucida: Reflections on Photography* (New York: Hill and Wang, 1980), 4.

86. Barthes, *Camera Lucida*, 90.

87. Barthes, *Camera Lucida*, 92. Barthes refers to photographers as agents of death: "All those young photographers who are at work in the world, determined upon the capture of actuality, do not know that they are agents of Death."

88. Barthes, *Camera Lucida*, 90.

89. Barthes, *Camera Lucida*, 116.

90. Azoulay, *The Civil Contract of Photography*, 129.

91. For more on this, please see Susie Linfield, *The Cruel Radiance: Photography and Political Violence* (Chicago: University of Chicago Press, 2010), 3–31.

92. Azoulay, *The Civil Contract of Photography*, 10.

93. Azoulay, *The Civil Contract of Photography*, 10.

94. Abigail Solomon-Godeau, *Photography at the Dock: Essays on Photographic History, Institutions and Practices* (Minneapolis: University of Minnesota Press, 1991), 176.

about hegemonic representations of "victims" and the power of the regime of representation—especially in terms of reproducing the prevailing status quo. Yet, in our argument about writing with light, there is not one act (the violence) that came first, the other (the image of the violence) following suit as a trace, reflection, or echo. The "double act of subjugation," if it is happening, is happening simultaneously: "images of war are images that wage war."[95] Moreover, the photograph—understood not as a stable site of self-evident meaning but as "a projective surface that never discloses anything in itself"[96]—does not always by depicting subjugation simply reproduce it. Conversely, a photograph that does not depict violence explicitly may have violence as its referent. The question, indeed, arises, whether the "threat of violation" does not "*always* hang . . . over the photographic act,"[97] even if it is especially acute in cases where the photographed person captured in an image has been refused any other means to self-representation.

Thus, the question we are struggling with in undertaking a practice of writing with light, or *photographìa*, in a time of permanent war and displacement, is the following: Is it possible to understand our relation to photographs depicting "the pain of others"[98] as involving not only responses of guilt or compassion, indifference or apathy, but a more complex schema of political relationships? And if so, what would that political relationship look like? Social structures, ideological apparatuses, and phenomenological conditions are the light in the darkroom of history which is captured by photography. Photographs, especially photographs of violence and conflict, have the capacity to evoke strong sensory and affective reactions. Perhaps this is what causes an *a priori* hostility of critical thinkers to photography, the unsettling capacity of images to evoke feelings.[99]

When the television news showed the US-NATO bombings of Belgrade, we remember we saw for the first time before the "hit parade"[100] of still images and videos of the war a warning flash across the screen, which read: "What follows contains graphic content, it is advisable not to leave children in the room." Yet, in the verbal analysis of the same event, no one felt compelled to warn viewers, and in particular parents, to take the same measures to remove their children from earshot. Perhaps this is because words depicting the horrors of war are not considered violent?[101] Images shock where words fail to? In fact, the word "graphic," which alludes to the force of the image, implies that words do not have the same capacity as do images to be striking, disturbing, or violent, even when relating acts and experiences of violence.

---

95. Abounaddara Collective, paraphrasing Serge Daney, in Fox and the Abounaddara Film Collective, "Representational Regimes."

96. Azoulay, *The Civil Contract of Photography*, 311.

97. Azoulay, *The Civil Contract of Photography*, 118–19, emphasis added; see also 390.

98. Susan Sontag, *Regarding the Pain of Others* (New York: Picador, 2003).

99. See Linfield, *The Cruel Radiance*, 5–31.

100. Azoulay, *The Civil Contract of Photography*, 306.

101. The practice of giving trigger warnings to readers and audiences of spoken word or written text describing situations of violence, based on the assumption that hearing or reading such descriptions could be retraumatizing to survivors of such violence, may indicate that this attitude has shifted in recent years.

Or, perhaps, this is a sign of the collective assumption that images depict realities, whereas words only refer to them.

Following this commonplace logic, one could claim that words are treated as nonrepresentational and nonimagistic, since words are not treated as shocking depictions, even when they describe the horrors of war and displacement. Or perhaps we tolerate, and to a certain extent fail to recognize, verbal violence because it leaves no visible signs of the violence enacted. "Seeing is believing," after all. The flip side of this logic considers images to be anti-theoretical, especially the ones produced in moments of crisis and conflict. If theory is the establishment of a point of view and analysis within a wider interrelationship of events, depictions of war usually disrupt our capacity to take a point of view.[102] Yet, we argue that images are anti-theoretical only when we contemplate the image of the thinker as someone who establishes a point of view by comfortably sitting while pondering on the mysteries and perplexities of our social worlds. Perhaps this particular visualization of the thinker is in itself anti-theoretical, this cruel radiance of this distant observer and the hard structures of academic institutions that reproduce compartmentalized ways of seeing, knowing, thinking, and feeling the world from a certain seated (and privileged) position. Instead, through the methodology of *photographìa*, we want to challenge this depiction, echoing Sara Ahmed's argument in *Queer Phenomenology*,[103] in which she suggests that we can begin inhabiting a perspective with a body that loses its chair, a body that is not at ease and at home in the world, a body that inhabits borderlands. It is through living in, and living with, such bodies that we attempt to see depictions in words and at the same time to make images speak.[104]

In collaboration with photographer Paul Halliday, Les Back explores how photography might widen understandings of the "real" by "listening with a wider range of senses."[105] Their work draws on Merleau-Ponty's argument against separations of mind and body, subjects and objects inherent in Cartesian dualisms, and they make a compelling argument for Merleau-Ponty's understanding of intertwining.[106] For Merleau-Ponty, "the look" does not produce distance between the viewer and the looked-upon. Rather the look produces a connection, or, to use their words, this process of intertwining occurs at the moment when the seer and the visible are connected.[107] It is made on the stage of everyday life, but it also possesses a specific relationship to time. In that fraction of a second when the aperture of the camera

102. Sontag, *On Photography*; Aylwyn Walsh and Myrto Tsilimpounidi, "Virtues of Violence: A Testimonial Performance or an Affidavit of Lies, Excuses, Justifications," *Cultural Studies—Critical Methodologies* 15, no. 3 (2014): 1–10.

103. Sara Ahmed, *Queer Phenomenology: Orientation, Objects, Others* (Durham, NC: Duke University Press, 2006), 53.

104. As Ariella Azoulay puts it, "It is our historic responsibility, not only to produce photos, but to make them speak." (2008), 122.

105. Les Back and Paul Halliday, "Inscriptions of Love," in *Cultural Bodies: Ethnography and Theory*, ed. H. Thomas and J. Ahmed (Oxford: Blackwell, 2004), 33.

106. Maurice Merleau-Ponty, *The Visible and the Invisible* (London: Routledge, 1968/2004).

107. Back and Halliday, "Inscriptions of Love," 27–55.

opens, a tiny slice of time is preserved in which the relationship between the viewer and the looked-upon is caught, albeit the time-lapse, and is held in place.[108]

As such, the method of *photographìa*, the material trace of writing/*grafì* with light/*phos*, becomes an important method for capturing, invoking, and analyzing all the messiness and complexity of our social worlds. Photographs are invaluable in that they have the capacity to invoke the multimodality of these worlds. Images reveal the unspoken, the unspeakable, the unsaid—not only the things we cannot speak about because they are forbidden, unacceptable, or unthinkable but also, and perhaps most importantly, those things that cannot be said because they are registered in the spectrum of action, embodiment, performance, affect. Writing with light is an attempt to go beyond stereotypical dualities, in a space where words affect our ways of seeing and images our ways of knowing, showing how in fact the visual and the discursive are mutually constitutive. As such, *photographìa* exposes the logocentricity of philosophical approaches that reduce all knowledge to text, while forgetting the sensory, the embodied, and the affective debts of knowledge forged in and about conditions of violence, loss, grief, and mourning. In bearing witness to such conditions, the eye is not only "the organ that sees, but the organ that weeps."[109]

The United Nations Secretary General regularly urges photojournalists to produce more images, particularly of atrocities that seem to exist in silence and demand urgent action.[110] Of course, some crises are more photogenic than others. Many years ago, Vilém Flusser argued that our imagination had been turned into hallucination: photographs "are supposed to be maps but they turn into screens."[111] Images, generally, are mediations between the world and human beings; they harness the power of imagination, which is the ability to abstract surfaces out of the three dimensions of space and time to the two surface dimensions, and vice versa.[112] What we aspire to achieve with *photographìa* in this book is not to circulate more images of the declared refugee crisis, but rather to question how images make up a "global image scenario," as Flusser puts it, "magically restructuring our 'reality'" and leading us to forget we created the images.[113] If we are to return to the potential of photography to act as a map, a map rich in revealing surfaces, social relations, normative affects, hegemonic ideologies, and political structures, we first have to change our relationship to our own lived experience. A *photographìa* reminds us that *we create the images*. The deeper

---

108. Back and Halliday, "Inscriptions of Love," 34.

109. Veena Das, *Life and Words: Violence and the Descent into the Ordinary* (Los Angeles: University of California Press, 2007), 62.

110. Roland Bleiker, *Visual Global Politics* (London: Routledge, 2018), 1.

111. Vilém Flusser, *Towards a Philosophy of Photography* (London: Reaktion Books, 1983/2000). According to Flusser, "human beings ex-ist, i.e. the world is not immediately accessible to them," and so images mediate this distance. Even though photographs—as images—have the potential to represent the world, their mechanical reproduction means that "images come between the world and human beings. . . . Instead of representing the world, they obscure it, until human beings' lives finally become a function of the images they create. Human beings cease to decode the images and instead project them, still encoded, into the world 'out there,' which meanwhile itself becomes like an image—a context of scenes, of states of things."

112. Flusser, *Towards a Philosophy of Photography*, 8.

113. Flusser, *Towards a Philosophy of Photography*, 10.

struggle is to return to the visual dimension of our lived experience its immediacy, to try to experience it in its immediacy without the images that mediate it, to see instead of always looking, or gazing, or looking past.

The remaining chapters of this book are structured around objects that became visual tropes and shortcuts in representations of the European refugee crisis, reproducing the refugee as the Other of the citizen. Each chapter constitutes a visual essay, a *photographia*, in order to attempt to engage in an act of collective *seeing*, unravelling the dimensions of time, movement, and stasis that exist in the still images of the visual essays. Our method is based on writing with light even as we often struggle to find a glimmer of illumination in these global nights of rising fascism and deepening xenophobia. We stage these acts of collective *seeing*, because it is our belief that the only way to grasp this light is in its reflections in multiple eyes.

"Digital-Reproduction"
Photograph by Myrto Tsilimpounidi.

"Writing with Light"
Photograph by Myrto Tsilimpounidi.

3

Life Jackets

The UN High Commissioner for Refugees observed recently, "At times, it even seems that refugees have become a commodity, traded between states."[1] Our point of entry to examine the commodification of refugees in this chapter is the concept of commodity fetishism. In capitalism, social relations appear as relations between things;[2] they acquire a "phantom objectivity."[3] Extending Karl Marx's argument about commodity fetishism—subjects appear as objects, and objects as subjects—Walter Benjamin articulates how our desire to grasp objects is mediated by reproductions: "every day the urge grows stronger to get hold of an object at very close range by way of its likeness, its reproduction."[4] But reproductions are not always likenesses: sometimes images reproduce objects that stand in for referents that are not immediately, explicitly, or obviously depicted in them.

Although we most often assume that representation, particularly representation of human beings, occurs through the reproduction of their likeness—such as a portrait—there is a second sense of representation on which we focus in this chapter: the proxy. In her seminal essay, "Can the Subaltern Speak?" Gayatri Chakravorty Spivak argues that if we are to account for the "micrological texture of power" that constitutes our subjectivities under global capitalism, we must attend to this

1. Filippo Grandi, "Opening Statement at the 68th Session of the Executive Committee of the High Commissioner's Programme," United Nations High Commission on Refugees, October 2, 2017, www.unhcr.org/admin/hcspeeches/59d1f3b77/opening-statement-68th-session-executive-committee-high-commissioners-programme.html.

2. Karl Marx, *Capital: A Critique of Political Economy, Vol. I*, trans. Ben Fowkes (London: Penguin/New Left Review, 1867/1976), 163.

3. György Lukács, *History and Class Consciousness: Studies in Marxist Dialectics*, trans. Rodney Livingstone (Cambridge, MA: MIT Press, 1920/1971), 83.

4. Walter Benjamin, "The Work of Art in the Age of Mechanical Reproduction," in *Illuminations*, ed. Hannah Arendt, trans. Harry Zohn (New York: Schocken Books, 1969), 5.

double meaning of representation.[5] Representation is simultaneously a political and a perceptual-cognitive-aesthetic practice. In the first sense, Spivak tells us, representation is "a speaking for," a proxy or substitution (*Vertreten*); in the second sense, representation is "re-presentation, as in art or philosophy," a portrait (*Darstellen*) (275). The two senses of representation are "related but irreducibly discontinuous," Spivak writes (275). And she enjoins us: "The complicity-in-difference of *Vertreten* and *Darstellen*, their identity-in-difference as the place of practice . . . is precisely what [we] must expose" (275). If we are to understand how macrologies of power are congealed through the "micrological and often erratic" (279) process of subject formation, then we must attend to the relationship between these two "irreducible" yet "complicit" senses of representation (275). The reference to "exposure" in Spivak's text makes us think that the complicity of the portrait and the proxy can be illuminated through producing, reproducing, and watching photographs: exposure, in photography, is a function of shutter speed, lens aperture, and lighting at the scene. An exposure is also a single shutter cycle, the process of the shutter opening, closing, and resetting—ready to open again.

In this chapter, we follow the circulation of an object, the life jacket, and images of this object in a visual economy wherein it has come to be branded as a proxy for refugees. The life jackets worn by people arriving in Lesvos and other shores in the Mediterranean have come to figure prominently in documentary photography, installation art, social media campaigns, solidarity protests, and charity gala events. As life jackets are reproduced as a visual shortcut for refugees, a metonymic relation between the proxy object and its referent emerges. The fetishization of the life jacket—its homogenization, substitution, and erasure of the subjects it is meant to signify—mirrors the reification of social relations embodied in the regime of borders, in the bodies of those forced to cross them clandestinely. Following this object and reproductions of it around enables us to glimpse the political economy of war. Our argument in this chapter thus builds upon critiques of "categorial fetishism":[6] despite their relegation to the noneconomic, we argue that "refugees" reproduce and are reproduced in economies dominated by the commodity form.

As life jackets travel beyond the scene of arrival—often crossing several borders their erstwhile wearers are denied the right to cross—their material is upcycled into commodities, such as fashionable shoulder bags, by social entrepreneurs. Activists and artists dump them in front of government buildings, or decorate public monu-

---

5. Gayatri Chakravorty Spivak, "Can the Subaltern Speak?," in *Marxism and the Interpretation of Culture*, ed. Cary Nelson and Lawrence Grossberg (Urbana: University of Illinois Press, 1988), 279; hereafter cited in text.

6. Raia Apostolova, "Of Refugees and Migrants: Stigma, Politics, and Boundary Work at the Borders of Europe," American Sociological Association Culture Section, September 14, 2015, asaculturesection.org/2015/09/14/of-refugees-and-migrants-stigma-politics-and-boundary-work-at-the-borders-of-europe/; Heaven Crawley and Dimitris Skleparis, "Refugees, Migrants, Neither, Both: Categorical Fetishism and the Politics of Bounding in Europe's 'Migration Crisis,'" *Journal of Ethnic and Migration Studies* (2017), dx.doi.org/10.1080/1369183X.2017.1348224. Extending our argument in chapter 1, we would contend that the binary between "refugees" and "economic migrants" rests on the economic/political border that naturalizes the categories fetishized in migration management and in migration studies.

ments with them, in protest of the violation of human rights. But life jackets also become a potent proxy in discourses hostile to refugees: a study statistically analyzing life jackets (in addition to rubber dinghies and other refuse) describes "illegal immigration" as a "new source of marine litter" in the Aegean Sea and on seashores.[7]

The proliferation of images of life jackets and their proxy structure for people who, by wearing them, did and did not survive, raise for us ethical and political concerns about representation. Many of the debates surrounding the representation of refugees question the ethics of depicting lifeless bodies, such as the photograph of the Kurdish Syrian toddler Alan Kurdi, whose family's asylum claim was refused by Canada and whose corpse washed up on the shore of Bodrum, Turkey, after they attempted to cross the Aegean in September 2015.[8] Arguably, though, ethical questions haunting representation are not done away with if human bodies (whether living or lifeless) do not, literally, appear in photographs that circulate in the visual economy of the "refugee crisis." Indeed, precisely because they register their absence, the iconic artefacts used as proxies for "refugees" raise ethical and political concerns about their representation and unrepresentability.

WAR IS A FACTORY

That capital is militarized and war is capitalized upon is simultaneously nearly a truism in our times and a highly obfuscated reality. But, "if war is a factory, what does it produce? Blood? Destruction? Or, perhaps, wealth and power?": this is the central question in *The Factory*, a play written by Mohammad Al Attar, recently staged in Berlin and Athens under the direction of Omar Abusaada.[9] Set against an impenetrable screen which comes alight with images of the landscape of war, newspaper headlines in the international press, and projections of the actors on the stage, *The Factory* narrates the story of a cement factory that opened in 2010 in Jalabiya, a city near Raqqa in the north of Syria, just before a peaceful revolution against the regime began. The repression of dissidents turned into the civil and proxy war that

---

7. Stelios Katsanevakis, "Illegal Immigration in the Eastern Aegean Sea: A New Source of Marine Litter," *Mediterranean Marine Science* 16, no. 3 (2015): 605–8.

8. See chapter 6.

9. See Ruhrtriennale Festival of the Arts, 2019, www.ruhrtriennale.de/en/agenda/30/Mohammad_Al _Attar_Omar_Abusaada/The_Factory/; Onassis Stegi, "The Factory," 2018, www.onassis.org/whats-on/ the-factory; see also Gouri Sharma, "'The Factory': Play Exposes Murky Nexus of Western Business and Syrian War," *Middle East Eye*, November 6, 2018, www.middleeasteye.net/news/factory-play-explores -murky-nexus-western-business-and-syrian-war. Al Attar and Abusaada also collaborated on a trilogy based on ancient tragedies by Euripides and Sophocles performed by nonprofessional refugee Syrian female actors: *The Trojan Women*, staged in Jordan (2013), *Antigone of Shatila* staged in Beirut (2014), and, lastly, *Iphigenia*, staged in Berlin (2018). The latter production, originally intended to be staged in Lesvos, encountered logistical obstacles: the asylum-seeking participants there could not yet legally work in Europe; so, the production moved to Germany, arguably "losing its resonance with the specific precarity of many Syrian refugees' lives in Turkey and then in Greece." Margaret Litvin, "Syrian Theatre in Berlin," *Theatre Journal* 70, no. 4 (2018): 448. See chapter 5 for a discussion of Al Attar's play, *Could You Please Look into the Camera?* (2012) also directed by Abusaada.

has resulted in the displacement of more than eleven million people (half the population), of whom more than five million people are displaced internally within Syria, while at least another six million people fled the country. In the midst of war, and at the heart of armed conflict, the multinational French company Lafarge-Holcim, which owned the factory, kept production running by paying a series of warring factions for protection. When Islamic State (IS) took control over the area at the end of 2013, LaFarge paid protection money to IS in order to keep the factory running. After journalist Dorothée Myriam Kellou reported on Lafarge's dealings with IS,[10] France opened a judicial enquiry to establish whether Lafarge was "financing terrorist enterprises"[11] in order to keep the factory running during the war. Lafarge admitted to paying protection money to armed groups in Syria in violation of its own policies; yet, while insisting it is not "a political organization," around the same time Lafarge defended its bid to provide cement for Donald Trump's border wall on the United States–Mexico border, precipitating a diplomatic crisis between Mexico, the United States, and France.[12] Indeed, the last scene of *The Factory* is set before an impassable cement wall sealing Syria's northern border with Turkey, across which one of the factory workers tries to flee war with his wife and child.[13] His translated words still echo in our ears (though we read them as they flashed across the screen): "that wall was the last thing I saw from Syria."[14]

War is said to "produce" refugees, who are "traded" by states, "managed" by supranational institutions, and "reproduced" by nongovernmental organizations. States have officially announced that we are living in permanent war. Austere capitalism has made a redundancy of the notion of "war by other means," as it increasingly relies on policing, the deployment of military power, and technologies of segregation and incarceration—walls, camps, prisons, ghettoes—inside, at, and beyond territorial state borders. Indeed, neoliberalism is a philosophy of economics legitimating waging war within a state's own territorial borders, as reflected in its own discourse of "social wars": the war on drugs, the war on crime—but also the war on cancer, the war on poverty, and so on. At the same time, from its nascence, neoliberalism has been crafted into, and globalized as, a regime of rule through imperialist war and occupation. Whole continents were transformed into laboratories of neoliberal rule through the imposition of dictatorships, the manufacture of financial crises, the

---

10. Dorothée Myriam Kellou, "Syrie: les troubles arrangements de Lafarge avec l'Etat islamique," *Le Monde*, June 9, 2016 [in French], www.lemonde.fr/syrie/article/2016/06/21/syrie-les-troubles -arrangements-de-lafarge-avec-l-etat-islamique_4955023_1618247.html.

11. France 24, "France Opens Inquiry into Lafarge Deals with Syrian Armed Groups," *France 24*, June 13, 2017, www.france24.com/en/20170613-france-judicial-inquiry-lafargeholcim-syria-terrorism -jalabiya.

12. France 24, "France Warns Construction Firm Lafarge over Offer to Build Trump's Wall," *France 24*, March 10, 2017, www.france24.com/en/20170310-france-warns-construction-firm-lafarge-over -offer-build-trump-wall-ayrault-hollande.

13. Though the "wife and child" are physically absent in the scene, we read this as a theatrical restaging of the, by now, iconic (heteronormative) representation of people crossing borders, drawn from the US Highway Sign, which we discuss in chapter 5.

14. Based on our memory of viewing the performance of *The Factory* at Onasis Stegi, Athens, November 11, 2018.

production of genocidal famines, and the exploitation of so-called natural disasters. In the arsenal of neoliberalism, debt colonialism—the restructuring of economies by transnational financial organizations (such as the International Monetary Fund and the World Bank) in alliance with supremacist nation-states, local elites, and multinational corporations, producing indebted national economies—has been a preferred weapon.

The reproduction of war is bound up with—even as it imperils—social reproduction. Economy has become war, and war economy. Thinking of war as something intimately connected to reproduction and not only as its antithesis discloses something important about the nature of war that has not so much been hidden from view but underexposed, bleached into the banal background: it's economy. This is the meaning of permanent war. Permanence requires reproduction. "War is no longer finite—no more a violent event 'out there,' but instead a vital presence permeating our everyday," argues Mimi Thuy Nguyen.[15] Since neoliberal empire fashions war as an "exceptional power" that will bestow the "gift of freedom"[16] on benighted societies (3–4) that are ostensibly trapped in an "anachronistic space" or "permanently anterior time" (16),[17] thereby bringing them into modernity, Nguyen suggests that "the transition between war and peace is rule by multiple and mutable means. Nor can we yet know this project in its totality (though we know that there are more refugees, and more deaths, being created through both war and peace making)" (xi).

Nguyen argues the figure of the refugee "fold[s] empire into debt" (31). Her account illuminates an "economy of indebtedness" (8) that links together in a nonmetaphorical way the social phenomena anchored to debt that are falsely bifurcated, divided into distinct "crises": that known as the "financial crisis" and that termed the "refugee crisis."[18] Central to this economy of indebtedness are "regimes of representation" (30), since the "stubborn remainder" of freedom's absence—its "trace"—becomes visible as "race or gender," as a "duration of the past as continuous subjection," which "does not subside with the passage of time" (18–19). Nguyen's account enables us to frame the compulsory gratitude that refugees are made to feel:[19]

---

15. Mimi Thuy Nguyen, *The Gift of Freedom: War, Debt, and Other Refugee Passages* (Durham, NC: Duke University Press, 2012); hereafter cited in text.

16. Nguyen defines the "gift of freedom" as "an assemblage of liberal political philosophies, regimes of representation, and structures of enforcement that measure and manufacture freedom and its others. To elaborate further: where the attachment to freedom appears an intuitive, universal issue, the implementation of its measure as such (as an absolute value) conceives, and consolidates, fields of knowledge and power whose function lies in the idea that freedom's presence cannot manifest in the present of some peoples and spaces for whom it is currently absent, and that produces a regime of control and interference that provides and defers its substantiation for an indefinite time. In the terms of our discussion, the attachment to freedom and its implementation through gift giving are therefore precisely the forms through which the encounter with the racial, colonial other can be appropriated, through an existing continuity with imperial discourse, into liberal empire" (12).

17. Nguyen, quoting Anne McClintock, *Imperial Leather: Race, Gender, and Sexuality in the Colonial Contest* (London: Routledge, 1995), 30.

18. See our discussion of "nesting crises" in chapter 4.

19. Dina Nayeri, "The Ungrateful Refugee: 'We Have No Debt to Repay,'" *The Guardian*, April 4, 2017, www.theguardian.com/world/2017/apr/04/dina-nayeri-ungrateful-refugee.

first for being gifted with "freedom" through imperialist war and occupation and then—forced to flee the scene of deadly intervention—being given "protection" by the receiving state, often, though not always, the same state which waged or profited from the war that made them seek refuge in the first place (23). Urging us to view "the gift of freedom as liberal war," Nguyen presses us to "imagine war as continuous with refuge" (35). Rather than the refuge constituting the terminus of, or the escape from war, we witness a war on mobility in which the granting of asylum functions like an elaborate, legalized protection racket.

Nguyen argues that "freedom may be experienced as 'thing, force, and gaze'" (9).[20] In this chapter, we attempt to unravel these three aspects of representations of displacement by examining how they are reified in the ubiquitous life jacket, a symbolic object that stands in for the figure of the refugee. Our point of departure is that "refugee" is itself an ossified category—itself a representation—that dehumanizes its proper objects as well as those whom it abjects through its delimitation, a process involving thingification, force, and the constitution of sociolegal, bureaucratic, humanitarian, military, and documentary gazes. In this task, of revealing how categorial fetishism lends itself to visual objectification, Nguyen's analysis guides us, particularly her reminder that "the gift of freedom calls for the realignment of heterogeneous social forms of organization with abstract categories and properties, rendered natural, ineffable, and inalienable, but also objectified, calculable, and exchangeable" (13).

The bordering between "political" refugees and "economic" migrants conceals the economies that surround the former and the politics that produce, exclude, and differentially include the latter. As we saw in chapter 1, the hegemonic attempt to contain and manage people on the move into differentiated populations and separate spheres of recognition, regulation, and control involves variable attributions of agency, choice, freedom, or their lack thereof, all of which silence the actual subjects transformed into objects of "migration management." The alignment of refugees with the political, is, paradoxically, depoliticizing: the border between economic migrants and political refugees rests on a set of dichotomies between, on the one hand, sovereignty/economic rationality/self-possession and displacement/vulnerability/dispossession on the other. Refugees are assigned to the realm of politics not because they are viewed as political agents but because they are divested of agency, which is conflated with the economic rationality of *homo economicus*, ascribed to those deemed not in need of protection but whose ostensibly self-interested calculations of economic costs and benefits lead them to cross borders. To put it another way, while "economic migrants" are the remainder or surplus population of asylum processes, refugees are "exiled" from the economy theoretically, and, in some jurisdictions, materially, being forbidden to work in the capitalist market. Nevertheless, the management of their displacement, mobility, and containment constitutes an economic sector. By way of an example (which only barely begins to graze the surface of this perniciously opaque economy), recall

---

20. Quoting Jean-Luc Nancy, *The Experience of Freedom*, trans. Bridget McDonald (Stanford, CA: Stanford University Press, 1993).

how an online vendor advertized on its website rubber dinghies (made in China) as "Refugee boats for sale":[21] available at US$300–$800, they were marketed as cheap, durable, yet also disposable vessels, an alternative to wooden boats for clandestine sea voyages.[22] These rubber boats are made in China, transported by containers to Turkey, Libya, or Malta, and used to traverse the Aegean and Mediterranean Seas. If their passengers survived the sea crossing, they may have ended up being put in containers themselves, at Moria or on one of the other island hotspots.[23]

It might seem like an obvious statement, even a truism, to say that the category of the refugee is defined through displacement—not only the violent displacement of the refugee from their home and their often permanent construction of being out of place in the society that grants asylum (from the point of view of that society) in return for eternal gratitude,[24] the "double absence," as Abdelmalek Sayad puts it,[25] but also the juridical displacement of illegalized others from the category of "the refugee." On the face of it, documentary photographs of anguished people arriving to something resembling safety on the shores of Lesvos did not make this discrimination between refugees and economic migrants. Those who saw these photographs as representations of people that ought to be welcomed generally viewed them as "refugees"—although in some social movement discourses, the term "migrant" was insisted upon precisely to refute the division between "forced" and "voluntary"

---

21. Will Horner, "'High-Quality Refugee Boats' for Sale on Chinese Website, Despite EU Criticism: The EU Has Taken Measures to Restrict the Sale of Boats in Libya, but Aid Groups Say the Sales Are Just a 'Symptom of a Wider Problem,'" *Middle East Eye*, August 8, 2017, www.middleeasteye.net/news/ high-quality-refugee-boats-sale-chinese-website-despite-eu-criticism; Jurgen Balzan, "Made in China: 'Refugee Boats' Available on Alibaba.com. China Is the Main Source of Rubber Dinghy Imports to Malta: Between 2012 and 2016, €1.3 Million in Merchandise Was Imported," *Malta Today*, April 24, 2017, www.maltatoday.com.mt/news/national/76525/made_in_china_refugee_boats_available_on _alibabacom#.XMw_OC2B3OQ.

22. Jovana Arsenijevic, Marcel Manzi, and Rony Zachariah, "Defending Humanity at Sea: Are Dedicated and Proactive Search and Rescue Operations at Sea a 'Pull Factor' for Migration and Do They Deteriorate Maritime Safety in the Central Mediterranean?" (Luxembourg: Médecins Sans Frontières, Operational Research Unit [LuxOR]), 2017), 18, searchandrescue.msf.org/assets/uploads/ files/170831-%20Report_Analysis_SAR_Final.pdf.

23. See chapter 4.

24. Nguyen argues that being stuck in time is imputed to the refugee not only because they are "stuck, stalled, and otherwise detained (by law but also in heart, in mind) for an unforeseeable duration" (35) through encampment, bureaucratic waiting, and detention (and, we might add, in some contexts, through forced unemployment, dispossession, and acute social and spatial marginalization), but also because they are constructed as coming from, and therefore embodying, a racialized anachronism, always already—long before they arrived at the hotspot, or the camp, or the detention center—living in the "imaginary waiting room of history" to which "colonial others are . . . consigned" (41). Quoting Dipesh Chakvrabarty, *Provincializing Europe: Postcolonial Thought and Historical Difference* (Princeton, NJ: Princeton University Press, 2007), 7–8. Interestingly, representations of Greece and its detention and humanitarian infrastructure as backward and non-European are driven by the same historicist, colonial narrative. Thus, it is unsurprising that constructions of Greece as a transit country riddled with its own problems—transitioning out of its "own, national" crisis—fed into a narrative of asylum seekers seeking to "go on to Europe." Here, refugees were stuck in a waiting room within a waiting room, to invoke the (problematic) figure of nesting crises, which we discuss in chapter 4.

25. Abdelmalek Sayad, *The Suffering of the Immigrant*, ed. Pierre Bourdieu, trans. David Macey (Cambridge: Polity, 2004), 126–27. See chapter 2.

migration in place since at least 1951.[26] The administrative-carceral gaze that trains itself on human beings in order to differentiate them into "populations" in and through the logic of the hotspot[27] effects a fourth kind of displacement: the displacement inherent in categorial fetishism, of human beings by juridical categories. This is redoubled by a fifth level of displacement, this one visual. Among predominant photographic depictions that at once purport to depict or refer to refugees, and render them invisible, the life jacket provides perhaps the clearest example of the latter form of displacement, as the *eidôlon* of the "refugee." Thus, it is not incidental or innocuous how frequently in photographic representations of "refugees" an object stands in for a category that is itself objectifying of the people it ostensibly stands in for.

Of these proxy objects for "refugees," perhaps the life jacket (and, to a lesser extent, other artefacts that survive sea crossings, such as rubber dinghies) is the most emblematic. But in the wake of the "refugee crisis," numerous research and artistic projects focused on retrieving and representing objects left on border crossings, along routes and trajectories (such as the Balkan route) taken by people on the move, all of which inscribe the presence of human beings as a function of their multiple absences.

VISUAL ECONOMY

The notion of "visual economy" turns on a double meaning: First, like the notion of a regime of representations, which we discussed in chapter 2 through the insightful works of cultural theorist Stuart Hall and filmmaking collective Abounaddara, it is a way of describing a system in which images are produced, reproduced, exchanged, circulated, and viewed through regulated processes of long historical duration. Here, we invoke the term "visual economy" to make an explicit link between the economy of representations and the economy of war. If, following Al Attar, we think of war as a factory, it is also a factory of images—images of war that wage war, as Abounaddara aptly reminds us.[28] A second sense of "visual economy" refers to the management of available resources, the sparing use of visuals—in particular, the use of visual shortcuts—to construct meaning. The life jacket as a proxy for "refugees" is such a visual shortcut, which comes to signify, and indeed reify, this category. Putting the two senses together, we can see how the visual economy in which refugees are reproduced relies on the frugal use of the proxy object to perform a restrained signification of an absent, yet immediately intelligible, referent.

---

26. Apostolova, "Of Refugees and Migrants"; Crawley and Skleparis, "Refugees, Migrants, Neither, Both."

27. Anna Carastathis, Aila Spathopoulou, and Myrto Tsilimpounidi, "Crisis, What Crisis? Immigrants, Refugees, and Invisible Struggles," *Refugee: Canada's Journal on Refugees* 34, no. 1 (2018): 29–38. See chapter 2.

28. Abounaddara Collective, paraphrasing Serge Daney, in Jason Fox and the Abounaddara Film Collective, "Representational Regimes: A Conversation with the Abounaddara Film Collective," *World Records Journal* 1, no. 10 (The Documentary Camera, 2018): 1–7. See chapter 2.

Elena Fiddian-Qasmiyeh's conceptualization of *repress*entation speaks to how the hypervisibility of "certain groups of forced migrants and certain identity markers (real, imagined, and imposed)" rely on the "concealment" of others "from public view."[29] The life jacket is a *repress*entation of "refugees" in Fiddian-Qasmiyeh's sense in that it makes hypervisible an objectified proxy for the "ideal refugee"[30]—as no one would "voluntarily" endanger their own life and that of their children by "putting them in a boat" if they were not absolutely forced to do so.[31] Polly Pallister-Wilkins points out that "time and again the experiences of people on the move across the borders of Europe, the experiences of displacement and life-seeking, are reduced to the dramatic image of the rubber dinghy approaching the shore with its human cargo of 'suffering Syrians,' 'desolate Afghans,' or 'helpless women and children.'"[32] Yet, Pallister-Wilkins claims that these "dramatic" images fail "to capture the full subjecthood, variegated vulnerabilities and complex needs of people on the move. . . . [C]omplex politics and long-running structural causes have been visually rendered and reduced to those dramatic images of boat arrivals in Lesvos that conceal more than they illuminate."[33] This reduction gains even greater abstraction by the visual reproduction of the life jacket as the shortcut to this emblematic scene of arrival, to these "bodies in boats" coming ashore. Even a photograph of a horizon—a line where sea and sky meet—in which a speck of orange is barely visible produces an intelligible meaning, through its circulation in this visual economy, of a discarded life vest that failed to save a body that never made it to shore.[34] Understood as *repress*entations, such images always illuminate precisely by concealing.

In her aforementioned reflection, Pallister-Wilkins rightly seeks to draw attention to "the things that often get lost" in dominant representations of the "refugee crisis": for instance, EU border policies that are elided in the "spectacle" of boats in the sea and their passengers arriving on shore.[35] Yet, images of life jackets and

---

29. Elena Fiddian-Qasmiyeh, "*Repress*entations of Displacement from the Middle East and North Africa," *Public Culture* 28, no. 3 (2016): 458.

30. Elena Fiddian-Qasmiyeh, *The Ideal Refugees: Gender, Islam, and the Sahrawi Politics of Survival* (Syracuse, NY: Syracuse University Press, 2014).

31. Here, we allude to Warsan Shire's poem "Home," which went viral and became a rallying cry and was widely referenced in sympathetic discourses at the height of the refugee crisis—not only in Europe but also in protests against the Trump administration's so-called Muslim ban in the United States and demonstrations in Israel against a proposed policy which would have led to the deportation of tens of thousands of African migrants. In particular, the verses that proclaim: "you have to understand,/no one puts their children in a boat/unless the water is safer than the land" were widely reproduced on placards, social media posts, and in speeches. Lily Kuo, "'Home': This Poem Is Now the Rallying Call for Refugees: 'No One Leaves Home Unless Home Is the Mouth of a Shark,'" *Quartz Africa*, January 30, 2017, qz.com/africa/897871/warsan-shires-poem-captures-the-reality-of-life-for-refugees-no-one-leaves-home -unless-home-is-the-mouth-of-a-shark/. See Warsan Shire, "Home," in *Teaching My Mother How to Give Birth* (London: flipped eye, 2011).

32. Polly Pallister-Wilkins, "There's a Focus on the Boats Because the Sea Is Sexier Than the Land: A Reflection on the Centrality of the Boats in the Recent 'Migration Crisis,'" The Disorder of Things, December 9, 2015, thedisorderofthings.com/2015/12/09/theres-a-focus-on-the-boats-because-the-sea-is -sexier-than-the-land-a-reflection-on-the-centrality-of-the-boats-in-the-recent-migration-crisis/.

33. Pallister-Wilkins, "There's a Focus on the Boats."

34. Eirini Vourloumis, Image 11.

35. Pallister-Wilkins, "There's a Focus on the Boats"; Lizzie Deardon, "Refugee Crisis: European Leaders Blamed for Record High Deaths in the Mediterranean. Exclusive: Report Author Says Politicians Have

other reified objects that stand in for "refugees" in this visual economy are, precisely, "things lost,"[36] or things discarded. At the same time, they are not images of things at all but rather shortcuts to subjects: human beings who, whether they survive the passage and are made into things through the categorial fetishism of asylum or lose their lives at sea, are objectified through the proxy object that ostensibly stands in for them. Visuals of life jackets (the objects themselves, and images of the objects) are so jarring to us because they not only indicate survival of the sea voyage but also conjure drowning: not only the affect of profound relief felt upon the removal of the life jacket once on shore but also the profound grief we feel (or, perhaps, incredibly, fail to feel) for those who never arrive, for those who with their absence haunt the spectacle of arrival. The life jacket, then, is also a *repres*entation in a second sense that we think is consistent with Fiddian-Qasmiyeh's initial parsing:[37] inherent in its representational structure is the absence of the subject—the person or people—it stands in for. This absence is, in the first instance, a function of its being a proxy for a certain category of human beings who experience social death and can never be represented by the category that they are made to perform in order to survive. In the second instance, absence is the consequence of the necropolitical use of the geography of the sea to ensure that people do not survive the journey, to bring about their literal death.

Another way to think about this inherent absence haunting the proxy object is through the notion of *eidôlon*, discussed in chapter 2.[38] Here, too, we find a double meaning: *eidôlon* is an idealized person or thing (perhaps, even, one we "idolize");

Been 'Wantonly Ignoring' Reality to Maintain Ill-Informed Government Positions," *The Independent*, November 2, 2016, www.independent.co.uk/news/uk/home-news/refugee-crisis-closing-borders-people-smugglers-human-trafficking-mediterranean-deaths-record-a7391736.html.

36. Pallister-Wilkins, "There's a Focus on the Boats."

37. Fiddian-Qasmiyeh, "*Repres*entations of Displacement from the Middle East and North Africa."

38. "Starting with a particularly violent image—or, perhaps we should say *an image corresponding to the everyday violence to which we have become accustomed*—found in the media and derived from current events, [Léa] Beloussovitch makes a copy, a double, an alternative. She subjects this image to a series of transformations that deconstruct it definitively. First, she reframes it, concentrating only on a detail, the scale of which will inevitably be modified in the final format. Next . . . she produces this new image on an unexpected surface: felt. Far from the glossy appearance of magazines or the slick effect of our screens, this fibrous material used since antiquity immediately summons a sensuality—or, we might say, a 'default corporality'—since it serves primarily to protect us from the cold. Finally, this material naturally degrades as the artist's pencil strokes cover its surface. From the clear and speckled original image, the resulting work becomes downy, velvety, almost powdery, forming clouds of color that melt into one another, to such a point that without knowing the origin, we would think that we are looking at a purely abstract image. These three operations—reframing, changing the surface and 're-materialization'—not only strip the images from their media context but also from their intended use. . . . These raw snapshots of current events, thrust into our gaze, include war scenes, images of refugees and attacks; most of the time, the artist selects them because they capture the victims candidly and unposed. What creates the mechanical or digital eye in the hands of the photographer is a theater, a stage that incorporates our emotional reaction at the forefront, in the fixed moment of an instant. Conversely, the long period of time that the artist dedicates to her activities, which entails first scouring the media to find these images and then transforming them into drawn works. . . . As if the time in the studio became a time to heal, a step back from the overly-visible, a form of economy—and maybe even *ecology*—of seeing." Gaël Charbau, "Léa Beloussovitch, EIDÔLON: 'Before My Gaze Thy Soul's Eidôlon Stands,'" Exhibition Statement, Galerie Paris-Beijing, April 2019, www.galerieparisbeijing.com/exhibition/eidolon-gaze-thy-souls-eidolon-stands/.

and it is also a spectre, phantom, ghost—an apparition of a person, dead or alive. Life jackets function as *eidôla* for refugees in both senses of idealization and spectrality. The banal materiality of the life jacket may seem at first glance to refute its spectrality, since, to recall Jacques Derrida's questions in *Specters of Marx*, "what is the *being-there* of a specter? what is the mode of presence of a specter?"[39] But the life jacket is a commodity in the war economy of the refugee crisis, which like any commodity "haunts the thing" (189). If "commodities must be realized as [exchange] values before they can be realized as use-values" (179), it is because they are produced by alienated, exploited labor exchanged for a wage.[40]

> These ghosts that are commodities transform human producers into ghosts. And this whole theatrical process (visual, theoretical, but also optical, *optician*) sets off the effect of a mysterious mirror: if the latter does not return the right reflection, if, then, it phantomalizes, this is first of all because it naturalizes. The "mysteriousness" of the commodity-form as presumed reflection of the social form is the incredible manner in which this mirror sends back the image (*zurückspiegelt*) when one thinks it is reflecting for men the image of the "social characteristics of men's own labor": such an "image" objectivizes by naturalizing. Thereby, this is its truth, it shows by hiding, it reflects these "objective" (*gegenständliche*) characteristics as inscribed right on the product of labor, as apparition of the inapparent the "socio-natural properties of these things" (*als gesellschaftliche Natureigenschaften dieser Dinge*). Therefore, and here the commerce among commodities does not wait, the returned (deformed, objectified, naturalized) image becomes that of a social relation among commodities, among these inspired, autonomous, and automatic "objects" . . . The specular becomes the spectral at the threshold of this objectifying naturalization: "it also reflects the social relation of the producers to the sum total of labor as a social relation between objects, a relation which exists apart from and outside the producers. Through this substitution [*quid pro quo*], the products of labor become commodities, sensuous things which are at the same time supersensible or social." (195–96)[41]

In capitalism, in order for an object's use value (its utility) to be realized, it has to be produced and to circulate on the market as an exchange value (a commodity sold for a price).[42] The spectrality of the commodity consists in the reflection, back to

---

39. Jacques Derrida, *Specters of Marx: The State of the Debt, the Work of Mourning and the New International,* trans. Peggy Kamuf (New York: Routledge, 1994/2006), 46; hereafter cited in text.

40. Fetishism is variously conceptualized as reification, alienation, false consciousness, and value—overlapping and interrelated concepts that, nevertheless, cannot be equated with each other. See Chris O'Kane, "Fetishism and Social Domination in Marx, Lukacs, Adorno and Lefebvre" (PhD diss., Center for Social and Political Thought, University of Sussex, 2013).

41. Quoting Marx.

42. This is a crucial genetic condition of commodity fetishism. A defetishizing critique thus has to attend to the subordination of use value to exchange value. On a Marxian account, there are no commodities, and no commodity fetishism outside the capitalist market. Tom Scott-Smith, in his otherwise interesting article on "the fetishism of humanitarian objects and the management of malnutrition," equivocates on this point, insisting that "humanitarianism, to be clear, is a different world from that of the market" (920). Although he draws on a marxian conception of commodity fetishism to analyze the concealment, transformation, and mystification of two humanitarian objects in particular (the MUAC band used in nutritional anthropometry to measure degrees of child malnutrition and Plumpy'nut, a therapeutic food

its alienated producers and consumers, of the social relations through which it was produced. In the commodity is the inverted image of the commodification (and exploitation) of labor, but it appears automatically, reified in the appearance of a naturalized object, autonomous from its producers. The commodity as apparition, as spectre, marks the "absence of body" (146), of flesh and bones; it is "not a living individual, . . . a real subject" (146), yet it appears as one.

This spectrality of commodities intensifies in late capitalism, as the relationship between use value and exchange value is increasingly mediated by the "society of the spectacle."[43] In the wake of the "refugee crisis," people were arriving in Lesvos wearing "fake life jackets" (an untold many wearing these jackets never arrived at their destination). The life jacket, already naturalized as an indispensable item in the "refugee's survival kit,"[44] is invested with hypervalue (maximizing profit) through the negation of its use value: filled with absorbent foam and other substances that would negate its basic function as a flotation device, the fake life jacket was and is sold in coastal points of departure in Turkey in the wake of the spectacle of the refugee crisis. Press reports reproduce the spectral substitution of objects for subjects: "Fake life jackets sold to refugees play a role in their drowning."[45] Not the manufacturers and retailers that profit from the production and sale of fake life jackets but the fake life jackets themselves are, in this parsing, endowed with responsibility for making refugees drown. The conditions of possibility for the extraction of hypervalue from the fake life jacket—an object with exchange value in the border spectacle—that is, the war on mobility that compels people to make the voyage, denying them safe passage, are even further removed from view.

As exchange values, we find that life jackets are "moving about freely" (191); they are "thing[s] in flight," or "bodiless bod[ies]" like a "silhouette of the sensuous

used to treat malnutrition in feeding programmes), his premise that a "voluntary ethos [as] opposed to the profit motive" drives humanitarianism (920) places an account of how these objects are valorized as commodities just beyond reach. Tom Scott-Smith, "The Fetishism of Humanitarian Objects and the Management of Malnutrition in Emergencies," *Third World Quarterly* 34, no. 5: 913–28.

43. Guy Debord, *The Society of Spectacle* (London: Rebel Press, 1967).

44. Choose Love, a pop-up shop in Soho, London, set up by Help Refugees, invites Christmas shoppers to buy survival kits to be sent to refugees: "Shop your heart out, leave with nothing, and feel the love." See Aamna Mohdin, "Choose Love: The Shop Where Customers Buy Gifts for Refugees," *The Guardian*, November 23, 2018, www.theguardian.com/business/2018/nov/23/choose-love-pop-up-shop-london-customers-buy-gifts-refugees.

45. World Health Organization, "Fake Life Jackets Play a Role in the Drowning of Refugees," *Bulletin of the World Health Organization* 94 (2016): 411–12, dx.doi.org/10.2471/BLT.16.020616, www.who.int/bulletin/volumes/94/6/16-020616.pdf. See also Yiannis Papadopoulos, "Fake Life Vests Soak Up Chances of Survival for Shipwrecked Refugees," *EKathimerini*, February 2, 2016, www.ekathimerini.com/205666/gallery/ekathimerini/special-report/fake-life-vests-soak-up-chances-of-survival-for-shipwrecked-refugees; BBC, "Migrant Crisis: Turkey Police Seize Fake Life Jackets," *BBC News*, January 6, 2016, www.bbc.com/news/world-europe-35241813; Samantha Turnbull and Joanne Shoebridge, "Syrian Refugees Being Sold Fake Life Jackets with Absorbent Foam, Volunteer Says," *ABC News*, January 18, 2016, www.abc.net.au/news/2016-01-18/volunteer-reveals-challenges-facing-syrian-refugees/7095006; Hannah Al-Othman, "Tricked into Death: 150,000 Migrants' Life Jackets—Many of Which Are Useless Fakes—Lie Piled on the Coast of Lesbos in Grim Memorial to Those Who Die Crossing the Mediterranean," *Daily Mail*, February 6, 2017, www.dailymail.co.uk/news/article-4196010/150-000-migrants-life-jackets-lie-piled-Lesbos-coast.html.

body"—or, we might say, with cruel literality in the case of the fake life jacket—an empty shell. The spectre of the life jacket as *eidôlon* is—to invoke both Derrida and Benjamin at once—mechanically reproduced (136). The life jacket is "an apparition . . . an appearance and *finally an image*, in the sense of *phenomenon* and in the sense of rhetorical *figure*" (147) for the "refugee crisis."[46] Imagined as a proxy for the "refugee," the life jacket is projected "on an imaginary screen where there is nothing to see" (125). Finally, the life jacket is a *revenant*: it "comes back" on the scene of consumption, the visual, or the political—whether through creative reuse, recycling, or as a stand-in for a double absence.[47]

How does the life jacket become a mobile signifier for people on the move, and specifically for refugees arriving in Europe? How does it become the material for symbolic interventions, and how is it reincarnated in new, useful objects? How does the life jacket mobilize people, compel them to action? How does the life jacket become an expressive medium, a canvas for reinscription? How does the life jacket end up doing things that its wearers cannot? Cross borders, gain recognition, speak and be heard.

A story is commonly told in answer to such questions. It may as well begin at the scene of arrival, which initiates a cycle of appearances. Here, life jackets are photographed as they enter the field of vision from the shore, in the distant horizon formed by the sea and the sky. As the electric orange blots come closer, their bearers come into view. Once safely on land, no longer having a purpose—but also no way to return to a place where they once had a purpose—the life jackets are discarded, together with other objects, including, often, the vessel itself. Because there are so many of them arriving—all at once—"a massive surplus of life jackets"[48] quickly pile up as waste on the beaches. Don't forget: over one million life jackets made the journey to Europe since the start of the refugee crisis. Concerned cosmopolitan citizens of the world come to visit them and vocally abhor their degrading conditions: "Our Greece trip has brought us to Lesvos where we witnessed how the coast—a place where many refugees arrive with hopes of a better life and a safer future—looks more like a graveyard of life jackets and broken boats. Although we had many positive experiences during our field trip in Greece, we still wanted to share these pictures with you too, as they show a part of the sad and sometimes hopeless situation refugees face here, not able to move back or forth. . . . Once you have seen, you cannot unsee."[49]

The life jackets, like other wasted lives, are eventually transported to a landfill on the side of a hill, where they are laid to rest in a graveyard, where no one can see

---

46. Emphasis in original.

47. As the translator, Peggy Kamuf notes, "a common term for ghost or specter, the *revenant* is literally that which comes back. We leave it in French throughout." In Derrida, *Specters of Marx*, 224n1.

48. Caters News Agency, "Thousands of Life Jackets That Saved Refugee Lives Are Converted into Laptop Cases and Bags. Masses of Life Jackets Worn by Syrian Refugees as They Crossed into Europe Are Now Providing Jobs for Their Former Wearers—as They Are Converted into Laptop Cases, Bags and Other Travel Accessories," *Caters News Agency*, n.d., www.catersnews.com/stories/latest-news/thousands -of-life-jackets-that-saved-refugee-lives-are-converted-into-laptop-cases-and-bags/.

49. Women Refugee Route, Facebook post, January 16, 2017, www.facebook.com/WRRoute/posts/370224510024648.

them—at least no one who has paid a not-at-all-insignificant sum and has the right passport to enjoy the natural splendour of the Aegean islands. But even there they do not find peace—even though a few thousand of them are, with much effort and genuine feeling, configured into a peace sign in one of the many political protests during which they will come to put their bodies on the line.[50] They become symbols—even martyrs—of resistance to the cruel regime of borders, which succeeds by failing to provide safe passage and even criminalizes those who try to mitigate its violence by engaging in sea rescue.[51]

The life jackets engage in artivism, some bravely scaling monuments, others staging occupations in front of parliaments,[52] still others—the most photogenic?— finding themselves on magazine covers[53] and sharing the limelight with socially conscious celebrities.[54] Supported by NGOs, celebrity artists, and radical activists, the "refugee life jackets" travel all across Europe to raise awareness of "countless lives changed by the crisis, with every single vest reflecting the individual life of a man,

50. "Dozens of Greenpeace and Médecins Sans Frontières (MSF) volunteers and local supporters teamed up to create the massive peace sign Friday on a hillside overlooking the small strait between Greece and Turkey that has become a main passageway for those fleeing to Europe. Made up of more than 3,000 life jackets and built by dozens of volunteers, the sign is a way to honor those who have made the journey and to urge peace in the new year, according to Greenpeace. Those involved in the project are calling for safe passage to those fleeing war, poverty and oppression. 'The peace sign is a symbolic gesture not only from MSF and Greenpeace but from the many volunteers who have been on the front line of responding to this crisis for many months already,' MSF spokesperson Sami Al-Subaihi told *Mashable*. 'Using the lifejackets of those who made it we remember the more than 3700 people who didn't.'" Megan Specia, "Refugees' Life Jackets Are Transformed into Message of Peace on Greek Island," *Mashable*, January 2, 2016, mashable.com/2016/01/02/refugee-life-jacket-greek-island/?europe=true.

51. "Activists congregate spontaneously in front of the Hamburg editorial office of German news outlet *Zeit*. Lifejackets were symbolically stored in the foyer. In speeches, they demanded an end to the criminalization of civilian sea rescue. Hamburg. Reacting to the opening of a 'pro' and 'contra' discussion on civilian sea rescue of fleeing people in the current issue of the weekly magazine *Die Zeit*, activists spontaneously gathered this Monday morning with a banner: 'There is no CONTRA for rescue—Against fortress Europe and its fans' in front of the editorial office in the Helmut Schmidt House in Hamburg. During the action of the nationalism is no alternative [NIKA] coalition, leaflets were distributed, speeches held and life jackets were symbolically placed in the entrance area of the publishing house. In addition, the activists put up a banner saying 'Ferries instead of Frontex.'" As reported in *Enough Is Enough*, July 16, 2018. Originally published by Indymedia DE at de.indymedia.org/node/22840. Edited machine translation by Enough Is Enough, enoughisenough14.org/2018/07/16/hamburg-seebruecke-theres-no -contra-for-sea-rescue/.

52. The International Rescue Committee organized volunteers who spent six months working towards a visual protest in London's Parliament Square with over 2,500 life jackets "shipped all the way from Greece," to coincide with the UN Summit on Refugees. According to one volunteer, "we're hoping to use these life jackets to get people to understand that these are human beings, these are families, these are parents, children, and give a platform to the refugees . . . who do not have a voice in this conflict, but are most affected by it." Lawrence Andrew, "Life Jackets in Parliament Square/International Rescue Committee," Newsflare, n.d., www.newsflare.com/video/86884/politics-business/life-jackets-in-parliament -square-international-rescue-committee#.

53. "Amnesty International Netherlands new refugee ad campaign ['Glamoria 2018'] is hyper sexualized, fetishized, 'American Beauty' style image of 'desirable' refugee women surrounded by life jackets. The 'humanize refugees' industry is the gift that keeps on giving." Twitter post by @shaistaAziz, December 15, 2018, twitter.com/shaistaAziz/status/1073889456720101376.

54. Lilly Waddell, "Penelope Cruz, 44, Cuts Ladylike Figure in Lovely Floral Dress and Heels at Glitzy Gala in Madrid," Mail Online, May 31, 2018, www.dailymail.co.uk/tvshowbiz/article-5792849/ Penelope-Cruz-44-cuts-ladylike-figure-feminine-floral-dress-heels-glitzy-gala-Madrid.html.

woman or child whose landing at Lesvos is just the beginning."[55] Yet, sometimes, overwhelmed by the scale of the problem, all the life jackets can seem to do is lie "in mute witness to tragic inaction on refugees."[56] Indeed, the majority unfortunately remains mute, passive, and stagnant, generally failing to find inventive ways to make a new life for themselves. The life jacket graveyard becomes an issue for the local population—who often lashes out against this community of uninvited guests constituting "refugee waste"[57]—but also for scientists, who seem to lend empirical support to the emerging consensus that the life jackets constitute pollution,[58] are simply garbage—if a very "special waste"[59]—and may even carry disease, posing a health risk to the native population. The local administration is charged with ineptitude. The solidarians and international creative class step in: they reveal the false dichotomy between life jackets and the environment and find inventive ways to help both at the same time.[60] They run workshops training others how to utilize the life jackets—or their constituent parts—in ways they could never have imagined

55. Ai Weiwei used fourteen thousand life jackets culled from Lesvos to decorate the six marble columns of the Berlin Konzerthaus (Concert House) for the Cinema for Peace Gala, held there on February 15, 2016 (discussed further in chapter 5). "Each life jacket represents a single refugee. The installation's scale is meant to draw attention to the number of human lives affected by the refugee crisis . . . Ai Weiwei's politically charged statement corresponds to his direct involvement on the Greek island. The sheer abundance of jackets used by the artist highlights the countless lives changed by the crisis, with every single vest reflecting the individual life of a man, woman or child whose landing at Lesvos is just the beginning." Nina Azzarello, "Ai Weiwei Wraps Berlin's Konzerthaus with 14,000 Refugee Life Jackets," *DesignBoom*, February 15, 2016, www.designboom.com/art/ai-weiwei-life-jackets-refugee -konzerthaus-berlin-02-15-2016/. See also AP Archive, "Ai Weiwei Turns Migrant Lifejackets into Art in Copenhagen," YouTube, June 30, 2017, www.youtube.com/watch?v=T3u2zTWXi4s; AFP News Agency, "Ai Weiwei Life Jacket Installation Highlights Refugee Plight," YouTube, July 13, 2016, www.youtube .com/watch?v=SEFQT5Q37hE.

56. Pasion Y Presion, "Life Jackets Lying In Mute Witness to Tragic Inaction on Refugees. #WithRefugees #lifejacketlondon," Newsflare, n.d., www.newsflare.com/video/86839/other/newsflare -edit-lifejackets-lie-in-mute-witness-to-tragic-inaction-on-refugeeswithrefugees-lifejacketlondon -httpstcogtcsn41rtl?a=on.

57. Marie Gillespie, "Refugee Waste: Death, Survival and Solidarity in Lesvos," in *A World Laid Waste? Responding to the Social, Cultural and Political Consequences of Globalization*, ed. Francis Dodsworth and Antonia Walford (New York: Routledge, 2018).

58. Katsanevakis, "Illegal Immigration in the Eastern Aegean Sea"; see also Jennifer Wagner-Lawlor, "Refugee Crisis Creates Ghostly Ocean Debris," Plastic Pollution Coalition, 2016, www.plasticpollution coalition.org/pft/2016/6/24/refugee-crisis-creates-ghostly-ocean-debris; Emily Creighton, "Environmental Impact of the Refugee Crisis," Planet Forward, March 2, 2017, www.planetforward.org/idea/environmental -impact-of-the-refugee-crisis.

59. Kounani and C. Skanavis, "Refugee Crisis: Greek Residents' Attitudes toward Waste Management in their Region" (paper, Protection and Restoration of the Environment XIV Conference, organized by Stevens Institute of Technology & Department of Civil Engineering and the Environmental Council, Aristotle University of Thessaloniki, Thessaloniki, July 3–6, 2018).

60. Al Jazeera, "Bags Made of Boats and Life Jackets," YouTube, March 8, 2016, 1:37 mins, www .youtube.com/watch?v=tbIyB_SXtFY. "The Chessboard of the World" is a giant outdoor art installation created by artist Fereniki Tsamparli and realized by a team at the University of the Aegean in Mytilene and TedXLesvos for World Environment Day. They constructed life-size chess pieces from salvaged refugee life jackets and paper discarded by university students. The chess board was made from material harvested from rubber dinghies. "Fereniki Tsamparli, the Artist Who Created the Giant Chessboard, Wished to Combine the Drama of the Refugee Crisis and Environmental Awareness by Recycling Life Jackets, Rubber Boats and Paper," *Al Jazeera*, www.aljazeera.com/indepth/inpictures/2016/06/making -giant-chessboard-refugee-life-jackets-160605103440023.html.

in their previous lives.[61] With a good design, a bit of skill, practice, and patience, life jackets can be repurposed, it turns out, to accomplish all manner of socially useful and beautiful things. "Nothing created, or destroyed, only transformed."[62] Social entrepreneurs enjoin savvy consumers: "Carry a product, carry a story."[63] Life jackets become transformed into messenger bags, laptop cases, but also "positive opportunit[ies],"[64] the raw material of sustainability and social inclusion, embodied in iconic designs—"fair warning though," thusly reincarnated, "we are not sure if they float!"[65] If they ever did, in the first place.

They may not float, but they surely inspire: life jackets trigger the senses, and not just the visual. "The refugee crisis was simply a set of numbers on the news. . . . But when I picked a jacket up, it stopped being just material. When you hold the jacket in your hand and you smell the sea, you look at things through a different prism and you realize that every jacket represents a human life."[66] And/or, perhaps, "each life vest is in effect a tombstone, a way of remembering the dead."[67]

---

61. "Safe Passage Bag Workshop, is an upcycling project where #bags are being created by refugees and locals living in #Mytilini. They are made from #lifejackets left on the #Lesvos shorelines, used by #refugees who have crossed the Aegean Sea from Turkey." Lesvos Solidarity, "Safe Passage Bags," 2018, www.lesvossolidarity.org/en/what-we-do/safe-passage-bags.

62. Five thousand life jackets were brought to the Netherlands by Makers Unite (makersunite.eu/production-process/). One of their designs using "life jackets upcycled into creative objects" is the laptop sleeve made by newcomers. "This unique design laptop sleeve from the MU Collection has made a long journey on its way to you. It started out as a life vest, helping people reach safety. Now in its new form, it is helping connect creative newcomers to the job market, leveraging their talents to build a new life in the Netherlands." Makers Unite, n.d., makersunite.eu/produit/sample-product/laptopsleeve/.

63. "When you become part of this movement, you don't only carry a product with a story. You create an impact and give stories a new beginning." Makers Unite, n.d., makersunite.eu/production-process/.

64. "Turning life-vests into positive opportunity. Orange is for being brave. Plus it's a design icon, as described by Dezeen, one of the top design solutions for refugees, the Makers Unite Totes are durable and high quality, making them perfect for braving the day." Makers Unite, n.d., makersunite.eu/produit/sample-product/eco-tote-bag/. Refugees themselves are enjoined to be makers, inventors, creators using the raw material of life jackets. To cite but two further examples: "Siba Obaid is 19-years old. Her father drowned at sea when he was escaping from Syria. So guess what? She designed a lifejacket with built-in GPS that sends an automatic alert, with location, to alert to the Coast Guard when others are drowning," @MuhammadLila, Twitter post, March 13, 2018, twitter.com/MuhammadLila/status/973614727736606720. "Exodus," an exhibition of artworks created by "unaccompanied young refugees" sponsored by the British Red Cross at the Huguenot Museum is advertized by a life jacket decorated with patches (hearts, crosses, peace signs, the Union Jack, and the words "freedom," "safety," "dignity," "unity," "humanity," "future," "health," "universality," "independence," and "vote.") huguenotmuseum.org/visiting/special-displays/.

65. Makers Unite, n.d., makersunite.eu/production-process/.

66. Achilleas Souras quoted in Emma Tucker, "16-year-old artist builds igloos from refugee life jackets for Moroso installation," *Dezeen*, April 6, 2017, www.dezeen.com/2017/04/06/achilleas-souras-builds-igloos-refugees-life-jackets-morosos-sos-save-souls-installation-milan-design-week/. Souras, an artist based in Barcelona, then sixteen years old, built an igloo installation from one thousand life jackets at Milan Design Week (April 2017), titled "SOS Save Our Souls." Souras cut and folded the jackets to resemble blocks of ice before assembling them. "The resulting waterproof structure is intended as both a shelter and a welcome point for arriving migrants."

67. Ben Quilty, speaking of his portraits of life jackets, which in effect are portraits of proxies: "Together the paintings constitute a memorial, as lugubrious and dour an epitaph as Australia's refugee policy." Quoted in Michael Desmond, "Ben Quilty: Life Vests 2016–2017," Deathscapes: Mapping Race and Violence in Settler States, 2017, buff.ly/2LZtGxh.

The capacity of life jackets to, simultaneously, bring to life and memorialize death, to register human presence through human absence, is, surely, evidence of their vivid spectrality.

A REFUGEE, NAME TO BE ANNOUNCED

The *quid pro quo* substitution of life jackets for refugees—imagined as "shipwrecked lives"—in visuals of the "crisis" reflects what Martina Tazzioli has termed the "politics of counting."[68] Here, efforts driven by solidarity with refugees that seek to make the deadly consequences of border regimes visible face a quandary: numbers (imagined to be even more "objective" than photographs) are used to represent the extent, scale, or scope of human suffering and loss; yet, quantification is an intense (if unintended) form of depersonalization, homogenization, and dehumanization. It is not incidental that, "reflecting upon border deaths, the first image that comes to mind for many of us is a list of numbers" (4). Tazzioli points out that "the daily alternation between death tolls and the bulletins of rescued migrants" issued by authorities "fashions us as spectators: migrants escaping wars become lives to save in the technical sense of being rescued at sea that 'we' can only observe and 'count'" (5). People attempting to cross the Mediterranean become "objects of a mapping gaze," reduced through the "scene of rescue" as forged by governmentality to "bodies to count and name" (5).

The life jacket, as a symbolic proxy for refugees—and as a mass-produced commodity mediating the razor edge of life and death in what is often imagined as a "transparent sea" (5) but is really, for "too many," a watery grave—is an easily apprehensible visual for the quantifying, evidentiary gaze, into which the global regime of migration management seeks to train citizens' ways of seeing. In that sense, it is not incidental that in its article announcing the publication of "The List: The 34,361 Men, Women, and Children Who Perished Trying to Reach Europe," *The Guardian* publishes a photograph of a life jacket captioned with the redundant explanation that "lifejackets have become a striking symbol of the refugee crisis."[69] Indeed, the

---

68. Martina Tazzioli, "The Politics of Counting and the Scene of Rescue," *Radical Philosophy* 192 (July/August 2015): 3, 5; hereafter cited in-text.

69. Alex Needham, "The List: The 34,361 Men, Women and Children Who Perished Trying to Reach Europe," *The Guardian*, June 20, 2018, www.theguardian.com/world/2018/jun/20/the-list-34361-men-women-and-children-who-perished-trying-to-reach-europe-world-refugee-day. See also Stephan-Andreas Casdorff and Lorenz Maroldt, "'The List' of Banu Cennetoglu: Artist Documents the Dying of 33,293 Refugees," *Der Tagesspiegel*, November 9, 2017 [in German], www.tagesspiegel.de/politik/die-liste-von-banu-cennetoglu-kuenstlerin-dokumentiert-das-sterben-von-33-293-gefluechteten/20558658.html. The List is a database compiled by volunteers since 1993 by United for Intercultural Action, a European network of 550 anti-racist organizations in forty-eight countries. See unitedagainstrefugeedeaths.eu and www.unitedagainstracism.org/campaigns/refugee-campaign/fortress-europe. It also forms one basis of the art practice of Istanbul-based photographer and cross-disciplinary visual artist Banu Cennetoğlu, who over the past sixteen years has sought to put it "out there in the world" as a "physical object" in various media, while insisting that "it is not art": "When you can hold it there's a way to relate to it that's better than an infinite scrolling experience. When there is a screen, you have somehow the power to isolate yourself." Cennetoğlu quoted in Charlotte Higgins, "Interview: Banu Cennetoğlu: 'As Long as I Have

politics of counting human beings shifts to the politics of counting life jackets. The pictured vest, we are told, "was one of 2,500 removed or discarded vests that formed a 'lifejacket graveyard' in [London's] Parliament Square to draw attention to the crisis in 2016."[70] As life jackets travel beyond the voyage in which they served as life-saving equipment and metamorphose into documentary, protest, commodity, charity, and artistic objects, they also become countable quantities, with origins, destinations, and political agency. Life jackets assemble, they draw political attention, they even live, die, and are "buried" in "graveyards."

Needless to say, the photograph of the life jacket which is credited to Hugh Peterswald (a photographer at Pacific Press) is itself a commodity: it belongs to the LightRocket collection of Getty Images, which owns the rights to the image. Standard editorial licence can be bought from Getty Images for €150 to €475, regular price, depending on the size of the reproduction.[71] The image, as it is reproduced in *The Guardian*, has been digitally altered. The green grass on which the life jacket once lay is erased, replaced with a stark white background. A shadow has been added underneath the object, the color saturation intensified, the contrast (the differential between light and dark) increased. The photograph is also reoriented, from portrait to landscape, so that the life jacket, which once stood vertically, is repositioned horizontally. This makes it more difficult in *The Guardian* reproduction for the viewer to read the label affixed to the life jacket: "C/F Boughaz, Tanger."[72] This is the name not of a person (for whom the life jacket stands in) but of a passenger ferry and its port of departure. The decontextualization of the object from the scene of its photographic capture, its displacement from a physical site of protest to a virtual site fashioned to resemble the scene of a mug shot—all happened at a price.

Like the discarded flotation devices, numbered as they are put to representational use—five thousand life jackets here, fourteen thousand there—all the counted deaths they failed to prevent circulate on condition of prior social deaths. The binary gender categories rotely assigned to the unnamed victims (men, women, and children), or the familial relationships meant to humanize them, or their (real or imputed) national origins form part of their depersonalization. This depersonalization takes place, first, in life.

A refugee, name to be announced. The title of this section is drawn from the programme of a conference that took place in 2017 in Mytilene, Lesvos, under the aegis of Lesbos Dialogues, a series of events jointly organized by the University of

---

Resources, I Will Make The List More Visible,'" *The Guardian*, June 20, 2018, www.theguardian.com/world/2018/jun/20/banu-cennetoglu-interview-turkish-artist-the-list-europe-migrant-crisis.

70. Needham, "The List."

71. See Getty Images, www.gettyimages.no/detail/news-photo/one-of-the-2-500-life-jackets-displayed-in-londons-news-photo/607856732.

72. The *C/F Boughaz* is a ship belonging to the fleet of Comarit-Ferry, "a Moroccan shipping company specialized in passenger transport. It maintains connections between the north of Morocco and the south of Spain and France. Its headquarters are located in the city of Tangier, one of the main ports of departure for its ferries. . . . The company is currently in financial difficulties with its fleet moored in the ports of Sète, Nador, Tanger, Almería and Algeciras." Wikipedia, "Comarit," September 24, 2017 [in Spanish, our translation], es.wikipedia.org/wiki/Comarit.

Agder (located in Kristiansand, Norway) and the municipality of Lesvos.[73] It is a phrase that haunted us since the moment we first read it. Attempting to understand its meaning and its significance has driven the argument in this chapter. According to the organizers' description, the aim of the Lesbos Dialogues was to "anchor . . . the relevant research and the dialogues on one of the main entrance points of refugees to Europe, giving at the same time the event the added value of the symbolic support of the academic and political Europe to the Greek islands and their citizens." The programme—comprising panels on "charting the current situation," "technology and social innovation," "mobile learning," "monitoring and modelling the crisis," and "crowdfunding"—details the names, institutional affiliations/organizations, professional roles, and presentation titles of speakers drawn from academics, INGO/ NGOs, foundations, and government. Following this information, at the end of each panel description, the phrase appears: "A refugee (name to be announced)." This placeholder may indicate the intention of organizers to involve "representatives of the refugees themselves" in cross-sectoral "discussions on charting the current situation and determining best practices to improve at least some of the issues related to their lives and their future." Despite the promissory nature of the utterance, the names never materialize.[74] Who are these "representatives"? Whom, precisely, do they represent? Who appointed or elected them? Behind the call to make them speak as and for refugees is the assumption of a homogeneous mass for which a proxy can stand in and speak on behalf of the others—reminding us, once again, of "the problem of speaking for others."[75]

If an object can come to represent a subject—and, indeed, act as its proxy—it is because that subject has, already, been objectified by things, forces, and gazes. The political and ethical issues of objectification, depersonalization, and silencing that arise around practices of counting refugees, we argue, are based in the prior issue of who counts as a refugee—ineluctably bound up in fetishism, which affects and naturalizes an ontological cut between populations consigned to death at various velocities. "Refugees are . . . 'fully labelled' in people's minds."[76] Does the categorial fetishism that attaches to refugees like a dead weight, pulling them under, leave any

73. "Technology and the Refugee Crisis," Mytilene, November 9–11, 2017. As reproduced on the website of the Observatory of the Refugee and Migration Crisis in the Aegean, University of the Aegean, refugeeobservatory.aegean.gr/en/technology-and-refugee-crisis-mytilene-9—11-november-2017; hereafter cited in text.

74. To be clear, on the programme as it appears on the project's website, which we found at the time of writing, the names of several panelists identified as "refugees" from various countries are listed. See lesbosdialogues .uia.no/technology. We are referring here to the reproduction of the programme as it appears in the depository of the Observatory of the Refugee and Migration Crisis in the Aegean, which was never revised to reflect the belated addition of refugee speakers' proper names, and, as such, reveals something important about the differential process through which refugees and citizens are asked or made to speak.

75. Linda Martín Alcoff, "The Problem of Speaking for Others," *Cultural Critique* 20 (Winter, 1991–1992): 5–32.

76. Roger Zetter, "Labelling Refugees: Forming and Transforming a Bureaucratic Identity," *Journal of Refugee Studies* 4, no. 1 (1991): 40. In this now-canonical article in forced migration studies, Zetter outlines the "conceptual tools of bureaucratic labelling—stereotyping, conformity, designation, identity disaggregation, and political/power relationships" (39).

space for self-representation? Does naming get away from the coloniality of the poli- tics of recognition?[77] In chapter 5, we examine calls to "say their names, hear their voices, see their faces,"[78] to represent through the portrait rather than the proxy in order to restore dignity and humanity to "refugees."

Yet, the portrait and the proxy are not locked in combat on either side of a divide between ethical and unethical representations. The one reproduces the other. The life jacket, a mass-produced object, circulates as a commodity in economies both visual and capitalist, with an unimpeded mobility that those whom it is made to represent, and indeed speak for, might look upon with irony. The reproduction of this proxy—resurrected from its grave, given new life, defended in its abiding util- ity, its striking symbolic power—might be understood as the recommodification of waste, of surplus matter out of place. The production of new value, through the reincarnation of the commodity (and reproductions of the commodity) in this case is possible only by virtue of its proxy attachment to those who consumed it, some of whom were, despite, in, and through it, consumed.

---

77. See Tazzioli, "The Politics of Counting and the Scene of Rescue," 5.

78. Ben Gidley, "Who Is Allowed to Be Human? 'Bare Life' in Aleppo and on the Mediterranean," *Wildcat Dispatches*, December 22, 2016, wildcatdispatches.org/2016/12/22/ben-gidley-who-is-allowed -to-be-human-bare-life-in-aleppo-and-on-the-mediterranean/; see also "Call Me by My Name: Stories from Calais and Beyond," n.d., www.migrationmuseum.org/exhibition/calaisstories; Lin Taylor, "London Art Gallery Showcases Calais Migrant Stories," Thompson Reuters Foundation, June 7, 2016, news.trust .org/item/20160607115545-fxflr/.

"Kurgan"
Photograph by Angelos Varvarousis.

"Narrow"
Photograph by Angelos Varvarousis.

"Greyve"
Photograph by Angelos Varvarousis.

What is at stake in a life jacket graveyard?

The reminder or the forgetting of a tragic event?

The identity of a place?

The history of a movement?

The future of those who use the few life jackets that have not been completely used up to secure the means to survive?

The photographs were taken at different moments during my two-year stay in Lesvos (2016–2018); they condense (incompletely) precarious fragments of a response to the above questions.

—Angelos Varvarousis

"The Mother"
Photograph by No Border Kitchen, Lesvos.

The Mermaid Madonna

Since February 2015, more than 850,000 recorded refugees have crossed over from Turkey onto the fifteen-kilometer stretch of coast on the northern side of the island of Lesbos, in the northeastern Aegean Sea in Greece. This project is titled after the book, *The Mermaid Madonna* (1955) by the acclaimed Lesbos-born writer Stratis Myrivilis.

The story takes place in the fishing village of Skala Sikaminias, one of the main entry points for refugees today. It is set in the 1920s, when this region witnessed its first wave of refugees during the forced population exchange between Greece with Turkey on the exact same coastline. At that time over fifty thousand Greeks settled on Lesbos, many of which have remained on the north side of the island.

A majority of the village population today descend directly from refugees from the above-mentioned population exchange. Due to the lack of imminent action from the Greek government and the European Union in 2015, the locals were the first to help refugees land safely and provide food and shelter. Their lives were severely disrupted as they were also forced to face the memories of their own family histories. This drove me to start a project driven stylistically by the magical realistic narrative of the text while examining the historical repetition of mass transitory movement on this coastline, and what role social memory plays in the permanence of landscape, questioning how physical environments may be continuous stages for different states of displacement.

—Eirini Vourloumis

"The Mermaid Madonna"

Photograph by Eirini Vourloumis.

"The Mermaid Madonna"
Photograph by Eirini Vourloumis.

"The Mermaid Madonna"
Photograph by Eirini Vourloumis.

Angelos Varvarousis

Born in 1983, Angelos lives and works in Athens and Barcelona. He is an urban planner, researcher, and activist who holds a PhD in urban political ecology from the Autonomous University of Barcelona. His research interests revolve around alternative lifestyles, the study of the commons, solidarity economies, and degrowth. He has published with prestigious publishers such as Polity Press, and he is an active member and academic lecturer at the Autonomous University of Barcelona. His work has been presented in many international conferences in Europe and the Americas. He has worked for international institutions, such as the British Council and the European Commission, and was a contributor to the Oslo Architecture Triennale 2019. His view on the commons is rather unconventional, as he focuses more on temporary experiences of commoning, investigating their liberating and transformative potential. In order to explain such moments of transgression and change, he is developing the framework of "liminal commons," in which he draws parallels between the archaic rituals of transition and the collective practices that develop in contemporary crisis-driven societies.

Eirini Vourloumis

Eirini was born in 1979 and raised in Athens, Greece, and is of Greek and Indonesian background. She began her career as a contributing photographer for the *New York Times* Metro section and is currently freelancing for various international publications from Greece, focusing on covering the ongoing economic and refugee crisis. Her current personal work has shifted from pure reportage and combines a documentary and conceptual photographic approach in which she explores social and political environments to reflect their dynamic within the context of the economic and refugee crises in her home country. Her reportage clients include the *New York Times*, *Wall Street Journal*, *New Yorker*, *Time*, *Le Monde*, *Businessweek*, and *The Guardian*, among others. She has exhibited at the Bozar Museum in Brussels, the Gropius Bau Museum in Berlin, and the Benaki Museum in Athens. Her photographs have been acquired by the Dakis Joannou Collection, and her first book, *In Waiting*, was released in 2017 by Hatje Cantz. Vourloumis is a member of the Greek Depression Era Collective.

4

Containers

A dockyard full of shipping containers forms a visual shortcut to imagining the successful mechanisms of globalization through the flows and distribution of commodities around the world. In the aesthetics of the European refugee crisis, containers became synonymous with the incarceration and detention conditions of thousands of "migrants" and "refugees." From carrying cargo around the globe, related to new spatial reconfigurations of power, and precarious working conditions in container ships and ports, to containing the "unwanted migrants and refugees"[1] in detention centers all around Europe,[2] these metal boxes reveal the intersecting connections between economies, flows of capital, war, and detention. In this chapter, we focus on containers in order to examine the multiple ways they have changed our lives; we contend that the unusual focus on metal boxes can be an invaluable research lens through which we can view some of the most pressing concerns of our era—namely, globalization, migration, urban deprivation, and new geometries of power.

The chapter begins by offering a brief critical history of containers—from their military use in the Vietnam War to the almost revolutionary effects of containerization—in order to reveal the mundane protagonists behind some of the most transformative phenomena of contemporary capitalism. We then examine the idea of containers as social landscapes by providing a short autoethnographic account of encountering containers and the multiple ways they altered the urban fabric of these places.[3] We focus, especially, on Greece and the processes through which "migrants"

1. Don Brown, *The Unwanted: Stories of the Syrian Refugees* (Boston: Houghton Mifflin Harcourt, 2018).

2. For example, in 2017, Hungarian Prime Minister Victor Orbán announced the construction of two converted shipping container camps on the country's borders with Serbia amid international criticism. See BBC News, "Hungary to Put Migrants in Converted Shipping Containers," March 17, 2017, www.bbc.com/news/av/world-europe-39301003/hungary-to-put-migrants-in-converted-shipping-containers.

3. This chapter is based on a research project entitled Imag(in)ing Containers as Social Landscapes, which was realized with the support of the University of Lincoln's research investment fund, principal

and "refugees" were being incarcerated in containers and were treated as sources of contamination by/to the local population. The containment of people on the move in containers and other physical infrastructures of detention and encampment materially enacts the schema of "nesting crises," a hegemonic discourse that positions the refugee crisis as an illicit "newcomer" that is contained within the sovereign debt crisis.[4] The discourse of a "crisis within a crisis" ultimately reifies the nation-state as a spatial container. Finally, we analyze how containers have been represented in art as aesthetic objects and variously fetishized and demystified in visual studies.

Containers appeared in the shipping industry more than sixty years ago. Since then, they have transformed the costs of transportation and handling of cargo and thus completely altered the dynamics of global trade. In essence, containers make loading and unloading cargo faster and cheaper; this mechanical, automated process has reduced socially necessary labor time[5] in port handling and transportation. In his historical overview, *The Box*, Marc Levinson argues that the shipping container "made the world smaller and the world economy bigger"[6] by generating logistical practices that introduced the new configurations of capitalist space and time. In other words, containers are part of an overlooked technological revolution that changed the face of trade and global connectivity. By minimizing the costs of transportation, containers opened up a whole new space of global trade routes, possibilities for new markets, and a new geography of precarious labor.

Containerization and its logistics began as a military enterprise. As Alberto Toscano and Jeff Kinkle remind us, pivotal to the accelerated use of containers in global trade was their successful utilization in the Vietnam War.[7] Malcolm McLean, who has been credited as the inventor of containers, secured a multibillion-dollar contract in 1967 for his transnational corporation Sea-Land to ship war material in containers from the port of Oakland to the port of Da Nang in Vietnam. Containers have since influenced the strategies and tactics of war; they are used to transport supplies for invading troops in territories where their militaries did not previously have bases. At this point, it becomes clear how a discussion about metal boxes is a meeting point of concerns regarding military invasions, war logistics, and economic struggles around the world.

The metal box at the heart of the phenomenon of containerization inherits a spatial logic inaugurated by European colonialism and transatlantic slavery. Following the container around enables us not only to trace the materialization of an economy based on plunder and exploitation in space but also to unravel how it reproduces

investigator Aylwyn Walsh and co-investigator Myrto Tsilimpounidi. The project took place in three cities (Athens, London, and Istanbul); this chapter is based on research conducted in Athens between December 2014 and October 2015 by photographer Zoe Manta and visual sociologist Myrto Tsilimpounidi.

4. Anna Carastathis, "Nesting Crises," *Women's Studies International Forum* 68 (2018): 142–48.

5. Socially necessary labor time refers to the average amount of time the average worker needs, using the prevailing technologies and tools, to produce a given commodity.

6. Mark Levinson, *The Box: How the Shipping Container Made the World Smaller and the World Economy Bigger* (Princeton, NJ: Princeton University Press, 2006), 1.

7. Alberto Toscano and Jeff Kinkle, *Cartographies of the Absolute* (Winchester, UK: Zero Books, 2015), 189.

colonial time, the temporality that came to dominate world history. Containers are the modern successors of the brutal efficiency of transatlantic slave ships, designed to cram in as many people as "possible"—abducted and forcibly transported from West Africa over the Atlantic to the Americas.[8] In this sense, containers are not a new invention; they do not suddenly appear in late capitalism. Rather, they contain a process of long historical duration. For centuries, wooden and metal boxes travelled the seas with stolen treasures. The container evokes the horror of spatialized experiences of dehumanizing oppression that mark modernity: captivity, suffocation, deprivation, anonymity, social death—"the topographies of cruelty" that characterize the age of Euroamerican Empire.[9] Achille Mbembe has argued that the spatialization of relations of power is the hallmark of early modern and late modern colonial occupation. Colonialism inscribed "a new set of social and spatial relations," a process of "territorialization": concretely, territorialization involved "the production of boundaries and hierarchies," the "subversion" of existing property relations, the classification of people, resource extraction, and the manufacture of cultural imaginaries—new ways of seeing the occupied landscape (25). Territorialization is the exercise of sovereign power, which in its modern and contemporary forms Mbembe calls "necropower" (26). Mbembe writes that space was "the raw material of sovereignty and the violence it carried with it. Sovereignty meant occupation, and occupation meant relegating the colonized into a third zone between subjecthood and objecthood" (26). The "revolution" in shipping—efficiency, standardization, homogeneity, volume, speed—that the container heralds actually reproduces the territorialization of the world, its necropolitical transformation (long before the "invention" of the container itself) into a world system. Today, containerization has "evolved into a global system comprising around 6,000 container ships and various air, rail, and road networks, which contingently supply those living in the rich North with an estimated 90 percent of everything."[10]

Moreover, as Caroline Knowles argues, the use of containers has resulted in "an ongoing reconfiguration of port geographies and choreographies of products in seaways and highways."[11] Transport costs are further reduced when the cargo inside containers is increased with more efficient packing of goods and products. Similarly, increased numbers of containers sailing in one ship drastically reduces the final cost of cargo transportations. We might think of this as the nested profits brought about through the expanded use of containers. The ships that sailed international seaways before the 1950s were too small for the revolution of containerization. The new, post-Panamax container ships have gigantic capacities and gained their name because

---

8. Unknown Author, "Diagram of a Slave Ship," pamphlet (London: James Phillips, 1787), www.bl.uk/learning/timeline/large106661.html.

9. Achille Mbembe, "Necropolitics," trans. Libby Mentjes, *Public Culture* 15, no. 1: 11–40; hereafter cited in text.

10. Thomas Birtchnell, Satya Savitzky, and John Urry, *Cargomobilites: Moving Materials in a Global Age* (London: Routledge, 2015), 1.

11. Caroline Knowles, *Flip-Flop: A Journey through Globalization's Backroads* (London: Pluto Press, 2014), 120.

their size makes it impossible to navigate the Panama Canal.[12] These gigantic ships required the building of special port facilities; since only a minority of global ports had adequate space, new port facilities had to be built to accommodate container ships, for which political support was required.[13] Approximately 90 percent of global trade today is transported by post-Panamax container ships:[14] this gives us a clear indication of the capitalist domination of choreographies of power, which, with containers, are also transported across borders.

In his film essay *The Forgotten Space*[15] and his photoessay *Fish Story*,[16] Allan Sekula, a filmographer, theorist, and critic whose body of work focuses on the material geographies of the advanced capitalist world, captures the economic struggles to lower labor costs and undermine the port, ships, and dock workers labor unions. With the advancement of containers and the automation of the handling of cargo, manual work was minimized on ports, signifying the end of the bustling port cultures of previous eras. Contemporary ports are portrayed in his work as empty, efficient, homogeneous, automated landscapes—aesthetically significant features of the era of late capitalism. At the same time, the working conditions of migrant manual workers in container ships are inhumane, invisible, and usually ignored "by many journalists whose own class status predisposes them towards fixating on white-collar and mental labor."[17]

Immanuel Wallerstein and Terence Hopkins, in their 1986 article, introduced the term global "commodity chains"[18] in order to describe the various links between raw materials, manufacturing processes, and transportation arrangements among the sites that would ultimately result in the final product. In the era of containerization, these links between production and consumption acquire such speed and urgency that they result in a redefinition of the global economy and international trade.[19] To put it differently, containers are a vehicle for commodity fetishism, whereby products that are the result of social relations—some of them very exploitative and vio-

---

12. The Panama Canal is an artificial eighty-two-kilometer waterway in Panama that connects the Atlantic Ocean with the Pacific Ocean. The Panama Canal, due to its location, has historically been a battlefield over control of global trade. France began work on the canal in 1881 but stopped due to engineering problems and a high worker mortality rate. The United States took over the project in 1904 and opened the canal on August 15, 1914. Colombia, France, and later the United States controlled the territory surrounding the canal during construction. The United States continued to control the canal and surrounding Panama Canal Zone until the 1977 Torrijos-Carter Treaties provided for handover to Panama. After a period of joint American–Panamanian control, in 1999, the canal was taken over by the Panamanian government.

13. Knowles, *Flip-Flop*, 121.

14. Allan Sekula and Noel Burch, *The Forgotten Space*, film essay, 2010, www.theforgottenspace.net.

15. Sekula and Burch, *The Forgotten Space*.

16. Allan Sekula, *Fish Story* (Dusseldorf: Richter Verlag, 1995).

17. Sandhu Sukhdev, "Allan Sekula: Filming the Forgotten Resistance at Sea," *The Guardian*, April 20, 2012, www.theguardian.com/film/2012/apr/20/allan-sekula-resistance-at-sea.

18. Immanuel Wallerstein and Terence Hopkins, "Commodity Chains in the World Economy. Prior to 1800," *Review (Fernand Braudel Center)* 10, no. 1 (1986): 157–70.

19. Gaey Gereffi and Miguel Korzeniewicz, *Commodity Chains and Global Capitalism* (Westport, CT: Praeger, 1994).

lent—are understood as objects for consumption in the capitalist market.[20] As such, containers become the emblematic objects of mobility, speed, global trade, and globalization—alongside their obverse processes: exploitation, war, and incarceration. As T. G. Demos puts it, containers became the "moving image of globalization,"[21] signalling a new era of connectedness and new territories for capitalist expansion, extraction, and exploitation.

Coinciding with the emergence of global commodity chains, in the beginning of the 1990s, many theorists rushed to celebrate an era characterized by the unprecedented mobility of people, capital, products, and ideas.[22] John Urry has made the study of mobility into a key study of modern life.[23] For Arjun Appadurai, mobility has become an emblematic concept of life within the globalized world, expressed in fluid terms of "flows" and "scapes."[24] Zygmunt Bauman's oft-quoted point about the "liquid" movement of modern life is instructive here: "what has been cut apart cannot be glued back together. Abandon all hope of totality, future as well as past, you who enter the world of fluid modernity."[25] In a more optimistic characterization, Ulrich Beck sees this new unprecedented interconnectedness of the world as an opportunity to create a new cosmopolitan vision in which nobody can escape this new kind of "collective consciousness."[26] These are, of course, important texts in social and political thought that open up wider questions of mobility, connectivity, capitalism, and social dynamics. Yet, we seek to move away from celebratory understandings of mobility in order to unpack the messiness of its implications on the social world, to move away from abstract theoretical constructions of flows, scapes, and fluids, toward a political commitment to make visible the lived realities of people on the move. For example, it is one thing to talk about the "flows" of immigration from northern Africa to southern Europe and a different thing to engage with the experiences of the 518 refugees travelling from Eritrea to Italy, whose boat sank in Lampedusa in 2013. It is not only a difference in scale (a macro- or microlevel analysis of migration) or a question of disciplinary lenses (international relations versus sociology, for example) but, rather, a question informed by politics. A political perspective that puts people over the market, social well-being over profits, lived realities over abstract theories, while critically examining the circulation of their representations.

20. More recently, online platforms and applications trace the commodity chains of different products in an attempt to promote ethical consumption. See, for example, followthethings.com and www .phonestory.org.

21. T. J. Demos, *The Migrant Image: The Art and Politics of Documentary during the Global Crisis* (Durham, NC: Duke University Press, 2013).

22. Zygmunt Bauman, *Liquid Modernity* (Cambridge, CT: Polity Press, 2000); Ulrich Beck, "Critical Theory of World Risk Society: A Cosmopolitan Vision," *Constellations* 16, no. 1 (2009): 3–22; John Urry, *Mobilities* (Cambridge, CT: Polity Press, 2007).

23. Urry, *Mobilities*; Anthony Elliot and Urry John, *Mobile Lives* (London: Routledge, 2010).

24. Arjun Appadurai, *Modernity at Large: Cultural Dimensions of Globalization* (Minneapolis: University of Minnesota Press, 1996).

25. Bauman, *Liquid Modernity*, 22.

26. Beck, "Critical Theory of World Risk Society," 3.

ENCOUNTERING CONTAINERS

Without containers, the tremendous and catastrophical expansion of global trade in the last sixty years could not have taken place. As Peter Drucker argues, this expansion is the "fastest growth in any major economic activity, ever recorded."[27] If containers are such important monuments to global capitalism—and to ecological collapse—it seems strange that, for a long time, one may have hardly ever encountered them in one's daily urban life. Containers travel the oceans in post-Panamax ships, reaching commercial ports that are usually far away from urban centers. From there, cargo trains and transporter trucks distribute them via national highways to storage facilities that are also, usually, located at the peripheries of urban centers. If, for most of the late twentieth century, in our everyday urban lives we were not familiar with the sight of containers, something shifted in the early decades of the millennium. Containers began to appear in urban centers, in architecture and art. Leading to the Containers as Social Landscapes project, this sparked an interest in the photographic documentation of containers in the three cities in which the researchers were spending a lot of their time: Istanbul, Athens, and London.[28] It was the first time that we encountered containers on our daily walks. This research project is the outcome of peripatetic observations, informal discussions, and everyday frustrations in the three cities.

To be more precise, our initial encounters with containers started in Istanbul. After the global financial crisis of 2008, Istanbul continued to multiply in size, and new gentrification and regeneration projects were visible all over the city center and on the wealthy outskirts. Prime Minister Erdoğan was announcing a new era of financial prosperity and Europeanization for Turkey, and Istanbul was the epicenter of this new chapter of modern Turkish history. The city was preparing for a bid to host the Olympic Games in 2012; the usual business of neoliberalization of public space and extreme gentrification that accompanies mega events such as the Olympic Games was evident. In our daily walks, containers were becoming a usual sight in Istanbul. After some initial discussion with friends in the city, we quickly became aware that most of those containers were used to house low-waged migrant construction workers, the silent heroes behind Istanbul's miraculous development. The conditions in the construction sites were very poor: up to eight workers (usually undocumented Kurdish migrants) were living in one container, their only residence. Often, the workers were moved inside the containers from one construction site to the next, and as a result they had no idea where they were located in the city.

Despite Istanbul's frantic preparations, London won the bid to host the 2012 Olympic Games. On our daily commute in the east part of London, we became accustomed to the sight of containers. Studios were marketed to hipsters under the brand name Container City. The 2012 Olympic Games in London left an irrevers-

---

27. Peter Drucker, *Innovation and Entrepreneurship* (London: Routledge, 2007), 28.

28. In 2013, Myrto was based in London at the University of East London; her research at the time was focused on public space and the mobilizations and resistance techniques exhibited in Gezi Park in Istanbul and on the streets of Athens.

ible mark on a city that was already unaffordable for most; once again, marginalized groups were pushed to the urban periphery of London. Some residents who could no longer afford their houses in East London decided to relocate to the container dwellings,[29] which were more affordable; housing, offices, theatre, and gallery spaces in containers near the river Thames were marketed as a new urban trend. Several container parks were developed into affordable housing for purchase in an attempt to deal with the housing crisis unfolding in the city.[30]

In the northern suburbs of Athens, containers are currently used as the makeshift detention center of Amygdaleza, incarcerating thousands of migrants in inhumane conditions. People detained there are locked into metal boxes with neither ventilation nor sanitary amenities. In early 2015, after a series of suicides and protests inside detention centers led to the then newly-elected SYRIZA government promising to shut down detention centers, a media spectacle was staged "exposing" what was hidden from view in Amygdaleza. The cameras entered the containers, and for a moment it seemed this government was going to answer the call to abolish the use of containers in immigration detention,[31] and, indeed, to end the *de facto* regime of indefinite detention.

In all three cities, the recommodification of containers to shift purpose and meaning nevertheless returns their contents to the status of objects or commodities, ready to be moved on, sold, or discarded. Three cities and one metal protagonist pointing towards issues and daily struggles that are interconnected, such as the neoliberalization of public space and the punitive containment of people whose movement is seen as unruly or whose labor can be hyperexploited.

In an era of "crisis," the study of markets and movement needs to be reimagined in relation to the human costs of capitalism, including precarious labor, dispossession, and migration management. Containers are objects on the move: they are floated across oceans on container ships, packed on transport lorries and driven down highways, streamed down rivers, and taken aboard cargo trains on railways. But in what follows, we focus on their stasis. Containers on the move might be the ideal metaphorical vehicles to examine a number of concerns. Yet, precisely because this research project was carried out in the milieu of crisis and stagnation, we wanted to know what happens when the container reaches stasis:[32] a momentary stop that

---

29. See, for example, www.containercity.com.

30. The UK's largest temporary housing development, a container village for homeless people, opened in 2019 in west London. Set up on derelict land next to an estate in Acton, the container village is the most ambitious effort yet to utilize the oblong, mobile units to help address the housing crisis. For more, see Adam Forrest, "UK's Biggest Shipping Container Village Opens up for Homeless People," *Big Issue*, December 7, 2017, www.bigissue.com/latest/uks-biggest-shipping-container-village-opens-homeless-people.

31. See, for example, the "Monitoring Moria" mission of Sea-Watch, October 12, 2017, sea-watch .org/en/monitoring-moria/; Yara Boff Tonella, "If You Want to Know the True Meaning of Fear, Hunger and Cold, Come Here," Amnesty International, March 15, 2018, refugeeobservatory.aegean.gr/en/"if-you -want-know-true-meaning-fear-hunger-and-cold-come-here"-amnesty-international.

32. The research project Containers as a Social Landscape was developed as a practice-led investigation in three locations (Athens, Istanbul, London), with a core objective to consider the place, purpose, and politics of the particular object: the shipping container. Three teams were formed using different applied research skills: in Athens (photography), London (architecture), and Istanbul (theatre). Each team undertook a year-long process of workshops and practical explorations. The intention was to allow the form of

punctuates its journey—not stillness as the absence of movement but as the collision of opposing forces.[33]

Exemplifying the imagery of consumption and waste, containers are used in architectural designs for a wide range of purposes. Craig Martin's book *Shipping Container*[34] considers the phenomenon of containerization and its repurposed use in architecture. Containers have determinate lifespans. When a container is damaged (compromising its stackability) or otherwise exceeds its lifespan, it "dies." But since they cannot easily be disposed of, and it is more expensive to have them shipped back to their origins, they are repurposed and given a second lease on "life." Containers in stasis have been converted into offices, homes, and galleries; used as emergency shelters to house homeless people and refugees; to form army bases; and to serve as detention centers. To paraphrase Demos, containers in stasis expose the otherwise hidden urban geographies of globalization. This is what geographer Deborah Cowen[35] debates in *The Deadly Life of Logistics*, an exegesis of violence of global trade; there, Cowen considers how logistics and infrastructure are foundational to economies of war, securitization, and national defence strategies as much as they are crucial to what narrowly gets defined as "trade" in the capitalist economy. As objects, containers simultaneously contain the much-celebrated revolution of global trade and the untold stories of precarious labor, the mobility of capital and the borderlands of exclusion, the neoliberalization of urban space and the punitive containment of certain groups of the population. It is of particular importance that these manifestations of mobility and containment are not contained as opposite dualities but as interdependent, mutually constitutive processes.

CONTAINERS AS SOCIAL LANDSCAPES

This metal box we started encountering in my urban walks is both the operator and a centuries-old symbol of regimes of exploitation. Yet, now in its stasis it contains living human beings, from the urban dwellers of London to the construction workers in Istanbul to the refugees in detention centers on the outskirts of Athens. If containers on the move concealed all the layers of extraction of raw material, exploitative labor exchanges, and processes of distribution that add up in order to make up the final product, then what processes and mechanisms were concealed in their stasis? If containers on the move are key operators of commodity fetishism, then what kind of

---

the artistic discipline to respond to, as well as be informed by, the research process. Photographia 2 is the outcome of the visual investigation in Athens.

33. Stasis as defined by Thucydides is a set of symptoms indicating an internal disturbance in both states and individuals. A moment in which forces are opposing: while they cancel each other, they provide a space for stillness. See more on the idea of stasis in Thucydides's work in Jonathan Price, *Thucydides and Internal War* (Cambridge: Cambridge University Press, 2009).

34. Craig Martin, *Shipping Container* (London: Bloomsbury, 2016).

35. Deborah Cowen, *The Deadly Life of Logistics: Mapping Violence in Global Trade* (Minneapolis: University of Minnesota Press, 2014).

fetishism is invoked in their stasis? Containerization is what Raymond Williams calls "the magic system"[36] through which commodities appear in high street department stores and supermarkets. But it is also the magic system through which discarded commodities disappear: garbage and waste is transported inside containers from their site of production in the global North to vast landfills in the global South.[37] People pick garbage, sort it out, and resell it.[38] This is a reminder of the hegemonic representations of a refugee crisis in 2015 and the "magic ways" in which people appeared on the shores of Europe. A representation that, as we discuss more extensively in other chapters, makes invisible the chains of war, exploitation, displacement, and agony that contributed to this appearance. This is also a painful reminder of the logic of Fortress Europe and the hotspot mechanism through which the same people disappear indefinitely in detention centers, going through the process of sorting out who counts as a refugee and who as an economic migrant.

The fieldwork for this project took place in Athens between December 2014 and October 2015, with the aim to create a visual testament to the aesthetics of crisis in the city and to austerity and Fortress Europe. Containers became our vehicles to a journey in globalization's backyard, to a European periphery after several years of economic crisis and on the verge of the refugee crisis. In the first stage of the investigation, we photographed containers from a distance at Amygdaleza detention center on the outskirts of the city.[39] In February 2015, the newly elected left-wing SYRIZA government in Greece pledged to close detention centers and transform them into open reception facilities. In a climate of enthusiasm and hope, we managed to enter Amygdaleza and were allowed to use our cameras for research purposes. We quickly became aware of the symbolic power of dominant representations—how images of this "crisis" were being used both "inside" and "outside" of Greece. We also felt the ethical burden and anxiety of what it means to add more images and representations to the mushrooming visual discourse of the unfolding refugee crisis.[40]

We followed the containers' trajectories around the city. Newly homeless people, victims of the economic crisis, were (if only the lucky) housed in containers by the crumbling welfare state. In the era of extreme financial and sociopolitical crisis, who gets contained? What are the limits between inside and outside? How can visual methods challenge the limits of what we know about the interrelationship between mobility and logistics? We posed these questions in a climate of increased pressure for the Greek government to appear to have control over its borders and migration.

---

36. Raymond Williams, *Border Country: Raymond Williams in Adult Education*, ed. John McIlroy and Sallie Westwood (Leicester, UK: National Institute of Adult Continuing Education, 1993).

37. Birtchnell, Savitzky, and Urry, *Cargomobilities*, 6.

38. Parasher Baruah, *Waste*, 2015, 37:53 mins, youtu.be/bNpQ9W94LmI.

39. Amygdaleza was Greece's first dedicated detention center for refugees and undocumented migrants in 2015 and consists of dozens of containers that were originally set up to house people displaced by earthquakes. See Karolina Tagaris, "Greece Pledges to Shut Immigrant Detention Centers," *Reuters*, February 14, 2015, www.reuters.com/article/us-greece-politics-immigrants/greece-pledges-to-shut-immigrant-detention-centers-idUSKBN0LI0MJ20150214.

40. A similar anxiety that I feel now reflecting on this process, an anxiety that Anna and I decided to inhabit and which motivated us to write this book.

A newly-elected leftist government was facing a delicate balance between a decade of economic crisis and stagnation and a rising conservative, racist, and xenophobic discourse in Greece and across Europe. In that moment, we felt the containers were the ideal protagonists in order to (visually) index the diverse meanings of the so-called nesting crises in Athens.[41]

By the end of the summer of 2015, the Greek government declared it was "experiencing a crisis within a crisis":[42] still neck-deep in financial crisis (and its disastrous effects on human lives), and with no end in sight, the Greek socio-economy could not absorb the new arrivals whose sudden appearance on the shores of the Aegean islands was said to constitute a "refugee crisis." When the United Nations High Commission on Refugees urged Greece to "take charge"[43] of this crisis—that is, to own and contain it—the rejoinder by Greece's then-deputy minister for Immigration Policy, Tasia Christodoupoulou, was that the EU member states had abdicated their responsibilities: "solidarity has been replaced by national self interest."[44] Yet who—or what—would be the subject of solidarity? Refugees, whom recalcitrant EU member states refused to relocate within their own borders, denying them refuge? Greeks, who had already "suffered enough"?[45] Or, perhaps, the Greek state itself, facing a problem with "dimensions that exceed the capabilities of our country," yet which, nevertheless, has made good of its "humanistic obligation to give of our remanence to these people."[46] The figure of "nesting crises" functioned to delineate the boundaries of national space and time. National space is constructed as a container. If the global economic crisis had already been made "ours" by being constructed as a problem inherent in the national economy—a sovereign debt crisis—the global war on migration became reinvented as "Europe's crisis" and then "Greece's." Moreover, the figure of nesting crises serves to distinguish the normative victims of what are seen as distinct, if overlapping, political phenomena (debt and migration), from those who parasitically share in, or indeed by their very illicit presence cause or contribute to, the continued suffering of the beleaguered national subject.

---

41. Carastathis, "Nesting Crises," 2018.

42. Christodoupoulou quoted in Phoebe Greenwood, Noah Payne-Frank, and Apostolis Fotiadis, "The Greek Island Sinking under Europe's Refugee Crisis," *The Guardian*, August 20, 2015, 14:47, www.the guardian.com/world/video/2015/aug/18/greek-island-leros-europe-migrant-crisis-video; prime minister of Greece, "Declarations of the Prime Minister A. Tsipras after the Conclusion of the Governmental Summit for the Management of Issues Related to Refugee Flows" (Athens: Office of the Prime Minister, 2015), www.primeminister.gov.gr/2015/08/07/13931 [in Greek, our translation; link is no longer functional].

43. William Spindler quoted in Stephanie Nebehay, "UN Urges Greece to Take Charge of Refugee Crisis," *Reuters*, August 18, 2015, www.reuters.com/article/us-europe-migrants-greece-unhcr/u-n-urges -greece-to-take-charge-of-refugee-crisis-idUSKCN0QN14920150818.

44. Christodopoulou quoted in Greenwood, Payne-Frank, and Fotiadis, "The Greek Island Sinking under Europe's Refugee Crisis."

45. Daniel Marans, "Greece's Economy Is Getting Crushed between Austerity and the Refugee Crisis," *Huffington Post*, July 25, 2017, www.huffpost.com/entry/greece-refugee-crisis-economy_n_56b 12f1de4b04f9b57d7b7d4?guccounter=1&guce_referrer=aHR0cHM6Ly93d3cuZ29vZ2xlLmNvbvS88& guce_referrer_sig=AQAAAAlrfah0jaiu5F6Mu9m06vloEmtWmAT5ev5sifh4UF6Wre_xc4ceWOivY11d WlSx-a4rCDjFz0DDB1wPiftRar3kkr8qp-GK6eUEBdDFXzBp3UY8rTHRrH-0eCURj3YkUl-RJGao qvgO1LgLPNRYhyDpRWZoX67nQqVr0V-cYjvw.

46. Prime minister of Greece, "Declarations of the Prime Minister A. Tsipras."

We did not want to fetishize the container as an object; rather, we aspired to treat metal boxes as intersections of different forms of exploitation and oppression. So, we stopped photographing containers as objects and we tried to capture their multiple meanings throughout the city of Athens. One of our concerns was to distance ourselves from a visual economy of art that uses the container as the "synecdoche for logistics, circulation and capital," obscuring its "relational properties" while becoming "mesmerized by its modularity, homogeneity and opacity."[47] We felt that this is also a statement against the ubiquitous use of containers as galleries, theatre spaces, pop-up exhibition, and performance venues, and all sorts of architectural trends that appropriate crisis-driven aesthetics. Departing from the Container City of London and focusing our study on the inhumane incarceration of people denied asylum or found to be lacking the "proper documents" in Athens, we were wary of reproducing a capitalization of the spectacle of crisis in our own container-related visual explorations. In a similar vein, for Shane Boyle, the prevalence and fetishization of "container aesthetics" often remain uncritically replicated in art contexts without sufficient attendance to the regimes of power and processes of capital accumulation towards which they point.[48] The same geopolitical and historical conditions that allow architects to repurpose a linchpin of international trade—the container—and to transform it into the physical infrastructure for exhibitions, reveals the embeddedness of the arts in the transnational global capital.[49] Art becomes a new terrain of the commodification of the container. As we saw in chapter 3 with respect to life jackets, the repurposing, upcycling, and reproduction of a commodity can be understood as a process of reincarnation or recommodification through which a "wasted" commodity is invested with new value.

Containers are represented as autonomous objects, moving around, as if on their own steam, while people remain outside the frame. Yet, containers may be moving around while containing people. Representations or reproductions of containers as aesthetic objects in visual arts are characterized by the absence or insignificance of human presence.[50] Homogeneity, standardization, repetition, modularity, and efficiency are functional and aesthetic features of containers. The essence of this terribly banal, dull, indifferent box is its substitutionality, its embodiment of capital's drive towards materialized abstraction.

Our aim was to defetishize containers in the midst of social phenomena reified as "economic and refugee crises." Jacques Rancière's analysis of container images

---

47. Toscano and Kinkle, *Cartographies of the Absolute*, 196.

48. Shane Boyle, "Container Aesthetics: The Infrastructural Politics of Shunt's 'The Boy Who Climbed Out of His Face,'" *Theatre Journal* 68, no. 1 (2016): 57–77.

49. An example of fascination with "container aesthetics" is Miroslav Balka's *How It Is*, commissioned by and exhibited at Tate Modern from October 13, 2009, until April 5, 2010. *How It Is* is described as a box of darkness, a black hole testifying to a number of incidents in recent Polish history. The Tate's description of the work is characteristic here: "by entering the dark space, visitors place considerable trust in the organization, something that could also be seen in relation to the recent risks often taken by immigrants travelling." See www.tate.org.uk/whats-on/tate-modern/exhibition/unilever-series/unilever-series-miroslaw-balka-how-it.

50. An example of this kind of work is Edward Burtynsky's photography of epic landscapes; see www.edwardburtynsky.com.

produced by Frank Breuer[51] suggests that the photographed container could potentially point towards the forgotten spaces—of the port, the factory—and the
invisibility of social relations of production:

> From afar the spectator perceived them as abstract scenes or reproductions of minimalist
> structures. Upon approaching, however, one discovered that the colored rectangles on a
> white background were containers stacked in a large deserted space. The impact of the
> series was down to the tension between this minimalism and the signification that it
> concealed. These containers were to be, or were to have been, filled with merchandise
> unloaded at Antwerp or Rotterdam, and probably were produced in a distant country,
> perhaps by faceless workers in Southeast Asia. They were, in short, filled with their own
> absence, which was also that of every worker engaged to unload them, and, even more
> remotely, that of the European workers replaced by these distant laborers.[52]

We might take issue here with the multiple levels of reification that the analysis itself
arguably reproduces in its objectifying representation of Southeast Asian workers as
"faceless," essentializing them as "absent," and, in the final analysis, using them as
an orientalist shortcut to lament the jobs that global North workers "lost" when the
jobs "migrated" to the global South through outsourcing, offshoring, production
shifts, and import competition in the era of so-called free trade. Rancière's reflection, as problematic as it is, made us think of the container's border policy: what
is inside, hidden, locked, transported, in motion, and what remains outside, in the
background, part of the passing landscape. When the border is secured, when the
container door is shut, the inside could be anything: flip-flops,[53] frozen pork chops,
a circuit board—useless now, but at the end of the chain it will meet other parts to
form a digital camera—cocaine, guns, or human beings. When the border is porous,
when the container door cracks open, the mystery of the merchandise is solved; according to Rancière, containers remain filled with their own absence, demystified as
they are, they expose the otherwise hidden trajectories of exploitation. This visual
reproduction of the logic of the border, between the inside and the outside, includes
the risk of defetishing containers too fast: "what appears to be a seamless technical
apparatus for distribution hides, beneath its blank metal surface, bodies in pain." [54]

---

51. Rancière refers to Frank Breuer's exhibition of cargo and containers presented during the 2005
Rencontres photographiques in Arles. A sample of this work can be viewed here: galleryluisotti.com/
images/containers-2002/.

52. Jacques Rancière, "Notes on the Photographic Image," *Radical Philosophy* 156 (July/August 2009),
www.radicalphilosophy.com/article/notes-on-the-photographic-image.

53. As is the case with Caroline Knowles, *Flip-Flop: A Journey through Globalization's Backroads* (London: Pluto Press, 2014).

54. Toscano and Kinkle, *Cartographies of the Absolute*, 207.

The following images were part of the exhibition "Containers as Social Landscapes," which was installed alongside extracts from our research diary in numerous venues in the UK (London and Lincoln), Turkey (Istanbul), and Greece (Athens). The exhibition consisted of thirteen iron panels (48 x 90 cm), each one a diptych of two images, captioned by an extract from the glossary of container shipping.[55]

55. Container Services International CSI Glossary: Useful Terms and Acronyms from the Container World, 2014, www.csiu.co/resources-and-links/glossary-of-the-container-world.

CONTAINER :

A REUSABLE STEEL RECTANGULAR BOX FOR CARRYING CARGO
THAT FIRST CAME INTO COMMON USE ABOUT 50 YEARS AGO.
THE SIZES OF CONTAINERS ARE STANDARDIZED SO THAT THEY
CAN EASILY BE MOVED BETWEEN SPECIALLY ADAPTED
CONTAINERS SHIPS, TRAINS AND TRUCKS.

BOX :

ANOTHER (LESS FORMAL) NAME FOR A SHIPPING CONTAINER.
THIS IS HOW THEY ARE OFTEN REFERRED TO IN THE INDUSTRY.

"The Box,"
Containers as Social Landscapes
Photograph by Zoe Manta and Myrto Tsilimpounidi.

Extract from Research Diary: Box

Container Terminology—Container
A reusable steel rectangular box for carrying cargo that first came into common use about fifty years ago. The sizes of containers are standardized so that they can easily be moved between specially adapted container ships, trains and trucks.

Container Terminology—Box
Another (less formal) name for a shipping container. This is how they are often referred to in the industry.

We are finally in Athens, or somewhere near Athens as we are never really in the urban parts that we can recognize and call Athens. We are driving mechanically from the northern outskirts where Amygdaleza detention center is located to the port of Piraeus chasing metal boxes. In Amygdaleza we cannot enter;, so we drive on the higher parts of the mountain in order to get a view down at the detention facility. White containers, one next to the other. Numbness. Down to the port of Piraeus, the locals complain that this part of the port is now sold to "a Chinese corporation" and the working conditions are awful and the unions completely powerless. They want to know about our research. They smile and call us "container spotters." In the COSCO-owned part of the port, we need special permission to go near the cargo containers, but there are many places for container spotting. Repetitive movements, boxes on top of boxes. Boredom.

Our equipment, our cameras, the clothes we are wearing, parts of the car we are driving up and down, all of them came boxed and know exactly how it is to travel inside these containers. Can we request an interview from our car battery? A mindful meditation on our lives' dependency on capitalism. In Amygdaleza we want to crack open the containers, these inhumane little prisons for the people the state now calls refugees. Our own trajectories so much implicit in their containment. Capitalism, fast consumption, commodities, war, displacement, and myriad stories contained in little boxes. We want to crack open the boxes governing our perception, our cameras the first small container.

"BCL Repair Criteria,"
Containers as Social Landscapes
Photograph by Zoe Manta and Myrto Tsilimpounidi.

Extract from Research Diary: Repair Criteria

Container Terminology—BCL Repair Criteria
Detailed repair criteria issued by the BCL that defines clearly which repairs should be performed on fleet containers. Damage Protection Plan (DPP) offered by containers lessors who are not "technically" allowed to offer insurance, which is a regulated market.

Containers, those celebrated boxes of global trade. Perhaps we made a mistake, a miscalculation brought us here. No grand narratives of the strong European market anymore, no capitalist fantasies to lull us into the logistically calculated lives of homeowners, family cars, and flat screens. What a beautiful thing the destruction of worlds. Greece is a regulated market and the epicenter of the financial crisis, debt piled up on more debt and a series of fragile governments. I remember writing somewhere that seasons here are not marked by falling leaves but between disbursements from the IMF, the European Central Bank, and the European Commission. Time passing is different in the epicenter of crisis; the linear contract of time is broken here. Time equals money, future time associated with progression is lost. What remains is empty time, a society waiting for something without knowing what that something might be. People waiting in containers indefinitely without knowing if they are ever going to secure the correct paperwork. Containers in Amygdaleza are the waiting rooms of history.

Repair criteria? Together with the colonial fantasies that Athens once was the birthplace of democracy and civilization. Time now goes back to the ancient past, the present of broken marble pillars and identities is not under a Damage Protection Plan. Yes, but a story from other times reminds us what happens to a society trapped in the myths of a glorious past.

"Detention,"
Containers as Social Landscapes
Photograph by Zoe Manta and Myrto Tsilimpounidi.

Extract from Research Diary: Detention

Container Terminology—Detention
Fees charged when containers are held outside the terminal longer than the agreed free time. All units will continue to be charged daily while in the custody of the consignee until returned to the shipping line.

A sign on the back of a truck reads "METAPHORES/ZONTA ZOA"; in Greek it means "transportation/living animals." Perhaps due to my dyslexia, maybe because I'm looking for a metaphysical sign, I understand the sign as the metaphor of living animals, an allegory of living animals in a truck near the sea in what has been called the "entrance gate to Europe for migrants and refugees." In my head, the voices from the people trapped in those containers in Amygdaleza repeating every now and then "We are not animals"; "People are not animals," repeated to us by one of the solidarians. I wanted to ask why all this fuss with equating people to animals? Is it not the problem that people are trapped in prison boxes, we do not know for how long, and all over Europe they are being portrayed as the source of a crisis. Or perhaps it is fine when animals are trapped, but now that humans are trapped it becomes a problem? It was not the appropriate time to ask these questions. Words detained, thoughts surveilled, what is freedom of expression in a moment when freedom of movement is criminalized? My words are never going to be free again.

"Blind Shipment,"
Containers as Social Landscapes
Photograph by Zoe Manta and Myrto Tsilimpounidi.

Extract from Research Diary: Blind Shipment

Container Terminology—Blind Shipment
When the shipper and receiver are not aware of one another, the freight shipment is called blind shipment. In such cases, the bill of lading lists the party that paid for the shipment as the shipper or receiver of the freight shipment.

Summer of 2015 in Athens, after a long time I have heard a reporter referring to it as the "summer of migration." As if I needed more evidence to be convinced that time in the epicenter of crisis is calculated differently. The summer of migration, what a sweet term, it could be the name of a summer retreat in the ideal paradise of the Greek islands. The crew of our luxurious yacht would take care everything for you as we migrate from one Aegean island to the other. Relax and let the beauty of the landscape sink in while we take care of you. Have you ever attended a presentation, an invited lecture, or a conference talk in which you heard (or said) "the Greek summer of migration"? Is this an accurate term for a time when people were murdered in the sea? A time when the sea passage between Greece and Turkey became an aqueous cemetery? Did it matter that it was summer, because we would have been sweating anyways. Yet, instead you listen to yourself politely asking the presenter, while sweating anyways, "Do you perhaps know when this term was used and why?" My words are never going to be free again.

It is a sunny morning on the shores of Lesvos, the Aegean Sea is beautiful and our cameras can capture myriad images for touristic purposes. This time, though, the tranquillity of the landscape was interrupted by the presence of boats on the horizon. The sea, the horizon, interrupted silences indicate the absence of words. The arrival, the moment that the shore is nearly there. No pictures taken for touristic purposes, but we were surprised to see that many of the newcomers were taking arrival selfies with their mobile phones.[56] A record that they made the journey, a picture to send back to their beloved ones, the beginning of a new life. A tourist or a refugee?

---

56. See chapter 5.

SWAP BODY:

USED FOR EUROPEAN ROAD AND RAIL TRANSPOR AND
NOT SEAWORTHY. CONSTRUCTED DIFFERENTLY TO
CONTAINERS AND WITH METRIC DIMENSIONS, THESE
ARE NOT STACKABLE AND SOME ARE FITTED WITH
RETRACTABLE LEGS.

"Swap Body,"
Containers as Social Landscapes
Photograph by Zoe Manta and Myrto Tsilimpounidi.

Extract from Research Diary: Swap Body

Container Terminology—Swap Body
Used for European road and rail transport and not seaworthy. Constructed differently
to containers and with metric dimensions, these are not stackable and some are fitted
with retractable legs.

*Fourth day at the port of Piraeus, we are waiting for the workers to occupy the port in
protest of its sale to China Ocean Shipping Company (COSCO Group). Through this sale,
the port of Piraeus became the second-largest Mediterranean facility for container ships.
Waiting, we become accustomed to the metallic aesthetics and the repeatability of containers
one stuck on top of the other. We craved the presence of human beings in our images next to
the containers, as though this would offer a more human scale. We waited, a container boat
arrives, cranes taking the containers from the boat to the side of the port. Storage. Container
trucks arriving taking some of the stored containers, moving towards one of the gates of the
port. New trucks arriving, more containers moving to the gate of the port. First day back at
Amygdaleza detention center. This time containers and humans in stasis. Nothing moves; we
feel that everything is waiting for . . . containers to be moved and humans to be classified in
different categories. We start to crave the repeatability of movement we witnessed at the port,
mechanical/nonsensical/monotonous. We begin to wish for the absence of humans next to the
containers; there is no human scale we could capture after all.*

*One person says that he feels as if he has no legs. In the whole journey, which took him eigh-
teen days of walking, the last three days without shoes, he could always feel his legs, but here,
in the detention, he started to feel as if he has no legs.*

"Nested,"
Containers as Social Landscapes
Photograph by Zoe Manta and Myrto Tsilimpounidi.

Extract from Research Diary: Nested

Container Terminology—Nested
A term used in less than truckload shipping in which materials are stacked so that one item goes inside another. Nested freight reduces the amount of space taken up and makes shipping more efficient as a result.

The same square in central Athens captured at different times of the day and night made us understand the schema of nesting crises in this city. In 2008, Athens was at the epicenter of the European economic crisis, news was spreading about the riots and the resistance movement in Athens, and myriad images of police brutality and tear gas made it to the international headlines. In 2015, it seems as if the economic crisis is an inescapable reality with silent victims visible all over the city, their concerns and their resistance no longer making headlines. When crisis becomes banal, can we still call it crisis? The spectacular moments of the square movement and the Indignados (Aganaktismenoi in Greek) and the resistant bodies occupying public space are not there anymore. In 2015, international media are not interested in the financial crisis, now we have the new round of crisis, this time called the "refugee crisis." Different formations of bodies occupy the central squares of Athens; different resistance movements and techniques are becoming visible. We want to question the spectacularity of crisis; we want to focus on the undeclared crises that will never make headlines. Different (declared or undeclared) crises, different formations of bodies on the same square.

Nested freight reduces the amount of space taken up and makes shipping more efficient as a result. Nested crises reduce the amount of social reaction as the social body is trying to recuperate from the multiple shocks, and as a result it makes more efficient the implementation of otherwise unthinkable measures. Nested bodies and resistant choreographies in the streets and squares reduces the risk of police brutality and neo-Nazi attacks; will solidarity find intersecting pathways of empathy along which to travel?[57]

---

57. See chapter 6.

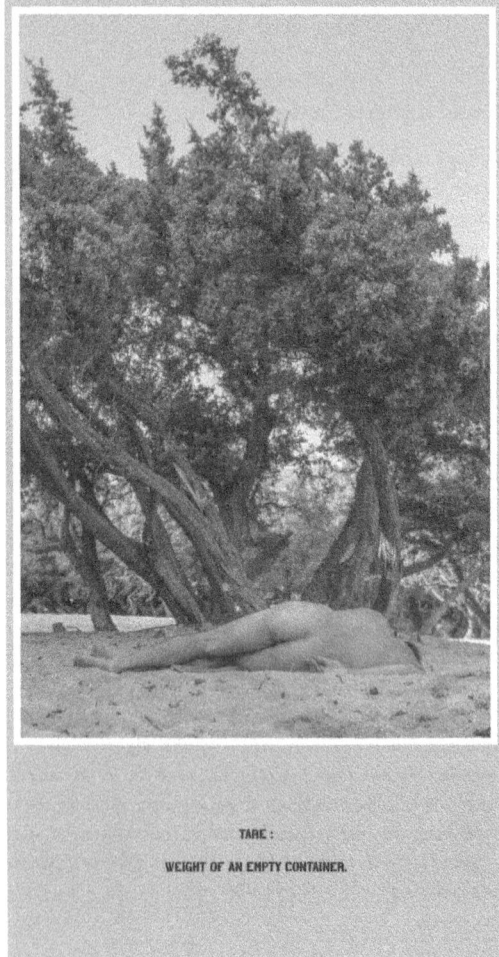

TARE :

WEIGHT OF AN EMPTY CONTAINER.

"Tare,"
Containers as Social Landscapes
Photograph by Zoe Manta and Myrto Tsilimpounidi.

Extract from Research Diary: Tare

Container Terminology—Tare
Weight of an empty container.

We create the images.

5

Survival Selfies

In 2013, the *Oxford English Dictionary* named "selfie" as its word of the year, acknowledging its omnipresence in popular media as a way of representing the self. Democratizing the once-elite genre of portraiture and popularized through urban youth cultures, the selfie has been celebrated as "the first and fundamental object of global visual culture."[1] The selfie, the act of capturing our own image—usually with a mobile phone camera—blurs the borders between the subject and the object of the photographic act; its representational power arguably derives from our imagined control over the ways we think we would like to look and to be perceived by others. This is the main reason the selfie has been celebrated as a sociocultural revolution in identity affirmation practices.[2]

The selfie is not an entirely new form of seeing oneself and others; it resonates with the long history of portrait painting and photography. Historically, the portrait was a marker of wealth and status of the person depicted, an interface of how we would like to represent ourselves and the ways others perceive us. The possibility of being able to look at a portrait of oneself was reserved only for the powerful; it was a form of power to be able to gaze at oneself, a reassurance of wealth and prestige. Mechanical reproduction made portraiture available to the masses and also transformed it into a tool of the nascent discipline of demography and, more generally, of social control through the use of portrait photography for passports, identity cards, and mug shots. With the advancement of mobile phone cameras, the selfie is a digitally reproduced form of self-portraiture intended for distribution on social media.[3]

---

1. Nicholas Mirzoeff, *How to See the World: An Introduction to Images, from Self-Portraits to Selfies, Maps to Movies, and More* (New York: Basic Books, 2016), 40.

2. Edgar Gómez-Cruz and Helen Thornham, "Selfies beyond the Self-representation: The (Theoretical) F(r)ictions of a Practice," *Journal of Aesthetics and Culture* 7, no. 1 (2015), doi.org/10.3402/jac.v7.28073.

3. See SelfieCity: Investigating the Style of Self-portraits (Selfies) in Five Cities across the World, selfiecity.net.

When a boat full of people safely arrives on the shores of Greece from Turkey, the first thing many of the passengers do is to unwrap the plastic film protecting their smartphone, turn their back to the sea, and take a selfie. If this gesture, in this context, seems dissonant with the urban youth culture of the selfie, what does it mean that "the selfie has been used as a recurrent media genre for the representation of migrants and refugees?"[4] If the so-called "European refugee crisis is the first of its kind in a fully digital age . . . the smartphone is the refugee's best friend."[5] Smartphones have proven invaluable not only for selfie-taking purposes, or (more generally) for communicating with loved ones but also for mapping clandestine routes across vast landmasses and finding relatively safer passages, for receiving advice from border-crossers sent through messaging applications, for transmitting GPS coordinates when in distress, and for accessing applications especially developed to assist refugees with finding housing, being reunited with loved ones, obtaining legal assistance, or interacting with international aid agencies. Social media–hosted sites urged people to "Smuggle yourself to Europe without a trafficker," using only a GPS-equipped smartphone.[6] Procuring local SIM cards, finding open Wi-Fi networks, and charging one's mobile battery became needs as urgent as food, shelter, and clothing.[7]

Being in possession of expensive smartphones was used as evidence of the undeservingness of refugees in the international media.[8] But it was also used to secure claims of the sameness, particularly of young, urban refugees, participating in a transnationally legible cultural practice—and therefore to structure empathetic relations with an assimilable Other with whom European publics could identify. Celebratory analyses of selfies tend to ignore the neoliberal underpinnings of subject formation that the global practice seems to (uncritically) reproduce—and, against this particular horizon of selfie-taking, the necropolitical conditions structuring the survival of the perilous journey. In this context, the selfie mediates the space between identity affirmation and testimony of survival. The material trace of the photograph—which, at first glance, may resemble a tourist's snapshot—is haunted by the proximity of death, its unrepresentability but also its affective and symbolic negation in a reaffirmation not only of identity but also of survival.

Selfies at the scene of arrival become reproduced as high art: Ai Weiwei's *Iphone Wallpaper* (2016) presents a collage of over 12,030 images taken by Ai on his phone

4. Lilie Chouliaraki, "Symbolic Bordering: The Self-representation of Migrants and Refugees in Digital News," *Popular Communication* 15, no. 2 (2017): 78–94, doi.org/10.1080/15405702.2017.1281415.

5. Patrick Witty, "See How Smartphones Have Become a Lifeline for Refugees," *Time*, October 8, 2015, time.com/4062120/see-how-smartphones-have-become-a-lifeline-for-refugees/.

6. Matthew Brunwasser, "A 21st-Century Migrant's Essential: Food, Shelter, Smartphone," *New York Times*, August 25, 2015, www.nytimes.com/2015/08/26/world/europe/a-21st-century-migrants-checklist-water-shelter-smartphone.html?_r=1.

7. Witty, "See How Smartphones Have Become a Lifeline for Refugees."

8. Dominic Lawson, "Smartphones Are the Secret Weapon Fuelling the Migrant Invasion," *Daily Mail*, September 28, 2015, www.dailymail.co.uk/debate/article-3251475/DOMINIC-LAWSON-Smartphones-secret-weapon-fuelling-great-migrant-invasion.html.

during his stay on the island of Lesvos (January to April 2016).[9] But, in his role as honorary president of the jury, Ai also urged celebrities who attended the Cinema for Peace Gala in Berlin in 2016 (for which he decorated the columns of the Berlin Konzerthaus with life jackets discarded on the shores of Lesvos)[10] to take selfies while ensconced in mylar blankets in support of #refugees. Decried as exploitative, even unfeeling, the celebrity selfies were widely viewed as "uncomfortable images from Berlin [which] showed people wrapped in symbols of misery while enjoying themselves."[11] Ai's Lesvos selfies were said to have a different affective appeal: "I know people who were volunteering on the Greek island at the time—unsung heroes who've worked for years to help asylum and refugees—and they were delighted to see the Chinese artist and to take selfies with him."[12]

As Anja Franck argues in her analysis "The Lesvos Refugee Crisis as Disaster Capitalism," selfies taken with refugees on the shores of Lesvos to power NGO crowdfunding campaigns "place the refugee body at the center of value extraction processes."[13] Similarly, Roopika Risam characterizes the "co-optation" of selfie-taking by refugees as "high-tech Orientalism."[14] She argues that the reproduction of photographs of "refugees" taking selfies—but not the selfies they took—by news media outlets "constitute the selfie-taking refugee as an object. . . . By circulating images of refugees taking selfies—rather than the selfies themselves—these news media articles deny both self-representation and agency to refugees."[15] Crucially, Risam "raises the question of how the agency of the selfies that are not circulated in news media may be recuperated."[16] The title of Risam's article, "Now You See Them," references the sleight of hand through which a magic trick is performed, whereby an object is made to disappear in front of one's eyes: now you see them, now you don't.

But, as we argued in chapter 3, the ethical questions haunting photographic representations of "refugees" do not wither away with the physical absence, nor do they arise merely due to the physical presence of people (or bodies) classified as such. Building on that argument here, we contest the notion that self-representation through portraiture necessarily interrupts the visual economy through which "refugees" are reproduced as objects of humanitarian, documentary, administrative, sociolegal, or other hegemonic gazes. We examine two assumptions underlying the debate

---

9. Ai Weiwei at Cycladic, Museum of Cycladic Art, Athens, 2016, cycladic.gr/en/page/ai-weiwei-at -cycladic#. The exhibit included portraits taken by the Photography Association of Mytilene (photographers who collaborated with Ai in his Lesvos-based project).

10. See chapter 3.

11. Emma Graham-Harrison and Tim Finch, "Was It Wrong to Get Celebrities to Pose Wearing Emergency Blankets for Refugees?" *The Guardian*, February 20, 2016, https://www.theguardian.com/ commentisfree/2016/feb/20/was-it-wrong-to-get-celebrities-to-pose-wearing-emergency-blankets-berlin -charlize-theron.

12. Graham-Harrison and Finch, "Was It Wrong," 2016.

13. Anja K. Franck, "The Lesvos Refugee Crisis as Disaster Capitalism," *Peace Review* 30, no. 2 (2018): 203.

14. Roopika Risam, "Now You See Them: Self-representation and the Refugee Selfie," *Popular Communication* 16, no. 1 (2018): 59.

15. Risam, "Now You See Them," 59.

16. Risam, "Now You See Them," 59.

about the visual dehumanization and humanization of refugees: first, that depictions of the face combat the objectification of human subjects, and second, that empathy and solidarity are enabled through representations of refugees as grieving, relieved, suffering, or grateful fathers, mothers, husbands, wives, children, or grandparents.

A recent content analysis of Australian media representations of refugees found that they were depicted in groups, from a distance, often in boats, with only 2 percent of images showing them as individuals with recognizable facial features.[17] In the Mediterranean "refugee crisis," some syndicated and independent photographers have attempted to counter "the visual dehumanization of refugees"[18] by employing different strategies. Indeed, in their analysis of photographs published in *CNN International* and *Der Spiegel* during the "long summer of migration," Xu Zhang and Lea Hellmueller found that 37 percent and 18 percent (respectively) were close-up shots.[19] Still, 25 percent and 40 percent of photographs (respectively) did not show refugees' facial expressions or emotions,[20] which—in addition to representing refugees as members of families—the authors argue "humanizes" them in the eyes of viewers participating in the "construction of the distant suffering."[21]

Photographs at close range that signify gendered, familial relationships become a primary visual trope in humanizing representations of "refugees," lending at least two interconnected senses to "close-ups": a tight frame around the subject (minimizing distance) and a tight embrace around the body (signifying intimacy). The close-up offers the viewer the perception of immediate proximity to the subject of the photograph; this perceived proximity is redoubled by the representation of refugees through reproductive frames. Representations of their (real or ascribed) participation in the heteronormative institution of the family becomes a tight frame, closing in around the figure of the refugee. Essentialized through their participation in an ostensibly natural form of organizing kinship relations—by being reproduced as husbands, wives, fathers, mothers, children—refugees become subjects of empathy; they are visually redeemed as the vulnerable or imperiled bearers of civil and political rights, including the right to international protection through their embodiment of reproduction.

Returning to the scene of photography in the era periodized, spectacularly staged, and reproduced as the refugee crisis leads us not only to question the desire to look at photographs of refugees but also opens up the possibility of asking of photographed persons, "Why are they looking at me?"[22] Why did they agree (if they did, indeed, agree) to be photographed? Ariella Azoulay (whose account of the "civil contract of

---

17. Roland Bleiker, David Campbell, Emma Hutchison, and Xzarina Nicholson, "The Visual Dehumanization of Refugees," *Australian Journal of Political Science*, 48 no. 4 (2013): 399, dx.doi.org/10.1080/10361146.2013.840769.

18. Bleiker et al., "The Visual Dehumanization of Refugees."

19. Xu Zhang and Lea Hellmueller, "Visual Framing of the European Refugee Crisis in *Der Spiegel* and *CNN International*: Global Journalism in News Photographs," *The International Communication Gazette* (2017): 12, 10.1177/1748048516688134.

20. Zhang and Hellmueller, "Visual Framing of the European Refugee Crisis," 13

21. Zhang and Hellmueller, "Visual Framing of the European Refugee Crisis," 17.

22. Ariella Azoulay, *The Civil Contract of Photography* (London: Zone Books, 2008), 18.

photography" we discussed in chapter 2) raises the possibility that subjects of photographs agree to be photographed not in order to be seen but in order to look. For Azoulay, consenting to or initiating the taking of a photograph, "even when suffering in extremely difficult circumstances," presupposes a shared recognition—among the parties to the civil contract of photograph—"that what they are witnessing is intolerable."[23] It allows us to shift theories of representation as these address photography from a focus on photographers as authors—or viewers as spectators—of photographs to subjects of photographs who are articulating a demand not only to be seen but to look and therefore to participate in a "sphere of political relations" not circumscribed by the state power that assigns them a noncitizen status.[24] On the face of it, given that it collapses the distinction between subject and object by turning the camera (often held in the palm of one's hand) towards oneself, the selfie as an act (and self-representation as the broader visual practice to which it belongs) troubles the dualism between being seen and looking, at the very moment of capture. Yet, celebrating self-representation (and selfies, in particular) as, straightforwardly and simply, an agentic rupture of a visual economy seems premature given that not all embodied gazes are equally empowered with "the right to the image."[25] Consider Azoulay's formulation of the fundamental question to be asked of a photographed subject in conditions of political violence in order to restore to them their political claim: "Why are these men, women, children, and families looking at me?"[26] Does the reproduced subject's gaze only come into view when the subject is reproductive?[27]

COULD YOU PLEASE LOOK INTO THE CAMERA?

Playwright Mohammad Al Attar, whose documentary play *The Factory* we discussed in chapter 3, collaborated with director Omar Abusaada on staging *Could You Please Look into the Camera* (2012). In the play, a filmmaker, Nura, invites young people who participated or were caught up in the protests that began in 2011 in Syria to

---

23. Azoulay, *The Civil Contract of Photography*, 18.
24. Azoulay, *The Civil Contract of Photography*, 19–20.
25. See chapter 2.
26. Azoulay, *The Civil Contract of Photography*, 17–18.
27. In relation to Azoulay's notion of the "citizenship of photography" that we discussed extensively in chapter 2, Adi Kuntsman talks about "selfie citizenship" to refer to claims that are made by "ordinary citizens via the use of their own networked self-portraits." Kuntsman here refers to the political use of selfies in social media: activists holding banners, various hashtag actions with people promoting them taking a selfie while holding a note, and selfies from protests and other mobilizations. These actions challenge the mainstream critiques of selfies as a narcissistic preoccupation, inherently apolitical and sometimes even antisocial (such as selfies in dating applications). At the same time, Kuntsman is aware of the danger of romanticizing such acts as providing new forms of agency, by recognizing that these acts are taking place against a backdrop of increased control of citizenship through biometrics that result in new forms of governance and violence. Thus, "selfie citizenship" refers to "particular forms of spectatorial intimacies and performative effects that can create or disrupt the sense of citizen collectivity through illusory proximity, and capitalize on individual visibility, at the time when citizenship itself is increasingly governed through biometric recognition." Adi Kuntsman, ed., *Selfie Citizenship* (London: Palgrave, 2017).

give testimony about their arrest and interrogation by the regime's security forces to a video camera set up in an improvised studio in an apartment.[28] Witnessing, testifying, representing, in front of cameras—that project actors' faces onto the cyclorama, some of them distorted to maintain anonymity, others visible, bringing them into closer, frontal view to the spectators—are emphasized visually as performative acts, which in both *Could You Please Look into the Camera* and *The Factory* address the audience to situate themselves vis-à-vis the otherwise austere stage (donned with mundane sets of domestic or bureaucratic/carceral spaces). The camera is central to this mode of address. Its obvious mediation of the reproduced image of actors on stage and off in the theatrical play, an image which visually dominates over the action on stage, may possibly generate reflection in viewers of their own situated acts of witnessing, testimony, and representation, and to question the often assumed relationship between documentary fact and moving image. What remains on the other side of the concrete wall, the projection screen, the border on which the spectacle is staged?

"The torture chamber is the paradigmatic space of the totalitarian regime," Hani Sayed states,[29] arguing that totalitarianism itself be understood as a politics of the image, not only in the narrow sense of the propagandistic use of images but in the deeper way in which totalitarianism shapes our most fundamental ideas about our individual identities, the space we inhabit, the forms of human interaction that are possible, and those that are impossible. "The ubiquitous symbol of regime propaganda has been the official photographs of Bashar al-Assad and his family," yet when the writer Zaher Omareen is himself suddenly arrested, he realizes: "There is no need for pictures in prison. Everything attests to the State's absolute dominance; this stark reality no longer requires symbols behind which to hide. On the outside the ubiquitous photograph of the Syrian leader has a purpose. It is there to make you think of one place, always: prison."[30]

The violence of the regime is not a means to an end; it is the system.[31] Thus, the prison might be a metaphor for Syria, if Syria had not been, as Al Attar states, for forty years "a large prison."[32] A report by Human Rights Watch published in the summer of 2012 documents the use of enforced disappearance, detention, and torture in un-

---

28. Mohammad Al Attar, Edward Blaise Ziter, and Lisa Wedeen, "Could You Please Look into the Camera?," *TDR/The Drama Review* 58, no. 3 (2014): 124–55, doi.org/10.1162/DRAM_a_00376; see also Edward Blaise Zitter, *Political Performance in Syria: From the Six-Day War to the Syrian Uprising*, 2014; "Theatre Review: Could You Please Look into the Camera," *The Scotsman*, www.scotsman.com/arts-and-culture/theatre/theatre-reviews-could-you-please-look-into-the-camera-write-here-1-2241412.

29. Hani Sayed, Untitled Lecture, Panel V, Abounaddara: The Right to the Image, Vera List Center for Art and Politics, New School for Social Research, October 25, 2015, livestream.com/TheNewSchool/abounaddara-the-right-to-the-image/videos/102806274.

30. Zaher Omareen quoted in Malu Halasa, "Malu Halasa on Art from within Syria's Prison Cells," Amnesty International UK Stories and Rights, June 16, 2014, www.amnesty.org.uk/blogs/stories-and-rights/art-within-syrias-prison-cells. See Malu Halasa, Zaher Omareen, and Nawara Mahfoud, eds., *Syria Speaks: Art and Culture from the Frontline* (London: Saqi Books, 2014).

31. Sayed, Untitled Lecture.

32. Mohammad Al Attar, Playwright's Note, "Could You Please Look into the Camera?," trans. Lisa Wedeen, introduction by Edward Ziter, *TDR: The Drama Review* 58, no. 3 (2014): 124–55.

derground prisons in Syria since the uprisings began in March 2011.[33] At around this time, Al Attar interviewed thirteen Syrians who had recently been detained, at first intending to use the interviews as the basis of a verbatim play.[34] A form of documentary theatre, verbatim theatre is constructed through the exact testimony of people interviewed about an event. Yet, as he worked on the play, Al Attar questioned his practice: "Should we write directly about this moment that runs like sand through our fingers? Or should we stand by and wait for a temporal distance to allow the necessary critical space that might enable a better apprehension of what is going on?"[35]

Indeed, the titular question, "Could You Please Look into the Camera?," repeated multiple times by the main character of the play, is less the polite phrasing of a direction and more so the reminder of the central problematic of the play: the question of the possibility of self-representation in the face of the destruction of selfhood, of the documentation of an "omnipresent but completely invisible"[36] reality: the torture chamber, the prison.

Sayed argues that the irrepresentability of torture, except as traces that remain on the body of the person subjected to it, is itself a means of control and discipline.[37] The uprising in Syria contested the politics of the image; the image became part of the struggle. YouTube was flooded with images of the tortured body. On the one hand, Al Attar's documentary theatre forms part of this movement, as Edward Ziter suggests: "Just as an army of amateur videographers has captured government atrocities, Al Attar apparently envisions a battalion of applied theatre practitioners who will help Syrians tell their stories to themselves and the world."[38] On the other hand, though, Al Attar puts into question the conditions of possibility of documentary representation, probing the boundaries between the "real" and the "imaginary":

My answer to all these questions and even my way of escaping them required that I betray the document in order to triumph on the side of the story; so I mixed real accounts with imaginary ones. I transferred all the questions that I could from my own heart and mind into the heart of the text. The text thus became a site for open-ended questions rather than a presentation of fully developed realities. I came to know that the meaning of documentary theatre ultimately lies in the way the text carries the complexities of the moment. It is a place open for questions about an unknown future and an unfinished narrative about what has already taken place.[39]

To ask someone (even oneself) to face a camera is to invite them to enter a frame: "To photograph is to frame. To frame is to define the boundaries of the real, of what

33. Human Rights Watch, "Torture Archipelago: Arbitrary Arrests, Torture, and Enforced Disappearances in Syria's Underground Prisons since March 2011," July 3, 2012, www.hrw.org/report/2012/07/03/torture-archipelago/arbitrary-arrests-torture-and-enforced-disappearances-syrias#_ftnref66.

34. Ziter, Introduction, "Could You Please Look into the Camera?," 126.

35. Al Attar, Playwright's Note, "Could You Please Look into the Camera?," 128.

36. Sayed, Untitled Lecture.

37. Sayed, Untitled Lecture.

38. Ziter, Introduction, "Could You Please Look into the Camera?," 126

39. Al Attar, Playwright's Note, "Could You Please Look into the Camera?," 129.

is representable, and what cannot be represented, in the dual meaning of what we are not allowed to represent, and what is not worthy of representation. And because of that the photograph . . . is *ab initio* implicated in its own interpretation."[40] The regulatory function of the image reproduces and is reproduced by our mundane acts of seeing—even when what we are seeing (and looking at) is ourselves. Every act of framing is an act of censorship, Sayed contends, where censorship is not only an act of state power but also of private power: thus, "images that circulate in the public sphere are always already censored."[41] Sayed also reminds us of a "less literal sense of framing": that is, the construction of reproducing, naturalizing norms.[42] For Sayed, Abounaddara's call to a right to the image[43] is a call to end private censorship, "to see the frame itself, to subject it to scrutiny and to critique."[44]

But how do we make the frame visible? In a Brechtian mode, Al Attar and Abusaada use photography—in particular, projected photographs and video of faces—to remind spectators of the constructedness not only of the play but also of images (or the lack of images) and of realities we confront or imagine. In *Could You Please Look into the Camera*, these faces are often distorted to protect their anonymity—but their voices are clear. This mirrors the dreams of Karim after his imprisonment and torture: "sometimes I see images from that time in my dreams, but the strange thing is I see the images but never faces, even though I hear people's real voices."[45] By contrast, the faces of the people—not the authorities but ordinary citizens—that caught her and her friends as they were leafleting and gave them up to security forces are emblazoned in Farah's memory: "What I cannot forget is the faces of those who gathered around us, beat us up, and dragged us. I remember them as if I had seen them less than half an hour ago" (138). If "the image is memory, a document" (143), its costs are revealed (and not revealed) at the end of the play: Nura, the filmmaker who set out to "document the experiences of detention" is detained in a security branch; what has happened to her interviewees is unknown. "I see all your stories, I see myself imprisoned all the time," (147) Nura had told Zayd—himself detained "for no apparent reason" (139)—foreshadowing this *fait accompli*. An unknown future and an unfinished narrative; "tears running silently down her face" that she "swiftly wipes . . . and stands up" (155).

FACING CRISIS

In July 2017, in Athens, we ran a photography workshop with a group called LG-BTQI+ refugees,[46] comprised of international and local activists, which we called Fac-

---

40. Sayed, Untitled Lecture. See also Judith Butler, "Torture and the Ethics of Photography," *Environment and Planning D: Society and Space* 25 (2007): 951–66.

41. Sayed, Untitled Lecture.

42. Sayed, Untitled Lecture.

43. See chapter 2.

44. Sayed, Untitled Lecture.

45. Al Attar, "Could You Please Look into the Camera?," 135; hereafter cited in text.

46. The organization has been anonymized.

ing Crisis. The initial aim of the workshop was to engage people in collective acts of self-representation through portraiture. Participants in the workshop were people who had been rendered entirely invisible in hegemonic and social movement discourses of the refugee crisis in Greece, Europe, and globally. Their lives, desires, and embodiments do not fit the narrative of the "deserving refugee," understood in terms of what Gayatri Chakravorty Spivak has called "reproductive heteronormativity."[47] In other words, they trouble the naturalized assumption that human lives and relationships gain value, significance, and meaning through ostensibly universal, heteropatriarchal structures of kinship and reproduction. In that sense, they trouble a fundamental condition of citizenship—and refuge. As Eithne Luibhéid has argued, sexual normativity is crucial to nation-state projects of "biological and social reproduction of the citizenry, but also for the cultivation of particular kinds of social, economic, and affective relationships."[48] Yet, sexual normativity also structures affective and social relationships in counterhegemonic social movements, in which LGBTQI+ refugees also found themselves violently marginalized.

Workshop participants were survivors of war, dictatorship, and racialized gendered violence, in their intersecting manifestations, understood not as "exceptional crises" but as the systemic underpinnings of global capitalism. Rather than simply offering a counternarrative of inclusion to hegemonic and activist representations of "deserving refugees," the workshop sought to intervene in the ways that inclusionary responses reproduce representational violence in rendering certain subject positions unthinkable, untranslatable, and, ultimately, unlivable. Our motivation in offering the workshop was a desire to enact "queer coalitions"[49]—that is, to find embodied ways of living and working together across and against axes of power and lines of belonging constituting our bordered reality, in which movements across space that contest the nation-state system are criminalized and those that threaten its foundational institutions, including the heteropatriarchal family, are violently punished.

We want to problematize the multiple forms of bordering in the countries of departure and arrival while at the same time unpacking the possibilities for queer responses to forced migrations. We suggest that, through the heteronormalization of refugees, the survival trajectories of refugees are perceived through framings not only of their own reproductive histories and futures (figurations of "family," "childhood," "maternity," and "paternity") but also of their (in)capacity to reproduce institutions—family, religion, nation—as a precondition of their social belonging. Survival and fugitivity as such become framed as questions of reproductive justice or reproductive danger, conditioning empathy, hospitality, and social integration on the one hand and indifference, hostility, and social exclusion on the other. In short,

---

47. Spivak in Nayanika Mookherjee, "Reproductive Heteronormativity and Sexual Violence in the Bangladesh War of 1971: A Discussion with Gayatri Chakravorty Spivak," *Social Text* 30, no. 2 (2012): 123–31, doi.org/10.1215/01642472-1541790.

48. Eithne Luibhéid, *Pregnant on Arrival: Making the Illegal Immigrant* (Minneapolis: University of Minnesota Press, 2013), 4.

49. Cathy J. Cohen, "Punks, Bulldaggers, and Welfare Queens: The Radical Potential of Queer Politics?" *GLQ* 3, no. 4 (1997): 437–65, doi.org/10.1215/10642684-3-4-437.

the survival of refugees is framed in reproductive terms—both in fascist discourses, which view them as a demographic threat, and in solidarity discourses urging their integration. The latter, while challenging the legitimacy of nation-state borders, nevertheless reproduce one of the most important institutional logics that constitute nation-states, what Spivak has termed "reproductive heteronormativity": the "assumption that producing children by male-female coupling gives meaning to any life"; "the oldest, biggest sustaining institution in the world, a tacit globalizer" that reproduces itself through "war and rape."[50] The effects of normalizing heterosexuality as the natural bond that affectively connects all human beings, or as a universal cultural trait inherent in societies in so-called refugee-producing countries, are many.

The scene of arrival becomes iconic of the crisis—and the survival selfie the iconic gesture of self-representation at the scene of arrival. This mediatized construction of the "crisis" does not allow us to fix our gaze on the destruction of bodies, spaces, and cities by a war machine driven by a fixation on power, profit, and Western ideologies. On the contrary, this representation of the "refugee crisis" habituates us into perceiving as the starting point of the crisis the arrival of dis-placed bodies on the shores of Europe.[51] Not a word for the unseen bodies who never made it through the journey and whose killings have transformed the Aegean Sea into an aqueous cemetery.

We want to juxtapose these widely reproduced images—of fathers, mothers, children, grandparents[52]—with a narrative of the kind of incident no one was there to photograph. This is Souma's story, a trans woman from Cairo, as she told it to a Greek journalist: "We arrived in Chios by boat having each paid 700 euro. All four of us LGBT people who had boarded the boat were for the entirety of the journey very discreet; in fact, I had covered myself almost completely in a niqab—it seems funny, but I was afraid to meet the same fate as another trans refugee; once her travelling companions realised she was trans, they threw her in the sea. Hours later the Turkish coast-guard collected her, but this whole torment, I learnt later, made her go mad."[53]

Who gets pushed overboard when survival becomes a question of reproduction?

What we are trying to challenge are our ways of seeing in the milieu of crisis, the notion of perspective in an era characterized by the proliferation of images, and the ways these affect our imagination and, thus, our reactions to the crisis. Representations of refugees are dangerous images, not only in the sense that the risk of objectification inheres in them but also because the material conditions that give rise to them are necropolitical ones. That survival—framed as reproduction—is apparently the subject of these images only means that the backdrop remains out of focus: the sea, the fear, the war, everyone left behind, everything destroyed, everyone fallen or pushed overboard.

---

50. Spivak in Mookherjee, "Reproductive Heteronormativity and Sexual Violence in the Bangladesh War of 1971," 125.

51. See chapter 1.

52. See chapter 6.

53. Souma quoted in Thodoris Antonopoulos, "Gay, Lesbian, Trans Refugees in Athens: One of the Most 'Invisible,' Dramatic but also Heroic Sides of the Refugee Issue," *Lifo*, November 8, 2016 [in Greek, our translation], www.lifo.gr/articles/lgbt_articles/120527.

DISPOSABLE CAMERAS

In recent years, photography has been heralded as an ideal medium for collaborative and participatory "refugee research." Holding the camera is seen to empower those who have direct experience of seeking refuge: as Caroline Lenette explains, "by framing and depicting their own lived experiences rather than being the 'object' of others' gaze and framing, Knowledge Holders can use photography as a means to challenge detrimental visual narratives of forced migration."[54] Participatory photography projects where refugees are the ones holding the camera have proliferated in Lesvos, Athens, and elsewhere since 2015. We found ourselves reproducing this logic when we ran a photography workshop with LGBTQI+ refugees in the summer of 2017, with the stated intention of disrupting the invisibility, the misrepresentation, and the coercive power of the image, to which, on their own accounts, the participants had been subject.

We called the workshop Facing Crisis. Our initial aim was to engage people who have been marginalized in this economy of representation, but also in the solidarity economy, in a collective process of self-representation. Confronted with a horizon against which things stop making sense, we selfishly wanted to find ways to keep imagining. Based on the premises of participatory photography methodologies, the workshops were designed around a series of discussions about issues of representation, intersectionality, identity, and belonging and aimed to give participants technical knowledge of framing, composition, visual language, and visual stereotypes. We chose portraiture because it was the most obvious inroad to self-representation, even though we wanted—and urged participants—to move from the stereotypical notion of the "face" (noun) to "facing" (verb)—that is, through taking a stance, to claim the visual as a space of resistance.[55] Against and behind hegemonic representations of crisis, we wanted to question who becomes the normative subject of crisis and who gets pushed out of the frame. Portraiture was thus the medium for bridging the metaphorical social body with the literal experiences and representations of embodiment of our participants, dwelling in the margins and contesting their marginalization against the backdrop of crisis. Our initial idea was to lead a series of practice sessions in various places in the city, giving each participant a disposable camera, and, at the end, to curate an exhibition of the works produced by the participants.

In the end, the photographs were taken not with disposable cameras but in a much more painstaking way using a digital camera, a collaboration between the students and the teachers (so to speak). This was because the workshop participants were keen to learn photographic skills that necessitate more sophisticated equipment. This took them out of the habit of taking snapshots (or selfies) and resulted in thoughtful framing, lighting, and other compositional choices. In the end, there

---

54. Caroline Lenette, "Visual Depictions of Refugee Camps: (De)constructing Notions of Refugeeness?," in *Handbook of Research Methods in Health Social Sciences*, ed. Pranee Liamputtong (New York: Springer, 2019), doi.org/10.1007/978-981-10-2779-6_47-1.

55. Susan Sontag, *On Photography* (New York: Picador, 1973).

was no exhibition (although we printed the photographs and the photographers shared them with each other). Indeed, in this chapter, we are not including any of the photographs that were taken during the workshop. In fact, as we reflect on the workshop, we want to problematize the ubiquity of projects that give cameras to refugees and exhibit photographs they take (of themselves, other refugees, etc.). Particularly when participatory photography is initiated not by the participants themselves but by researchers, photographers, solidarians, or artists (who of course may have multiple identifications and disidentifications with participants), the questions arise, for us (recalling the words of Spivak):[56] What anxieties do we mask in seeking to make the subaltern visible? Make the subaltern show its face? Asking the subaltern to take a selfie perhaps is an attempt to resolve on the level of representation the violent hierarchy that exists in virtue of the nation-state system. Do we have a romantic investment in a subject of struggle? We want representations that make us feel that this hierarchy can be eliminated in our personal relationships, and in the perceptual and affective relationship of the viewer to an image, particularly an image of a suffering other.

The primary way in which the suffering other becomes relatable in the image is through familiality: they become familiar by being familial. This is because our primary way of understanding relationship as such is through the institution of reproductive heteronormativity.[57] This is a question of violence. But we realized that, while they refused this visual discourse of suffering, and the subject positions and affects assigned to refugees—gratitude, despondency, resilience—the photographs that were taken during the workshop engaged in a stereotypical counterdiscourse, of camp gayness, replete with hegemonic standards of beauty. In that sense, they were all too relatable, familiar if not familial, homonormative if not heteronormative. But the point is not to replace one normativity with another, to create an ideal model of the LGBTQI+ refugee to counter the "bring your families" narrative.[58]

Facing Crisis, then, comes to mean something else as we consider the dynamics of power that center a subject, constructing them as an exemplar or even seeking to capture their individuality. Portraiture has always oscillated between these seemingly contradictory aspects of the subject. On the one hand, the portrait historically sought to represent the status, class, or power embodied in the sitting subject. On the other, the portrait ineluctably reproduced the individuality of the subject: the face. Yet, the refugee is not a subject; it is a state category. And as such—despite ever proliferating calls to do so—it cannot show its face. By being made visible as refugees, people are rendered invisible as subjects.

The "refugee" is not simply someone seeking refuge or fleeing violence; it is someone who qualifies for what is called "international protection," someone recognized

---

56. See chapter 3.
57. See chapter 1.
58. See chapter 6.

by a state as a legitimate supplicant. The obverse of the refugee is the "economic migrant," and indeed, what constitutes the refugee crisis for Europe is the logistical difficulty that ostensibly large numbers of people arriving present to the procedures designed to distinguish between the two. For example, (at the time of writing) on the logic of "refugee-producing nations," people arriving from Afghanistan, Yemen, Somalia, and Nigeria are not usually considered refugees and as such are not given the opportunity to claim asylum in Europe; they are slated for deportation. Whose crisis is declared and visible and whose remains undeclared and invisible? The category of the "refugee" is a crystallization of normative ways of viewing crisis, which makes people's experiences of fleeing violence legible only to the extent that they converge with state and supranational interests. Under this light, we cannot possibly reproduce portraits of "refugees."

So, the second stage of the Facing Crisis workshop was to reproduce the reproductions, returning to the scene of photography to stage the same photographs that we had collectively decided were "the best ones," but with their subjects absent. We could have photoshopped the images in order to remove the subjects,[59] but our aim was not to aestheticize; we could have laid a censor bar over the eyes or pixelated the faces of the subjects to anonymize them (as is commonly done in photographs of demonstrators or of children to protect their identity), but our aim was not to be grotesque, either. Taking the photographs again seemed important, not least of all because it required us to meticulously reproduce the photographer's perspective—to set the same frame, to set the camera just as they had, to remember the reasons they gave for their choices, what they had sought to make visible. But, further, the choice to revisit the sites of these photographic situations and restage the images was motivated by our own desire to make visible the structures of substitutionality—the familial and the familiar—that condition empathy (or its lack thereof). We wanted to underscore that the subject is always absent in reproductions of "refugees"—not only in the sense that the viewer of a photograph will always project their own categories of perception on an image, framed by that label, but also in the sense that the category is dehumanizing, and desubjectifying, whether one is made to wear it or is denied its protection.

Our participants did not aspire to be represented as "refugees"; some identified as "international travellers"; others reflected they often felt like "sacks of potatoes with legs." Although they were activists, their aim was not to become exemplars of "queer refugees" in Europe. Although we had their consent to use the photographs they took themselves of themselves, they made us deeply aware of the fact that these were, for them, dangerous images: that it was not safe for them to be visible as LGBTQI+ refugees. They didn't want the photographs exhibited in Athens, though they were sure no one would find them in an obscure, academic book. Indeed, they had experienced photographs being weaponized against them, the threat of

---

59. See Khaled Barakeh, The Untitled Images, 2014, Private collection (Germany); The Chartwell Collection (New Zealand), indd.adobe.com/view/fe2c943d-9089-4c9b-8549-9b7638b09397.

exposure to "community" or "family" looming over them; they had experienced being tokenized as "subalterns" called to represent themselves in international contemporary arts exhibitions. Photographs and video of them already circulate in news media and in lens-based art; some of them aspired to be models—of fashion and of movements.

We did not restage the images in order to protect the participants no longer visible in them. Had this been our motivation, we would be just like the asylum officers who (eventually) decided they were worthy of—and needed—protection in/ by Europe. Rather, we restaged the images to frame the Eurocentric gaze. We felt that by reproducing these dangerous images (by printing them in this book) in what is a highly regulated visual economy, we would be contributing to an exoneration of Europe, its colonial history, and the continuity of that history into the present through its "border imperialism."[60] On the one hand, European states are selling munitions and waging wars that produce refugees, and, on the other hand, Europe (and supranational organizations such as UNHCR and IOM) congratulates itself for "welcoming" refugees by circulating celebratory images of their survival, resilience, flourishing—even as it obfuscates the material conditions to which they are subject and actively attempts to quash their resistance.[61] Even Angela Merkel takes "selfies with refugees."[62]

In this context, giving "refugees" cameras to represent themselves elides the process of representational and political violence that congeals in the category of the refugee. Moreover, we want to move away from the discursive violence that refugees are facing on a daily basis as they become the subject of scholarly research and of artistic representations. We are disciplined into circulating these kinds of images, not only in research and art practice but also in social media, as evidence of our moral concern for refugees. In place of an abstract discussion of the ethics of representing violence, with the photographs below we invite the viewer to face it.

Instead of "them" facing "us," their faces being literally exposed, we want to destabilize the comfort of the viewer and eliminate any possibility of celebratory consumption of these images. In this sense, the images are banal and everyday and may even seem boring, portraying only the backdrop of Athens, apparently with no subjects present. Yet, by choosing to remove the subjects from the frame, our intent is to bring subjectivity into the light—both that of the viewer whose desire to see the refugee (in this case the LGBTQI+ refugee) is frustrated but also that of our participant photographers through whose eyes these frames were initially constructed.

Facing Crisis, then, means turning our attention to what usually remains in the background, what is unsaid, or what remains unheard while our attention is focused

60. See Harsha Walia, *Undoing Border Imperialism* (Oakland, CA: AK Press, 2013).

61. See chapter 6.

62. Stephanie Ott, "How a Selfie with Merkel Changed Syrian Refugee's Life," *Al Jazeera*, February 21, 2017, www.aljazeera.com/indepth/features/2017/02/selfie-merkel-changed-syrian-refugee-life -170218115515785.html.

on the spectacular and hegemonic representations of crisis. Facing Crisis engages with different ways of seeing the lived, everyday, and banal manifestations of crisis on the social fabric, on the social body. In our own creative/theoretical practice, the workshop was a moment of crisis that spurred us to reflect, argue, and take a stance on the politics of representation and on our own collective struggle of engaging with these representations in ways that do not reproduce precisely that which they set out to transform.

"Facing Crisis"
Photograph by Anna Carastathis and Myrto Tsilimpounidi.

We are at the National Technical University of Athens on a very warm summer day of 2017. In this space, right in front of this building, the Polytechnio, in 1973, the revolution against the junta took place. We share these stories as we walk around the space of the university; we add layers of stories and we interview walls, as the space is saturated by street art and political slogans. We chose this space as the main site of the Facing Crisis workshop, as universities are asylum spaces in Greece,[63] after the murder of students revolting against the fascist regime in 1973, which happened in this very place. Our participants tell us they feel unsafe in most places in the city, even those claiming to welcome refugees, because they are being harassed by Greeks and other refugees.

On the top stair, lying in front of the imposing door of this building, imagine a topless man smoking his shisha, enjoying the play between sun and shade. The frame was chosen as we discussed the traps of Hellenist representations of Greece—with doric columns and whitened marble making for small Acropulises everywhere—while the subject plays with Orientalist representations of Syria as he blows smoke circles. As a cloud of smoke obscures his face, the photographer captures his image. Can we ever disassociate ourselves from the myths of our national heritage and the hegemonic representations that build national identities?

---

63. In August 2019, as this book was going to press, the Greek parliament (specifically, lawmakers belonging to the governing New Democracy party and the fascist Greek Solution party) abolished the asylum status of universities.

"Facing Crisis"
Photograph by Anna Carastathis and Myrto Tsilimpounidi.

One of the participants shares the story of his journey to Athens, the crossing, the violence, the discrimination against his—according to him—obvious homosexuality. With the help of the other participants, he paints this violence on half of his face, while the other half he decorates with vibrant make-up. He stands some distance down the path from the camera and stares directly at it, almost facing it down. Where there is oppression there is also resistance, he tells us; this photograph is meant to inspire people to get out of abusive situations. He says that there is always a light at the end of the tunnel; you can see this light illuminating his figure.

"Facing Crisis"
Photograph by Anna Carastathis and Myrto Tsilimpounidi.

A trans woman gets inspired by this street art piece on the walls of the university. She places her body between these two figures in a pose drawn from a fashion magazine. Posing in front of them, she says she wants to highlight the contradiction between the two serious, stiff, male figures and her own self. She talks about capitalist exploitation and the financial crisis in Morocco and Greece; she identifies these two figures as bankers or politicians fixated on money and profit making. As the image is taken, she is seductively staring at the camera, while a few seconds after the shot we discuss the refugee economy in Europe and how this sometimes becomes a new form of capital in the milieu of crisis. Our participants get angry; they say that they encounter such figures whether in the form of border guards or politicians who are responsible for the destruction of their homelands. This is a long conversation; the second image against this wall is shot after sunset, with no daylight. One of the participants dusts his hand with glitter and gives the graffiti the finger. Ai Weiwei would be proud.[64]

---

64. This is a reference to Ai Weiwei's photography series "Study of Perspective" (1995–2003) in which the artist is giving the finger to monuments and symbols of authority around the globe.

"Facing Crisis"
Photograph by Anna Carastathis and Myrto Tsilimpounidi.

To take this photograph, the photographer struggles to get the right angle. The subject is lying down, his head amid the two hearts painted on the pavement. He is wearing a white tulle veil, which covers his face, affixed to his head by a plastic bedazzled tiara. Still, through the veil you can see that his eyes are closed. This is the last photograph we shoot that night; its meaning (from the point of view of the subject, who orchestrated it) is not discussed, as we were mainly focused on the formal challenge presented by taking a photograph when the subject is below us, not at eye level. As he stands up, he says he wants to title this photograph "Love Wins."

"Arrival Selfie"
Photograph by Nick Paleologos.

"Survival Selfie"
Photograph by Nick Paleologos.

Nick Paleologos

Nick (b. 1983) is a photojournalist and editor, born and raised in Athens, Greece. He worked for Icon Press Agency in Greece, from 2005 until 2013, covering all the major social and political events that took place in the country during this period. Also, as a member of the Phasma2 photographic collective, he took part in a number of projects and exhibitions, the most prominent one being The Vovousa Project. In 2014, he co-founded SOOC Agency together with an elite team of photographers who strived to combine news photography via visual storytelling. He is also a collaborator of Al Jazeera English. Through his work for SOOC and AJE, he had the opportunity to cover, among others, the refugee crisis, following the flow of people from Lesvos and Chios islands and throughout Greece all the way to central Europe.

6

Refugees Welcome

They said it was a photograph that sparked the movement.[1] We heard it again and again, often with that photograph projected behind the speaker, who would sometimes be arguing for or against the ethics of reproducing such photographs. The story goes that after media outlets published Nilüfer Demir's photograph of Alan Kurdi's lifeless body washed up on the shore of Bodrum, on September 2, 2015, the photograph of the three-year-old went viral on social media with the hashtags #humanitywashedashore and #refugeeswelcome.[2] Not visible in the frame are Alan's mother, Rehanna, and his brother, Ghalib, who also drowned, along with a dozen other people,[3] when the overcrowded fishing boat capsized in the waves just minutes after they had started the 4.5-kilometer journey from Akyarlar, Bodrum, to the island of Kos. According to Abdullah Kurdi, Alan and Ghalib's father, and the sole surviving member of the family, all the passengers were wearing life jackets, but they were fake.[4] On seeing the

---

1. Photograph by Nilüfer Demir, Doğan News Agency (since acquired by the state-controlled Demirören News Agency). Demir is a photojournalist based in Bodrum.

2. Alan Kurdi's name was initially reported as "Aylan Kurdi," the Turkish variant of his Kurdish name. According to figures reported by the BBC, #HumanityWashedAshore (#KiyiyaVuranInsanlik) was repeated in 500,000 posts in Turkish and Arabic alone; #RefugeesWelcome was repeated 1.5 million times in English-language posts. Mukul Devichand, "Kurdi's Aunt: 'My Dead Nephew's Picture Saved Thousands of Lives,'" BBC Trending Blog, *BBC News*, January 2, 2016, www.bbc.com/news/blogs -trending-35116022.

3. The precise number of people who drowned in the shipwreck is unknown to us (the authors) since reported figures of the total number of passengers, the number who perished, and the number who survived vary widely. With the exception of Rehanna and Ghalib, the other victims' names, identities, and biographies have not (to our knowledge) been published. In relation to the politics of counting discussed in chapter 3, it is worth reflecting on how the most reproduced photograph of the "refugee crisis" has functioned in an anti-documentary fashion, or as an anti-signifier in relation to the other simultaneous, individual deaths of people who drowned that day, including Alan Kurdi's own brother and mother.

4. Heather Timmons, "The Father of Syrian Toddler Aylan Kurdi on the Boat Ride That Killed His Family," *Quartz*, September 4, 2015, qz.com/495211/the-life-jackets-we-were-wearing-were-all-fake-the

photograph, which was reproduced millions of times, it is said that "Europeans" began "mobilizing the largest humanitarian voluntary effort since the second world war."[5]

Journalists celebrated "the power of a single photograph . . . to stir our collective conscience, even in the age of . . . selfie-fuelled narcissism."[6] Does this narrative refute or confirm the sceptical account of photographs anaesthetizing spectators who are less witnesses to than consumers of distant Others' suffering?[7] As an iconic image, the embodiment of humanitarian crisis, the photograph of Alan Kurdi has been compared to Huynh Cong (Nick) Ut's "The Terror of War," the 1973 photograph of Phan Thi Kim Phúc running naked among other children fleeing the United States–South Vietnamese napalm bombing of the village of Trang Bang, Vietnam;[8] and to Kevin Carter's "Starving Child and Vulture," which, taken in Ayod, Sudan, in 1993, documents the devastating famine, induced by macroeconomic restructuring and civil war.[9] Ut's photograph was touted as having "led to the end of the Vietnam war";[10] Carter's photograph is said to have led to his suicide (the fate of the photographed child is obscured). As images of arrival began to proliferate from the shores of Lesvos, this photograph of Alan Kurdi's corpse—which captured the aftermath of a lethal attempt at crossing the Aegean Sea to the nearby island of Kos—is said to have sparked a social movement to "welcome refugees" in Europe. It was preceded by the denial of asylum by a settler nation another ocean away.[11] As Tima Kurdi,

---

-father-of-syrian-toddler-aylan-kurdi-on-the-boat-ride-that-killed-his-family/. See chapter 3.

5. Liz Fekete, "Introduction," *Humanitarianism: The Unacceptable Face of Solidarity* (London: Institute of Race Relations, 2017), 1. See Helena Smith, "Shocking Images of Drowned Syrian Boy Show Tragic Plight of Refugees," *The Guardian*, September 2, 2015, www.theguardian.com/world/2015/sep/02/shocking-image-of-drowned-syrian-boy-shows-tragic-plight-of-refugees?CMP=share_btn_tw.

6. Sean O' Hagan, "The Photographs That Moved the World to Tears," *The Guardian*, September 6, 2015, www.theguardian.com/commentisfree/2015/sep/06/photograph-refugee-crisis-aylan-kurdi. See chapter 5.

7. Judith Butler, "Photography, War, Outrage," *Theories and Methodologies* 120, no. 3: 822–27; Susan Sontag, *On Photography* (New York: Picador, 1973).

8. The photograph, for which Ut was awarded a Pulitzer Prize, is variously called "Napalm Girl." See Time, "The Terror of War," *Time 100 Photos*, n.d., 100photos.time.com/photos/nick-ut-terror-war. See Mimi Thi Nguyen, "Chapter 2: Grace, the Gift of the Girl in the Photograph," in *The Gift of Freedom: War, Debt, and Other Refugee Passages* (Durham, NC: Duke University Press, 2012), 83–132.

9. Kevin Carter was awarded a Pulitzer Prize but also faced widespread criticism for staging the notorious photograph—waiting twenty minutes for the vulture to approach the child, who was struggling to walk to an international aid agency's feeding center and not intervening to help the child—also called "The Vulture and the Little Girl" and "The Struggling Girl," published in the *New York Times* on March 26, 1993. Carter committed suicide the following year. See 100photos.time.com/photos/kevin-carter-starving-child-vulture.

10. Even by the photographer himself. See Sarita S. Balan, "My Picture Led to the End of the Vietnam War: 'Napalm Girl' Photographer Tells TNM," *The News Minute*, March 9, 2018, www.thenewsminute.com/article/my-picture-led-end-vietnam-war-napalm-girl-photographer-nick-ut-tells-tnm-77703.

11. Alan Kurdi's family had fled from Kobane, Syria, to Turkey, deemed a "safe country," so they were ineligible for asylum under the Canadian laws prevailing at the time. The Canadian government denies ever receiving an asylum application from Alan Kurdi's parents, Rehanna and Abdullah. Still, following the photograph's viral reproduction, asylum procedures and Canada's refugee resettlement policies became an election issue. Liberal Party prime minister Justin Trudeau, who won the election, introduced #WelcomeRefugees, a policy commitment to resettle forty thousand Syrian refugees in Canada by the end of 2016. See Government of Canada, "#WelcomeRefugees: Key Figures," February 27, 2017, www.canada.ca/en/immigration-refugees-citizenship/services/refugees/welcome-syrian-refugees/key-figures.html; see

Alan's aunt, who unsuccessfully tried to sponsor her family members to come to Canada under the private sponsorship scheme for refugees, reportedly said, "We heard thousands of stories, we saw thousands of pictures of kids dying" before Alan Kurdi's photograph; "his older brother [Ghalib, five years old] lying beside him on that beach, nobody even took a picture of him, nobody even talks about him. . . . It was something about that picture, God put the light on that picture to wake up the world. . . . We are so proud of this picture [which] saved thousands of refugees."[12]

Why did this image affectively move people when others (before and since) failed to? Was it because the little child was light-skinned, "dressed for the west—in trainers and red t-shirt"?[13] Was it because he was pictured alone, reversing visual narratives of refugees (and migrants) as "hordes," "influxes," "crowds," and "threats"? Was it because the photograph is shocking without being graphic? Alan Kurdi "isn't maimed, he isn't bloodied, he looks like he could be sleeping except for the context."[14] Or was the image striking precisely because of the context? "This picture wasn't taken in a warzone, it wasn't taken in Syria. . . . The fact that this happened on a beach in Turkey has made people sit up and look."[15]

The photograph of the toddler killed by borders might be compared with the photograph of the toddler who barely survived war—that is, the image taken of five-year-old Omran Daqneesh, captured as he was sitting in an ambulance in shock, covered in ashes and blood, having just survived an airstrike in Aleppo.[16] In some reports, the impact of each photograph was measured—in true capitalist fashion—by the donations raised to provide humanitarian aid: these mushroomed in the case of Alan Kurdi, yet, in the case of Omran Daqneesh, donations only saw a brief spike the day the image was published but quickly "trickled off."[17] On this logic, the "civil contract

Patrick Kingsley and Safak Timur, "Stories of 2015: How Alan Kurdi's Death Changed the World," *The Guardian*, December 31, 2015, www.theguardian.com/world/2015/dec/31/alan-kurdi-death-canada-refugee-policy-syria-boy-beach-turkey-photo.

12. Mukul Devichand, "Alan Kurdi's Aunt: My Dead Nephew's Picture Saved Thousands of Lives," *BBC News*, January 2, 2016, www.bbc.com/news/blogs-trending-35116022.

13. Roy Greenslade, "Will the Image of a Lifeless Boy on a Beach Change the Refugee Debate?," *The Guardian*, September 3, 2015, www.theguardian.com/media/greenslade/2015/sep/03/will-the-image-of-a-lifeless-boy-on-a-beach-change-the-refugee-debate.

14. Joel Gunter, "Alan Kurdi: Why One Picture Cut Through," *BBC News*, September 4, 2015, www.bbc.com/news/world-europe-34150419.

15. Joel Gunter, *BBC News*, September 4, 2015: It is worth noting that this perspective elides the war being waged by the Turkish state against Kurds inside its territorial borders, which was not lost on those reproducing or commenting on the photograph of Kurdi in Turkish-language posts, whether they were expressing pan-Kurdish solidarity or making nationalist claims. See Cigdem Bozdag and Kevin Smets, "Understanding the Images of Alan Kurdi with 'Small Data': A Qualitative, Comparative Analysis of Tweets about Refugees in Turkey and Flanders (Belgium)," *International Journal of Communication* 11 (2017): 4064.

16. Mahmoud Raslan/Anadolu Agency/Getty Images, 2016. His statement, shared with the Syria Campaign, can be read here: web.facebook.com/TheSyriaCampaign/photos/a.608812989210718.1073741828.607756062649744/1118057038286308/?type=3&theater&_rdc=1&_rdr. A video of the rescue of Omar and his family from the bombed building was posted by the Aleppo Media Center, August 17, 2016, youtu.be/7cfBmRW3isc.

17. For instance, Mercy Corps received $2.3 million in donations in the month after the photograph of Alan Kurdi was first shared (compared to $4.5 million in the prior four years); by contrast, Mercy

of photography"—and accordingly, our responsibility as viewers of images—is supplanted by an economy of images at the nexus of humanitarianism-militarism. The photographed circulates through their commodified image as a subject needing rescue (or as one who can no longer be saved, as a proxy for other subjects who still can); the viewer of the photograph, by consuming the image, is urged to valorize it by converting the affects it rouses into philanthropy: a means of reproduction of capitalism as a system and of acutely marginalized groups within it.

It is according to this logic, in which photographs are reified—in their singularity and uniqueness—as containing the possibility of "changing the world" or "ending the war," that the bearers of affects disappear as embodied agents behind or facing the image, which is fetishized as the agent of social transformation. Spectators of photographs are constructed as the passive recipients of their meanings; "strong images"[18] are said to trigger affects through a unidirectional causal process, the aetiology of which absolves the subjects involved in the photographic situation of political responsibility for these feelings. Susana de-Andrés, Eloísa Nos-Aldás, and Agustín García-Matilla analyze the photograph of Alan Kurdi as a "socially transformative" image that "provoke[s] a strong 'e-motion,' in the etymological sense of an 'impulse that induces action.'"[19] They suggest that a photograph's power to mobilize is that it breaks "rigid" visual stereotypes of refugees and restores to refugees "their names, tells a story of a life cut short and generates projection and identification" (35). Indeed, they argue that this "image is transformative because it contains a new discourse" (35). Any claim to the power of this image to move us seems to rest on other images failing to do so. Does this "horde" of images fail to move us because, following this argument, they merely reproduce stereotypical vision? Or is it rather due to our own failure to watch photographs, take responsibility for their meaning, and make them speak to us? Photographs valorized as commodities have the capacity to initiate exploitation processes that, at the nexus of militarism and humanitarianism, are often uncritically conflated with activism.

While much of the debate around the photograph of the deceased Alan Kurdi focused on whether it should be reproduced or not, drawing on Hani Sayed (whose account of framing we examined in the previous chapter), we suggest that the appear-

Corps received $50,000 in the first twenty-four hours after the photograph of Omran Daqneesh was published, but the donations quickly "trickled off." See Malaka Gharib, "Photo of Omran Daqneesh, the Boy in Aleppo, Syria: Will It Help End the War?," NPR, August 19, 2016, www.npr.org/sections/goatsandsoda/2016/08/19/490679863/the-little-boy-in-aleppo-can-one-photo-end-a-war. See also Paul Slovic, Daniel Västfjäll, Arvid Erlandsson, and Robin Gregory, "Iconic Photographs and the Ebb and Flow of Empathic Response to Humanitarian Disasters," *PNAS* 114, no. 4: 217, 640–44, doi.org/10.1073/pnas.1613977114.

18. Marta Zarzycka, discussing the World Press Photo contest, considers the operative definition of "strong images" in that competition, which has to do with its capacity to "represent . . . an issue, situation or event of great journalistic importance, and does so in a way that demonstrates an outstanding level of visual perception and creativity." World Press Photo awards cited in Marta Zarzycka, "The World Press Photo Contest and Visual Tropes," *Photographies* 6, no. 1 (2013): 177–84.

19. Susana de-Andrés, Eloísa Nos-Aldas, and Agustín García-Matilla, "The Transformative Image. The Power of a Photograph for Social Change: The Death of Aylan," *Comunicar: Revista Científica de Educomunicación* 24, no. 47 (2016): 30; hereafter cited in text.

ance, publication, and dissemination of the photograph (like that of any reproduced photograph) depends on the censorship of other images: "images that circulate in the public sphere are always already censored."[20] Here, the image itself was the event. So, although some media outlets opted not to publish "the more harrowing photograph of the washed-up body"[21] (which had already gone viral), choosing instead another one of Demir's photographs, which shows Kurdi being carried by an officer of the Turkish coast guard, the referent is neither (at least not only or not primarily) Kurdi's death, nor the drowning of his brother and mother (whose bodies are never depicted, except in family photographs from their interrupted lives) and the other passengers who lost their lives, nor the war they fled and the war that followed them in flight. The referent of its reproductions (given this scene of reception) is the event of an image being reproduced. Moreover, since proponents of censoring the photograph showing Alan Kurdi face down in the sand argued it was dehumanizing, preferring to publish the alternate image—of his body being cradled in the arms of the coast guard officer—it is worth asking: Who is humanized by the latter image—the boy or the borders?[22]

The photograph inspired and was cited in countless reproductions—by artists, editorial cartoonists, writers, and activists. Two of the most literal reproductions involved the proxy structure of representation, whereby another person's body stood in for the body of the deceased child. Ai Weiwei was photographed by Rohit Chawla for *India Today* in Lesvos assuming the position in which Alan Kurdi's corpse was photographed, in "tribute to the tragic and everlasting image of [the] three-year-old Syrian refugee."[23] Thirty protesters in Rabat, organized by actress Latifa Ahrar, re-enacted Demir's photographic encounter with the deceased Alan Kurdi: dressed in jean shorts and red T-shirts, they lay face down in the sand. Although their horizon was formed by the Atlantic Ocean, a representative, journalist Rachid el-Belghiti, turned his gaze in the direction of the sea in which the small child drowned: "We are here to say that the Mediterranean should remain a space for sharing and exchanges, not a barrier for those who are victims of dictatorships, civil wars and terrorism."[24] Elsewhere, portraits of Alan Kurdi—in the position in which he was photographed—were constructed: in Gaza, children gathered with placards around a sculpture formed out of sand. On some accounts, the reproducibility of the image hinged on the universal possibility of identifying with Alan Kurdi: "alone, facedown, and faceless, he could have been anyone's son."[25] Khaled Hosseini's short story, inspired by the photograph

20. Sayed, Untitled Lecture. See chapter 5.

21. Greenslade, "Will the Image of a Lifeless Boy on a Beach Change the Refugee Debate?"

22. Greenslade, "Will the Image of a Lifeless Boy on a Beach Change the Refugee Debate?"

23. Gayatri Jayaraman, "Artist Ai Weiwei Poses as Aylan Kurdi for *India Today* Magazine," *India Today*, February 1, 2016, www.indiatoday.in/india/story/artist-ai-weiwei-poses-as-aylan-kurdi-for-india-today-magazine-306593-2016-02-01.

24. Natalie Evans and Richard Wheatstone, "Aylan Kurdi's Death Recreated by 30 People Dressed as Syrian Boy on Moroccan Beach," *Mirror Online*, September 10, 2015, www.mirror.co.uk/news/world-news/aylan-kurdis-death-recreated-30-6415214.

25. Ellan Baron, "Seven Sketches Inspired by Athens' Refugee Squats—in Pictures," *The Guardian*, September 8, 2016, www.theguardian.com/global-development-professionals-network/gallery/2016/sep/08/seven-sketches-inspired-by-athens-refugee-squats-in-pictures.

of Alan Kurdi, seems to rest on this familial substitutionality projected onto the photograph. His "Sea Prayer," commissioned by UNHCR (for which Hosseini has acted as a Goodwill ambassador since 2006), is told from the perspective of a father who, having fled Homs, anticipates a sea crossing from Turkey to Greece the following morning. He fears that he and his son won't survive the crossing. He whispers to his son, "You are special cargo, Marwan; the most precious there ever was. I pray the sea knows this. Inshallah. How I pray the sea knows this."[26]

In this chapter, we ask how reproductions of crisis can induce crisis in those who watch photographs. Under what conditions can photographs move us to act, not merely to reproduce but to transform social relations depicted (and obscured) in them? As we saw in chapter 1, both "crisis" and "reproduction" are polysemic concepts, with multiple layered meanings. Crisis can be understood as a state of emergency or exception, a dangerous rupture, or turning point, an event that threatens or breaks with normality—but crisis also refers to the faculty of judgement. The question arises how ruptures in normative time indicated by crisis open possibilities or spaces for reflexivity or critique. As Athena Athanasiou argues,

> if crisis is hegemonically conceptualized as the quintessential conjuncture of untimely critique, then critique means thinking, imagining and desiring against the times . . . against the self-evidence of current political time as a politics of emergency. Critique means subjecting to questioning the very authoritarian and anti-democratic premises about the times that declare critique untimely. Since the constitution of subjects itself is performed under conditions of crisis, crisis brings critique: it becomes a condition of critique with respect to how the borders of the intelligible and the sensible are inscribed. Besides, the ultimate goal of critique is to produce a crisis at the heart of processes that define the borders of the intelligible and the sensible. The vulnerability of our lives, as this is revealed, above all, at the moment of crisis, defines our subjectivity (as, one way or another, vulnerable, eccentric, and non-sovereign); simultaneously, it opens it up transformatively to others, generating conditions for new political communities, beyond the hegemonic "commonplaces."[27]

We are particularly interested in how images move: how they mobilize movements across and against borders, or how stills (stasis) urge us to take stances (stasis). Being affectively moved resulted in physical movement as people came to "ground zero" (not Bodrum or Turkey but Lesvos and Greece) and joined an amorphous move-

26. Sea Prayer, www.youtube.com/watch?time_continue=3&v=LKBNEEY-c3s; "Now Everyone Can Enjoy Virtual Reality Journalism," *The GuardianVR*, www.theguardian.com/technology/ng-interactive/2016/nov/10/virtual-reality-by-the-guardian#; Saeed Kamali Dehghan, "8,500 People Lost in Mediterranean since Death of Three-Old Alan Kurdi," *The Guardian*, September 1, 2017, www.theguardian.com/world/2017/sep/01/alan-kurdi-khaled-hosseini-mediterranean-refugees-sea-prayer. Alan Kurdi also gave his name to a rescue ship operated by the German charity Sea Eye, in a ceremony attended by his father, Abdullah, and aunt, Tima. See InfoMigrants, "German Rescue Ship Named After Drowned Toddler Alan Kurdi," February 11, 2019, www.infomigrants.net/en/post/15085/german-rescue-ship-named-after-drowned-toddler-alan-kurdi.

27. Athena Athanasiou, "Critique in Times of Crisis," in *Crisis as a "State of Emergency"* (Athens: Savalas, 2012), 92–98 [in Greek, our translation].

ment, standing with refugees; they bridged the spectatorial distance, gaining an immediate experience, becoming not only viewers of images but also participants in the scene of photography, the scene of rescue, the scene of solidarity.[28] In a sense, then, solidarity can be viewed as a gesture of stepping into the frame. Images mobilized people to stand in solidarity, to open their homes as hosts to refugees, to take to the streets to demand open borders, to make donations to self-organized volunteer efforts, sweeping down on the scene of the humanitarian emergency.[29] But we are also interested in how images are made of solidarity movements, of political stances, and how these images naturalize reproduction as the ground of collective survival.

SELF-REPRODUCING MOVEMENTS

Refugee solidarity movements in Europe since 2015 have primarily taken the form of what Silvia Federici calls "self-reproducing movements"—that is, movements that prioritize the day-to-day survival of their members and their constituent communities, who are "daily confronting crises in their lives."[30] In early 2016, a housing occupation movement emerged, particularly (though not exclusively) in the urban centers of Athens and Thessaloniki, contesting the state policy of segregating refugees on hotspot islands and remote camps, demanding, instead, their integration into the urban social fabric. Greece was widely represented as a haven of solidarity, drawing people from across Europe and many other places in the world who felt moved to come here and participate in the solidarity movement: "58 percent of Greeks responding to a February 2016 public opinion poll [said] that they had actively expressed their solidarity with the refugees in one way or another."[31] This representation—and, particularly, variants of it that attribute solidarity to ostensibly Greek values of "hospitality" (*filoxenia*), or to their own "refugee DNA"—sits uncomfortably alongside statistical representations of the prevailing "public opinion" three years in: in a recent poll (2018), 69 percent of Greeks interviewed said they supported "taking in refugees fleeing war and violence"—significantly below the European median of 77 percent. Moreover, reflecting the internalization of categorial fetishism in the

28. In light of the discernible rise of fascism in the aftermath of the refugee crisis, Julie Melichar argues that the counter-legacy to anti-migrant populism and white supremacy is the movement of "volunteers" doing "humanitarian response work." Julie Melichar, "The Political Legacy of the Refugee Crisis Volunteers," *Refugees Deeply*, May 1, 2018, www.newsdeeply.com/refugees/community/2018/05/01/the-political-legacy-of-the-refugee-crisis-volunteers?utm_campaign=coschedule&utm_source=facebook_page&utm_medium=Refugees+Deeply.

29. These were quickly supplanted by philanthropic organizations and NGOs. See Jessica Elgot, "Charity Behind Migrant-Rescue Boats Sees 15-fold Rise in Donations in 24 Hours," *The Guardian*, September 3, 2015, www.theguardian.com/world/2015/sep/03/charity-behind-migrant-rescue-boats-sees-15-fold-rise-in-donations-in-24-hours.

30. Silvia Federici, *Revolution at Point Zero: Housework, Reproduction, and Feminist Struggle* (New York: Autonomedia, 2012).

31. Leonidas Oikonomakis, "Solidarity in Transition: The Case of Greece," in *Solidarity Mobilizations in the 'Refugee Crisis,'* ed. Donatella della Porta (London: Palgrave, 2019), 65–66.

economic/political binary,[32] 82 percent of Greeks interviewed felt that fewer or no immigrants should be allowed into the country; 74 percent reported their belief that immigrants are a "burden"; and 59 percent blamed immigrants for crime (compared to non-immigrants).[33]

Some found it remarkable that people reacted in the ways they did. Yet, when placed in the context of intersecting crises, and the global wave of resistance to austere capitalism that in chapter 1 we trace to 2011, the reactions of people seeking to welcome refugees—whether travelling across continents and oceans, or stepping across the threshold of their front door to do so—reveal a historical process of the emergence of a collective subject of struggle against and beyond borders. The survival of groups pitted against each other by the state, by ethnonationalist, white supremacist, and class power, actually depends on breaking down the borders between their ascribed identities and reconstituting themselves as a coalition of mutual care and collectivized reproduction. On a utopian reading of the Refugees Welcome movement in Greece, a collective, heterogeneous subject—crosscut by lines of privilege and oppression, belonging and exile—sought to transform an economy of scarcity (intensified by the debt crisis) into an economy of generosity.[34] Further, for those identified as Greek citizens, locals, or members of long-standing migrant communities, solidarity in and against Fortress Europe was grounded in their own interpellation as, historically migrants or refugees,[35] secured mainly through "ethnicized economic bonds,"[36] family genealogy, but also through traumatic memory—including cross-generational trauma, memories repressed through official or hegemonic histories. For instance, international media outlets (and UNHCR) reported on the reproductive activism of Panayiota Vasileidou, an eighty-two-year-old resident of

32. See chapters 1 and 3.

33. Pew Research, EU Citizens' Views, 2019, www.pewglobal.org/2019/03/19/europeans-credit-eu -with-promoting-peace-and-prosperity-but-say-brussels-is-out-of-touch-with-its-citizens/.

34. Julia Ramírez Blanco inspired this point in her analysis "Activist Aesthetics in Madrid's 2011 [Puerta de Sol] Camp" (keynote lecture, Rebel Streets: Urban Space, Art, and Social Movements, May 28, 2019, Université de Tours).

35. It should be emphasized that although the agents of the European Refugees Welcome movement have been widely represented as European citizens in stasis, even a cursory observation of solidarity activism in the wake of this declared crisis reveals a different picture that disrupts this unidirectional and hierarchical construal of solidarity. On Syrian refugees as solidarians with impoverished Greeks, see, for instance, Al Jazeera English, "Syrian Refugees Helping the Homeless," January 12, 2017, buff.ly/2p5lMDn; on settled refugees welcoming newly arrived refugees (in the context of Canada), see Leyland Cecco and Annie Sakkab, "Refugee Given Second Chance in Canada Helps Syrian Family to Find Safety," UNHCR, January 3, 2017, trib.al/Lvbj7Fo. These representations are not unproblematic and could be analyzed with respect to the notions of the gift—and the debt—of freedom discussed in chapter 3 following Mimi Thuy Nguyen's theorization of neoliberal war and refugee passages.

36. Fatima El-Tayeb, *European Others: Queering Ethnicity in Postnational Europe* (Minneapolis: University of Minnesota Press, 2011), 23. El-Tayeb argues that "unified Europe manifests itself increasingly through ethnicized economic bonds, belonging to the EU primarily means having access to economic privileges not available to non-Europeans. In order to prevent or control the access of those non- (or in the case of the East not quite yet) Europeans, the continent's external borders are increasingly fortified. 'Fortress Europe' in turn means that non-Europeans may break the law—and accordingly may be treated like criminals—simply by being present. This requires an increased policing of Europe's internal as well as external spaces, in order to detect and remove illegitimate presences" (23).

Idomeni (a village of 150 people) while over ten thousand people were stuck (in stasis) when North Macedonia closed its border with northern Greece in 2016. Living on a monthly pension of €450, Panayiota Vasileidou daily cooked for dozens of people who would walk by her house, and she eventually hosted five of them who became her "company":[37]

> They didn't come to ask me for help. But when I saw them passing by down this street, every day I would make sandwiches, I made avgofetes [french toast], as we call them, I made little cheese pies. . . . Now, I feel for them, because I've been through it. If I hadn't been through it, I wouldn't understand. I lived it, in my skin. I felt the cold, the hunger, all of it. I sit here alone in the evening, alone with the television, all of that going around and around in my mind. And then I start crying. . . . To the politicians: open the borders. Let all these people go . . . let them live.[38]

One of five surviving siblings, Panayiota Vasileidou was seven years old when her home and her village, Chamilo, was burnt to the ground by the Nazis and their Greek collaborators in World War II, and she became an internally displaced person.[39] "Again with this war!" she exclaims. Then, and now, "the people are not to blame for anything."[40]

Some accounts of welcoming refugees construct the refugee crisis as a scene of what Kaja Silverman might call "idiopathic identification," an "assimilative form of identification" whereby a privileged subject "imaginarily occupies the position of the other, but only in the guise of the self or bodily ego. This kind of identification is familiar to all of us through that formula with which we extend sympathy to someone less fortunate than ourselves without in any way jeopardizing our *moi*: "I can imagine myself in his (or her) place."[41]

Although media representations constructed Panayiota Vasileidou as "The Refugees' Grandmother," or as the "Generous Greek Grandmother" who "opens her home to Syrians," who have "become her family," in the interviews she gave, Panayiota Vasileidou never refers to herself either as "Greek" or as a "grandmother"; the people she shared her home with, she called her "company" (as in, her companions); neither "Syrians," nor even "refugees": to refer to them (and to herself), the nouns she uses are "people" and "human beings." Women of her age in Greece (and elsewhere) are made to assume the culturally circumscribed role of grandmother, a gendered and age-specific reproductive identity enmeshed with duties of care (unto

37. UNHCR, "Greece: The Refugees' Grandmother in Idomeni," YouTube, April 8, 2016, www.youtube.com/watch?v=Hb_Hdjy4CVw.

38. Panayiota Vasileidou quoted in BBC News, "Generous Greek Grandmother Opens Her Home to Syrians," BBC News, April 25, 2016, youtu.be/szKREhVcbAs, our translation. Incidentally, in the interview, Panayiota Vasileidou never refers to herself as "Greek" or to the people she shares her home with and who become her "company" as "Syrians," or even "refugees." The words she uses are "people" and "human beings."

39. UNHCR, "Greece: The Refugees' Grandmother in Idomeni."

40. UNHCR, "Greece: The Refugees' Grandmother in Idomeni."

41. Kaja Silverman, *The Threshold of the Visible World* (New York: Routledge, 1996), 25; hereafter cited in text.

death) from which relatively few (particularly of her generation) have ways to escape. Framing Panayiota Vasileidou's reproductive activism through the naturalized figure of the grandmother reproduces at the representational level what is likely a lifetime of compulsory, unwaged reproductive labor (reflected in her reported pension).

In that sense, rather than subjecting Panayiota Vasileidou to critique for how she views the people she came to care for, we find it more germane to ask, how do we—through media representations of her—view Panayiota Vasileidou? Why are we encouraged through familial framings to naturalize her gendered exploitation in a heterosexual economy (as a grandmother), when, in her own fragmentary narrative, she emphasizes her subjectivity as a survivor of war and displacement? "The look is under cultural pressure to apprehend the world from a preassigned viewing position, and under psychic pressure to see it in ways that protect the ego," writes Silverman (3).

> Even before we become conscious of having seen something, that image has already been processed in all kinds of classificatory ways, which help to determine what value it will assume. We can look at an object a second time, through different representational parameters, and painstakingly reverse the process through which we have arrogated to ourselves what does not belong to us, or displaced onto another what we do not want to recognize in ourselves. Although such a re-viewing can have only a very limited efficacy, and must be repeated anew with each new visual perception, it is a necessary step in the coming of the subject to an ethical or nonviolent relation to the other. (3)

To be sure, representations of charitable acts that sometimes get folded into the Refugees Welcome movement are replete with idiopathic modes of identification: "images of families sleeping in the open squares on chilly winter nights have made [Greeks] forget their own problems," comments one journalist in his report showing Greeks "turn[ing] up in droves with bags of food and medicine" in central Athens: "We could be in their position, and if we were, we would need a helping hand," says one.[42] But the heterogeneous movement to stand in solidarity with refugees was not, we would suggest, primarily driven by "crude empathy," to invoke Bertold Brecht's term for the appropriation of the other's experience by the self.[43]

---

42. Mohammad Adow, "Greeks Doing What They Can to Help Refugees," *Al Jazeera English*, March 5, 2016, www.youtube.com/watch?v=rX-sXUb-A04.

43. See Janna Houwen, "An Empty Table and an Empty Boat: Empathic Encounters with Refugee Experiences in Intermedial Installation Art," *American, British, and Canadian Studies* 27, no. 1 (2016): 49, www.degruyter.com/downloadpdf/j/abcsj.2016.27.issue-1/abcsj-2016-0018/abcsj-2016-0018.pdf. Perhaps a textbook example of crude empathy is the "Ration Challenge," a campaign recently promoted by a UK charity, which urges presumably food-secure citizens to "eat rations like a refugee: get sponsored and show refugees that we're with them, not against them." Concern Worldwide UK, www.rationchallenge.org.uk. The Ration Challenge was started in 2014 by two Australians while they visited refugee camps on the border of Thailand and Myanmar. They have since "partnered" with Oxfam and most recently Concern Worldwide UK to run the challenge. "Challengers" are sent a week's standard ration box "exactly like" that given to Syrian refugees in Jordan: 420 grams of rice, 170 grams of lentils, 85 grams of dried chickpeas, 120 grams of tinned sardines, 400 grams of tinned kidney beans, 330 ml of vegetable oil. However, "challengers"—unlike refugees—who are "vegetarian or vegan, or have a food allergy . . . can substitute any items [they] can't eat for an alternative ingredient (use the same weight) e.g. swap sardines for tofu." Academics

Instead of naturalizing solidarity as a practice of reproducing an inherent cultural or humanistic value, or even as the automatic outcome of an historical or lived experience, we view the expression of solidarity as a political stance in an invidiously divided political field. On the one hand, the solidarity movement with refugees coheres with the directives of UNHCR to global civil society, that "we need to be welcoming these people into our communities."[44] However, in their best instances, solidarity efforts disrupt the hierarchical host-guest relationship and the naturalization of national belonging that such dictates seem to reproduce. On the other hand, as we discuss later in the chapter, solidarity has, increasingly, been met with state efforts to suppress it through strict regulation, criminalization, violent evictions, deportations, and incarceration. Moreover, the terms and conditions through which communities are imagined, constituted, and reproduced as welcoming are not pure of dynamics of power or exclusionary and oppressive ideologies—even as these ideologies and power relations are explicitly constructed as the constitutive exterior against which these self-reproducing movements are battling. Indeed, rhetorics and organizing practices which romanticize welcoming communities as "family" represent one of the most problematic—if generally unproblematized—reproductions of naturalized power.

Perhaps the most well-known example of the self-reproducing movement to "welcome refugees" is the City Plaza Hotel in central Athens, which was squatted in the spring of 2016 and run by a committee of the Network of Social Support for Refugees and Migrants.[45] City Plaza is a once-abandoned, bankrupt hotel in Athens that was occupied in April 2016 by a group of activists who repurposed its one hundred rooms to house refugees. Otherwise known as the "best hotel in Europe"[46] and "the largest grassroots solidarity effort in Europe," the hotel houses over four hundred refugees at a time (who have come from Syria, Afghanistan, Iran, Iraq, Palestine, Pakistan, Ghana, Eritrea, and elsewhere), as well as volunteers and activists, who share the daily tasks of cooking, cleaning, and security as well as education projects, cultural activities, and political organizing. Particularly in international media and transnational solidarity networks, the project quickly became an exemplar of antiracist organizing, if not the epicenter of struggle for refugee rights in Greece—garnering visits and support from luminaries of left

---

Victoria Canning, Monish Bhatia, and Omar Tofighian wrote an open letter to Concern UK, available here: twitter.com/DrMonishBhatia/status/1128703276998905856.

44. See for instance, UNHCR, "'We Need to Be Welcoming These People into Our Communities': Theo James Travelled with Us to Meet Refugees in Greece," Twitter post, February 1, 2017, twitter.com/Refugees/status/826907345833836554.

45. On July 10, 2019, as this book was going to press, and just a few days after the election of the New Democracy majority government, the thirty-nine-month-long occupation of City Plaza ended, and its residents were reportedly transferred to safe buildings elsewhere in the city. See City Plaza, "39 Months of City Plaza: The Completion of a Cycle, the Beginning of a New One," July 10, 2019, http://solidarity2refugees.gr/39-mines-city-plaza-oloklirosi-enos-kyklou-archi-enos-neou/ [in Greek].

46. "No pool, no minibar, no room service but still the best hotel in Europe" campaign, https://best-hotel-in-europe.eu.

intelligentsia, such as Judith Butler, Wendy Brown,[47] David Harvey,[48] Sandro Mezzadra,[49] and Angela Davis.[50]

Could one of the reasons that City Plaza has emerged as such a successful paradigm—both within and beyond the territorial borders of Greece—have to do with the representation that "all the families [t]here live like one family"?[51] Could the cultural essentialism through which family becomes naturalized as the primary institution of societies constructed as anachronistically patriarchal—an Orientalist construction, which views gender and sexual politics as static or uncontested, particularly in Muslim-majority societies subjected to imperialist war—render solidarity with refugees as reproductive of heteronormative kinship structures? In other words, if refugees are always already represented as reproductive, is solidarity always already heterosexual?[52] Could it be that "[solidarity] does not work, or does not qualify as [solidarity], unless it assumes a recognizable family form"?[53] Arguably, the emphasis on family in solidarity discourses aims to assert the commonality between "populations" divided by borders, to call for reproductive justice in the face of necropolitical power, and to humanize "refugees," whose reproduction is constructed as dangerous by xenophobic, racist, and white supremacist nationalisms. Still, the problem arises that, "if we engage the terms that these debates supply, then we ratify the frame at the moment in which we take our stand. And this signals a certain paralysis in the face of exercising power to change the terms by which such topics are rendered thinkable. Indeed, a more radical social transformation is precisely at stake when we refuse, for instance, to allow [solidarity] to become reducible to 'family.'"[54]

Although the best known, City Plaza was not the first building squatted by activists expressly for the purpose of housing refugees in the wake of the refugee crisis: in

---

47. Video of Judith Butler and Wendy Brown's visit to City Plaza: www.youtube.com/watch?v=Zi5E FUOfWcY&feature=youtu.be&fbclid=IwAR1Qigx2P898p1iqzVGhBpMiSXQP7PbzHUXkHIMeKiN nozejkaF2s08E9BY.

48. Video of David Harvey's visit to City Plaza: www.facebook.com/watch/?v=1695077274117942.

49. Poster from Sandro Mezzadra's workshop The New European Border Regime: www.facebook.com/ cityplazaathens/photos/gm.882752071831319/1561537244141110/?type=1&theater.

50. Video of Angela Davis's visit to City Plaza: www.facebook.com/watch/?v=1800691056889896.

51. Yiannis Baskakis, "All the Families Here Live Like One Family," *Efsyn*, April 22, 2017, www.efsyn .gr/ellada/koinonia/107693_oles-oi-oikogeneies-edo-zoyn-san-mia-oikogeneia [in Greek, our translation]. Early on in the housing occupation, City Plaza began to represent its "400 residents" as "100 families" (implying a nuclear model of family). See for instance, City Plaza, "Support the City Plaza Refugee Accommodation and Solidarity Center in Athens," June 13, 2016, solidarity2refugees.gr/support-city -plaza-refugee-accommodation-solidarity-center-athens-greece; "What Is City Plaza?" leaflet, June 14, 2016, solidarity2refugees.gr/city-plaza-leaflet/. The representation of City Plaza as offering its residents "a house and a family" is reproduced in the photography project by Mara Scampoli and Mattia Aluni Cardinali, "We'll Come United," *ByLine*, December 19, 2017, www.byline.com/project/81/article/1973.

52. Here, we are, of course, riffing on Judith Butler, "Is Kinship Always Already Heterosexual?," *Differences: A Journal of Feminist Cultural Studies* 13, no. 1 (2002): 14–44.

53. Butler, "Is Kinship Always Already Heterosexual?" 14. We have replaced the word "kinship" with "solidarity" to generate reflection on this question but also on the ways in which the reproduction of heteronormative political communities seems to escape critical notice when those involve people who have been constructed as belonging to anachronistic temporalities and spatialities even through leftist antiracist and feminist ideologies.

54. Butler, "Is Kinship Always Already Heterosexual?" 40.

September 2015, the Refugee Housing Occupation Assembly of the Anti-authoritarian Movement (AK) started a squat in Exarchia (in central Athens), which eventually moved to a disused building belonging to the Ministry of Labor, Social Security, and Welfare at Notara 26.[55] Their motto, "solidarity has a home," represents a (much-debated) shift in the terrain of anti-authoritarian politics to a politics of care, or "solidarity in practice."[56] Dozens of autonomous squats have reclaimed empty school buildings, shuttered hotels, abandoned and sometimes derelict houses, and closed hospitals. In this sense, the solidarity infrastructure overlaid the ruins left by crisis and austerity: the city of Athens, in particular, gutted by the structural adjustment of the national economy, was transformed into an urban landscape beset with empty and often crumbling houses and apartments (and an astronomical rise in homelessness), padlocked shops, and public buildings abandoned by the rapidly shrinking welfare state.[57]

By the time the refugee crisis was declared in Greece, seven years of austerity for most people had meant drastic reductions of income, long-term or intermittent unemployment, and two-thirds of children living in or "at risk of" poverty, while basic goods like heat, food, and medicine were beyond reach.[58] In June 2015, the UNHCR declared an emergency in Greece, and the EU mobilized its humanitarian response unit for the first time inside Europe.[59] But it was not the first time that a humanitarian emergency had been declared in Greece. Five years earlier, in 2010, Doctors of the World declared a humanitarian crisis in the center of Athens; street clinics and social pharmacies were set up to compensate for a health care system cut to ribbons by austerity.[60] Self-organized solidarity clinics, community kitchens,

---

55. Melpomeni Maragkidou, "Anarchists Have Taken Over a Building in Athens to House Refugees," *Vice News*, September 28, 2015, www.vice.com/en_uk/article/xd7vj4/anarchists-have-taken-over-a -building-in-athens-to-house-refugees-876.

56. As Hector Uniake argues, the crucial difference between practical solidarity—in an anarchist or anti-authoritarian register—and state-sanctioned humanitarianism or philanthropy lies in the will [of the former] to grant autonomy to those it supports." Hector Uniake, "You Can't Evict a Movement: A Story of Squatting and Migration in Athens," *Open Democracy*, March 21, 2017, www.opendemocracy.net/en/ can-europe-make-it/you-cant-evict-movement-story-of-squatting-and-migration-in-athens/.

57. In emphasizing these particular dynamics, we are in no way claiming that the emergence of this movement is a phenomenon unique to Athens or Greece or Europe. Nor do we wish to reproduce a temporal exceptionalism that sees the declaration of the refugee crisis as its starting point. Admittedly, a thorough discussion of these issues lies beyond the scope of this chapter. For a discussion of refugee solidarity and squatting movements, see Pierpaolo Mudu and Sutapa Chattopadhyay, *Migration, Squatting, and Radical Autonomy* (London: Routledge, 2017); Óscar García Agustín and Martin Bak Jørgensen, *Solidarity and the "Refugee Crisis" in Europe* (London: Palgrave Macmillan, 2019). Indeed, what must be stressed is that even in one particular location—such as central Athens—these solidarity movements are always already transnational, and their reproduction relies on transnational solidarity, for instance, the Solidarity Caravans that regularly come to Exarchia with supplies, medicine, food, and spirit from other parts of Europe to support anti-authoritarian squats.

58. Graham Satchell, "Impact of Greek Austerity Measures on Ordinary People," *BBC*, October 13, 2011, www.bbc.com/news/av/world-europe-15286028/impact-of-greek-austerity-measures-on-ordinary -people.

59. Daniel Howden and Apostolis Fotiadis, "The Refugee Archipelago: The Inside Story about What Went Wrong in Greece," In *Refugees Deeply, News Deeply*, March 6, 2017, www.newsdeeply.com/refugees/ articles/2017/03/06/the-refugee-archipelago-the-inside-story-of-what-went-wrong-in-greece.

60. In 2009, austerity-mandated cuts to the public health budget resulted in the first malaria outbreak since the 1970s, hundreds of deaths from West Nile Virus, and other infections after infectious

clothing swaps, and free shops emerged in the neighborhoods of central Athens. We might say that one effect of the financial crisis was the development of a solidarity infrastructure. There was also a pre-existing anti-authoritarian squatting movement, though not one articulated clearly to the acute social injustice of homelessness. These movement infrastructures have been instrumental to people's survival during the first years of the refugee crisis. Before (and after) international NGOs landed, it was local, small-scale organizing, established migrant and antiracist networks, anarchists with squatting know-how, and so-called ordinary people on the seashores and in city squares who not only rhetorically but also practically welcomed those whom the state was now calling "refugees." The veritable absence of the Greek state in the months (and years) leading up to the declared refugee crisis, and its commission of nothing short of infrastructural torture since the institution of the island hotspots and mainland camps, was justified in terms of its financial—and not its moral—bankruptcy: as this widely reproduced fallacy goes, "there is little the state can do to help refugees, so civilians and charities have had to step in."[61]

But should survival, revolution, and human flourishing be understood through the register of reproduction? Is reproduction an inherently conservative concept? Is it an inherently heteronormative concept? As we argued in chapter 1, strains of social reproduction theory (SRT) retain a kernel of the natural from which the social unfolds. SRT and its political imaginary stage a struggle at the "boundaries" of "capitalism's constitutive institutional divisions: where economy meets polity, where society meets nature, and where production meets reproduction."[62] On the one hand, the politicization of social reproduction has the potential to challenge "capitalism's rapacious subjugation of reproduction to production"; on the other hand, it remains, for us, an open question whether "reinventing the production/reproduction distinction" is a sufficient condition for "reimagining the gender order" (36).

We do not have a cynical perspective on the social movement response to the phenomena that the "refugee crisis" does and does not name. We do have a critical perspective that is also critical of ourselves, over the passage of time, for certain reactions we had, as have most people who have been implicated in the human and social relations of this time. We wonder which subjects our own efforts in engaging in acts of solidarity and resistance have marginalized, rendered invisible, or may even have pushed overboard.[63] As we have discussed in the introduction, we are not only looking at the crisis landscape from a distance but also close up. In that sense, any critique

---

disease and spraying programmes against mosquitos were cut. The sudden rise of new HIV infections was attributed by epidemiologists to sharing needles; between 2010 and 2011 intravenous heroin use was reported to have risen by 20 percent, coinciding with a rise in homelessness. David Stuckler and Sanjay Basu, *The Body Economic: Eight Experiments in Economic Recovery, from Iceland to Greece* (New York: Penguin Books, 2013).

61. Adow, "Greeks Doing What They Can to Help Refugees."

62. Federici, *Revolution at Point Zero*, 35–36.

63. See chapter 5 for a discussion of Souma's story, which, for us, encapsulates the necropolitical articulation of reproduction and survival and inspires this phrase. See the introduction for our discussion of our conscious choice not to discuss our own political activism in this book, following methodologies of refusal.

we elaborate is quite personal, and we are directly implicated in it as products—and not merely dispassionate observers—of the crisis.

BRING YOUR FAMILIES

As a highly mediated phenomenon, the solidarity movements intervening in the refugee crisis often reproduced the categories of gender, "race," nation, religion, and age, through which images were invested with urgency and meaning. To the extent that the main register of humanizing representations of "refugees" naturalizes the nuclear family as the site of care, connection, and collective survival in conditions of crisis, "community" emerges in social movement discourses as isomorphic with or as a substitute of "family." This renders the exiles of the institution of the family as outsiders or interlopers in communities naturalized around compulsory hetero-sexuality, patriarchy, religion, and nationalism. For instance, conditions not only in state camps and detention centers[64] but also in housing squats have proven hostile to LGBTQI+ people who are seeking refuge. The Greek police, military, but also religious NGOs, certain solidarians, and some members of their "own" communities "replicate the persecution [LGBTQI+ refugees] fled in the first place."[65] Against the backdrop of intersecting crises—that is, multiple, overlapping, declared, and undeclared crises, the targets of which are pitted against each other—LGBTQI+ people of various origins and trajectories struggle for their survival in the increasingly militarized urban space of Athens and the carceral spaces of Lesvos and other hotspot islands, mainland camps, and detention centers.

"Flight" (2015) was an installation in the St. James Church in London: "a frail rubber dinghy, overturned as if sinking down into the depths. Three orange lifejackets are falling from its safety into the void: two adult-sized and one a child's. The child's has fallen further into the abyss, almost out of reach of desperate parents."[66] Citing the image that has become iconic of the Refugees Welcome movement—with

64. Lesvos LGBTQI+ Refugee Solidarity, "LGBTIQ+ Refugees at Grave Risk of Exposure, Violence and Death as Conditions Worsen on Lesvos: Statement from Lesvos LGBTQI+ Refugee Solidarity," November 4, 2017, www.facebook.com/permalink.php?story_fbid=309129119494411&id=286931478380 842.

65. LGBTQI+ Refugees, "Our Own Home: Fighting for Safety, Stability, and Choice as LGBTQI+ Refugees in Greece," *Arts Everywhere*, February 5, 2018, www.artseverywhere.ca/2018/02/05/lgbtqi-refugees/; Matt Broomfield, "Queer Refugees on Lesvos Are Crying Out for Help," *The New Arab*, November 10, 2017, www.alaraby.co.uk/english/indepth/2017/11/10/queer-refugees-on-lesvos-are-crying-out-for-help?utm_source=twitter&utm_medium=sf.

66. Ariella Dorman, "Flight," 2016. See www.theguardian.com/artanddesign/2015/dec/20/flight-by-arabella-dorman-review-relic-of-a-rough-crossing-illustrates-refugee-crisis. Dorman followed this with "Suspended" (2016): an installation, in the same venue, of seven hundred items of refugees' clothing salvaged from Lesvos, to remind the world of the life and death plight of displaced people. "From afar, the clothes hang in a mass like a ghostly chandelier adorning the nave of the church. But the artist, who has worked in Gaza, Afghanistan and Iraq, wants worshippers to look closer and reflect on the individuals who once wore the garments. Refugees are not numbers, they are people." See "Suspended," an installation by Arabella Dorman, 22:46, January 31, 2018, www.youtube.com/watch?v=uXcm73cLTK0.

the added value of the *eidôlon* of the life jacket[67]—this installation reproduces the primary visual trope through which "refugees" are represented in humanizing terms: as "men, women, and children"—*in that order*. The order matters: the power of this trope lies not only in the relationships, kinship, intimacy, or love which bind together human lives but, rather, stems from the inviolable universality of patriarchal order. In that iconic image we see a man leading a woman who holds a female child by the hand, all of them running (the child almost being dragged off her feet). Underneath the image we read: "bring your families."[68] Not only the gendered/age-based hierarchy and composition but also the size of the "family" matters to the iconicity of this image: the nuclear family is institutionalized under late capitalism and is privileged in legal and policy definitions of family underlying relocation, family reunification, and other processes of state-controlled movement of refugees and asylum seekers.

The image was reproduced on banners and placards at demonstrations, stencilled on walls in many cities, worn on T-shirts, and displayed on stickers to mark heterotopias,[69] spaces friendly toward refugees. Despite its reappropriation by a movement that called (to lesser or greater degrees, given its heterogeneity) for open borders, or no borders, it is important to acknowledge the origins of the image: it is the nation-state. And not just any nation-state but the United States of America, where at one of the most violently policed borders in the world, between the United States and Mexico, after hundreds of people were killed by cars from 1987 to 1990 while crossing along Interstate 5, the US transportation authorities commissioned John Hood to design a highway sign warning drivers of "border crossers." Hood, a Navajo artist, has stated that he wanted to elicit US citizens' empathy with migrants crossing the borders, hence choosing to represent them, in his design of the immigration sign, as a fleeing family in whose place any American could substitute their own.[70] The sign was placed near the border fence that was by the mid-1990s still under construction and that now seals a large swath of the United States–Mexico border.[71] Despite/because of this fencing, and current calls to "build a wall," making it more imporous and the crossing more hostile, this border remains, in the words of Gloria Anzaldúa, "una herida abierta [an open wound] where the Third World grates against the first and bleeds."[72] Used widely in the United States by pro-immigration

---

67. Discussed in chapter 3.

68. From Another Europe Is Possible: Maxresdefault, December 1, 2017, https://www.anothereurope .org/defend-refugees-and-free-movement-back-amendment-332/maxresdefault/?_escaped_fragment_.

69. Michel Foucault, "Of Other Spaces: Utopias and Heterotopias," *Journal of Architecture /Mouvement/ Continuité*, October 1984, web.mit.edu/allanmc/www/foucault1.pdf.

70. Scott Gold, "The Artist Behind the Iconic 'Running Immigrants' Image," *Los Angeles Times*, April 4, 2008, www.latimes.com/local/la-me-outthere4apr04-story.html; Victor Morales, "Iconic Sign Evokes Connection to Long Walk," *Indian Country Today*, October 12, 2008, indiancountrymedianetwork.com/ news/iconic-sign-evokes-connection-to-long-walk/.

71. Sections of the United States–Mexico border have been fenced or walled, while other sections have not yet been. In 2019, 1,053 kilometers (654 miles) of the border had been fenced; 2,058 kilometers (1,279 miles) are not. See www.businessinsider.com/us-mexico-border-wall-photos-maps-2018-5). For an interactive map of the border and the different kinds of barriers in place at different sections, see www .usatoday.com/border-wall/us-mexico-interactive-border-map.

72. Gloria Anzaldúa, *Borderlands/La Frontera: The New Mestiza* (San Francisco: Aunt Lute, 1987), 25.

movements, the image was popularized globally through a stencil by the street artist Banksy, which meant to subvert the negative connotations of the warning sign by emphasizing the hopefulness and agency of those undertaking migration trajectories.[73] By 2015, the iconic image was lifted from the immigration sign and used as the trademark of the Refugees Welcome protest movement across Europe in the wake of the so-called refugee crisis.

This image, its circulation, and its political underpinnings illustrate what we termed in chapter 1 the heteronormalization of the "refugee crisis": "refugees," whether they are seen as the normative victims or the harbingers of this crisis, are presumed to be reproducing heteropatriarchy—whether this is seen as a positive or negative thing. It is through their ostensibly universally socially legible kinship relationships—as fathers, mothers, children—that they are positioned as deserving supplicants or as threats to the biological or cultural continuity of the host nation-state. On the one hand, refugees are welcomed into the affective economy they are seen to reproduce, as members of families and of the so-called human family. Such sympathetic representations depend on the transcultural legibility of their participation in family and kinship structures and on their being gendered as men/fathers, women/mothers, and boys and girls/children. On the other hand, nationalist and fascist ideologies which construct refugees as a demographic problem also focus on the reproductive threat they pose: refugee women are constructed as excessively procreative; refugee men are constructed as sexually predatory or improperly patriarchal; refugee children are actually not children at all but imposters, themselves of "reproductive age." "Reproducing refugees" are seen as threats to the continuity and coherence of a racialized national subject—understood in terms of inheritance, blood, and property.

Within anti-authoritarian movements in solidarity with refugees, we have seen the reproduction of (state and supranational) institutional categories of migration (the family, the unaccompanied minor, the single man, the pregnant woman, etc.), all of which are based on reproductive heteronormativity. These categories are used (consciously or unconsciously) to construct hierarchies (on the representational and material levels) of respectability, deservingness, and belonging. In other words, self-reproducing movements in the midst of the refugee crisis rely on representations of refugees as reproductive even when they would not ideologically align themselves explicitly with patriarchal, sexist, homophobic, or transphobic views.

If heteronormalization structures the state of emergency (the humanitarian crisis) to which social movements then seek to respond with socially reproductive and discursive interventions, then part of what such movements are reproducing is heterosexuality. To be clear, heterosexuality in this sense is not a sexual preference but an institution and—in most places in the world—a compulsory form of social life, which is violently enforced: in war zones, on the route of escape,[74] in detention

---

73. Jorge Rivas, "Bansky Transforms Migrant Road Sign into DREAM Crossing," *Colorlines*, February 22, 2011, www.colorlines.com/articles/banksy-transforms-migrant-road-sign-dream-crossing.

74. Jane Freedman, "Sexual and Gender-Based Violence Against Refugee Women: A Hidden Aspect of the Refugee 'Crisis,'" *Reproductive Health Matters* 24, no. 47 (2016): 18–26.

centers and camps,[75] on food lines run by Christian NGOs,[76] and in housing squats occupied by solidarians.

SOLIDARITY IS NOT A CRIME

Not only solidarity activism but also nongovernmental humanitarianizm is operating in a "shrinking space within a bordered debate," as states heightened the criminalization of solidarity with people on the move.[77] Giving lifts to people walking hundreds, or even thousands, of kilometers was construed as "facilitating illegal transit." Inviting people home for a meal or shower or offering them a place to stay became "harboring." "Smuggling" (often conflated with the distinct crime of "human trafficking") was a charge attached to a range of activities, including sea rescue or helping people to cross land borders. Communicating coordinates of boats in distress to rescuers was tantamount to "facilitating illegal immigration."[78]

Martina Tazzioli argues that the criminalization of self-organized solidarity and nongovernmental rescue activity paved the way to the militarization of humanitarianism. In the Central Mediterranean, the criminalization of sea rescue, in conjunction with the EU-Libya Deal,[79] has resulted in "a spatial rerouting of military

---

75. See Lesvos LGBTIQ+ Refugee Solidarity, "LGBTIQ+ Refugees at Grave Risk of Exposure, Violence, and Death as Conditions Worsen on Lesvos," Press Release, November 4, 2017, tinyurl.com/LesvosLGBTIQ; Matt Broomfield, "Queer Refugees on Lesvos."

76. Since late 2015, after most NGOs withdrew from the Moria camp in Lesvos in protest, housing and other services have been mainly coordinated by the NGO EuroRelief, the humanitarian arm of Hellenic Ministries, an international evangelical Christian missionary organization incorporated in the United States. In the summer of 2016, the NGO was publicly accused of using its position in the camp to religiously convert refugees. Patrick Kingsley, "Aid Workers Accused of Trying to Convert Refugees," *The Guardian*, August 2, 2016, www.theguardian.com/world/2016/aug/02/aid-workers-accused-of-trying-to-convert-muslim-refugees-greek-camp-detention-centre-lesvos-christianity. According to refugees and frontline volunteers, "EuroRelief allegedly use food, clothes, travel permits, and even access to WiFi, to coerce vulnerable refugees into converting to Christianity." Matt Broomsfield, "The Abusive American-Christian NGO with a Stranglehold over Refugees' Lives," *The New Arab*, May 1, 2018, www.alaraby.co.uk/english/indepth/2018/5/1/the-abusive-ngo-with-a-stranglehold-on-refugees-lives. Although proselytism is a crime under Greek law (due to the influence of the state religion of Greek Orthodoxy), of which the founder of Hellenic Ministries had been convicted in the 1980s (the conviction was overturned), at the time of writing EuroRelief has not, to our knowledge, been investigated by authorities. EuroRelief workers and volunteers have reportedly referred to LGBTQI+ refugees as "sinners" and the NGO's religious views preclude the provision of condoms or contraceptives. See Broomfield, "Queer Refugees on Lesvos." See also Are You Syrious, "EuroRelief: Evangelical Organization Providing More Harm Than Aid to Refugees," *Are You Syrious Daily Digest*, January 11, 2018, medium.com/@AreYouSyrious/ays-daily-digest-11-01-2018-eurorelief-u-s-807717ec51f8.

77. Fekete, "Introduction," 2–3. The report published by the Institute for Race Relations in 2017 discusses twenty-six cases involving forty-five individuals prosecuted under anti-smuggling and/or immigration laws since 2015, yet they are but a drop in the ocean compared to the crackdown on solidarity activists, sea rescuers, and ordinary people who found themselves facing serious criminal charges for assisting other people.

78. See Institute of Race Relations, *Humanitarianism: The Unacceptable Face of Solidarity* (London: Institute of Race Relations, 2017).

79. See European Commission, "EU Action in Libya on Migration," European Commission, December 7, 2017, ec.europa.eu/home-affairs/sites/homeaffairs/files/what-we-do/policies/european

humanitarianism, in which migrants are paradoxically *rescued to Libya*"—that is, to the site of embarkation on the dangerous sea crossing.[80] In other words, "the politics of rescue, conceived in terms of not letting people die, has been re-shaped as a technique of capture."[81] Tazzioli points out that the "criminalization of refugee support activities cannot be separated from the increasing criminalization of refugees as such: not only those who are labelled and declared illegal as 'economic migrants', but also those people who are accorded the status of refugees. Both are targets of restrictive and racialized measures of control."[82]

Why is solidarity so threatening to nation-states across Europe? A study published by Open Democracy gathered data from media sources in relation to convictions of solidarians. In fourteen European countries, more than 250 people were arrested, tried, and charged for supporting refugees. Most cases occurred in Greece, Italy, and France, and the majority of the "crimes" involved the provision of food, transport, and shelter to "migrants without legal papers."[83] In Greece, the case of the nonprofit organization Emergency Response Center International and the arrest and detention of four of its members in 2018 has raised concerns over the direct criminalization of solidarity and sea rescue in the country. The crimes of which the activists are accused carry punishments of up to twenty-five years in prison. Human Rights Watch claims that the felony charges are unsubstantiated and the prosecution seeks to criminalize the act of solidarity and of saving lives.[84] In Italy, the newly elected far-right government prevented the disembarkation of the migrant rescue ship *Aquarius* on November 2018 over fears that the passengers of the ship and their clothes could be contaminated by HIV: referring to the passengers, "prosecutors from Catania, eastern Sicily, alleged that the waste was illegally labelled by the ship's crew as 'special waste' rather than 'toxic waste.'"[85] In France, in December 2018, police with batons, tear gas, and plastic bullets cleared the refugee camp of Calais and arrested activists who were transporting people to hospitals, sending a clear message of zero tolerance.[86]

-agenda-migration/20171207_eu_action_in_libya_on_migration_en.pdf; Michael Asediu, "The EU-Libya Migrant Deal: A Deal of Convenience," *E-International Relations*, April 11, 2017, www.e-ir .info/2017/04/11/the-eu-libya-migrant-deal-a-deal-of-convenience.

80. Tazzioli, "Crimes of Solidarity," 8.

81. Tazzioli, "Crimes of Solidarity," 8.

82. Tazzioli, "Crimes of Solidarity," 8.

83. Alexander Nabert, Claudia Torrisi, Nandini Archer, Belen Lobos, and Claire Provost, "Hundreds of Europeans 'Criminalized' for Helping Migrants—as Far Right Aims to Win Big in European Elections," *Open Democracy*, May 18, 2019, www.opendemocracy.net/en/5050/hundreds-of-europeans-criminalised -for-helping-migrants-new-data-shows-as-far-right-aims-to-win-big-in-european-elections/.

84. Human Rights Watch, "Greece: Rescuers at Sea Face Baseless Accusations: Prosecution Seeks to Criminalize Saving Lives," *Human Rights Watch*, November 5, 2018, www.hrw.org/news/2018/11/05/ greece-rescuers-sea-face-baseless-accusations.

85. Lorenzo Tondo, "Italy Orders Seizure of Migrant Rescue Ship over HIV-Contaminated Clothes," *The Guardian*, November 20, 2018, www.theguardian.com/world/2018/nov/20/italy-orders-seizure -aquarius-migrant-rescue-ship-hiv-clothes. See chapter 4 for a discussion of rhetorics of contamination and containment of refugees.

86. Mark Townsend, "Police with Batons and Teargas Force Migrants to Flee Calais Camp," *The Guardian*, December 1, 2018, www.theguardian.com/world/2018/dec/01/french-police-step-up-calais -refugee-evictions.

The criminalization of solidarity is happening in a climate of rising xenophobia, racism, and far-right politics in the European Union; it can be seen as an attempt by state and supra-state authorities to forcefully remind activists who is in control over migrants' survival. At the same time, this intense criminalization of practices of active solidarity "highlights a 'politicization of humanitarianism' that offers spaces of intervention that movements and transnational solidarity forces cannot waste to achieve a radical transformation of the existing order."[87]

In this context, perhaps it is more appropriate to talk about social stasis rather than social movements.[88] In a context where numerous borders, both inside and outside the nation-state, put a stop to people's movement, we urgently need to make stasis into a political category. The Greek meaning of stasis moves past the idea of inertia. Rather, stasis provides the space to pause, to reflect. It is about taking a stance: it suggests the corporeal, affective, and ideological positioning of the self (*stasi zois*). Stasis, as defined by Thucydides, is a set of symptoms indicating an internal disturbance in both states and individuals[89]—a moment in which forces are opposing, while they cancel each other out, and as such provide a space for stillness. Thus, even if stasis suggests stillness, it is a disruptive stillness. Stasis also means "standing up against," or "uprising." A further meaning of stasis is a single photographic "exposure" or a single cut in a negative strip (as in a single station in a roll of film). In this sense, stasis also opens up the capacity for representational resistance in its multiple intertwined senses.

The initial, visual meaning is generated from the tendency of protesters to gather symbolically together in occupations of public space. There is a deeper point to make regarding the contemporary manifestations of protest movement in which mass demonstrations tend to have as their function the (largely still) gatherings in front of monuments or parliaments. In prior struggles, there was a greater function of visibility, gaining support, and mobilizing publics in the pre-gathering marches which indeed constituted a growing movement of people towards a predetermined endpoint. In contemporary struggles, since 2011, occupations create of public spaces sites of static contestation (for example, city squares); movement occurs as a result of police attack or violent dispersal techniques. As such, stasis becomes a productive counterpoint through which we might understand the social kinetics of solidarity and uprisings. The very presence of bodies in public spaces (despite their often conflicting agendas in heterogeneous assemblies) forces a recognition that representative democracy is in crisis.

The driving insistence of progression that is inherent in the "movement" model of social movements is, arguably, closely aligned with the neoliberal paradigm. Instead,

---

87. EuroNomade, "Criminalization of Solidarity, Right to Escape, Solidarity Cities," April 5, 2018, www.euronomade.info/?p=10517.

88. Giorgio Agamben, *Stasis: Civil War as a Political Paradigm* (Stanford, CA: Stanford University Press, 2015); Costas Douzinas, "Stasis Syntagma: The Names and Types of Resistance," in *New Critical Legal Thinking: Law and the Political*, ed. M. Stone, I. Rua Wall, C. Douzinas, pp. 32–45 (London: Routledge, 2012).

89. See chapter 4.

as Athena Athanasiou suggests, "the very practice of stasis creates both a space for reflection and a space for revolt, but also an affective comportment of standing and standpoint. It is such a corporeal and affective disposition of stasis that derails, if only temporarily, normative presuppositions about what may come into being as publicly intelligible and sensible in existing polities."[90]

In this sense, stasis does not presuppose stillness, as such, but also implies there is a productive potential to the disruption that happens when the flows of progress, capital, and trade are stopped. If capitalism is all about the circulation of commodities and mobility of capital, then a truly subversive and revolutionary act is to disrupt, to pause, or to dismantle the pre-existing pathways that have led to dogmatic obeisance to capitalism's rules. A strike, for example, is considered successful when it puts a stop to the inevitable functioning of the factory. The point is not to generate a way out but to force political attention (from those in power and the public) to the issue. This forced attention does not gain political urgency from being spectacular but from its staying power. As Sandro Mezzadra claims, the refugee housing occupations in Athens (and surely not only in Athens) "politicize a specific border that is becoming more and more important in migratory experiences—the temporal border, the temporality of waiting, of living suspended in holding camps, 'hotspots,' and other structures—and they [solidarians] transform it into a chance for a new democratic invention and imagination."[91]

In other words, squats, public occupations, and solidarity infrastructures are different moments of stasis in which the "waiting for" could be transformed into a politicized "standing for." Moreover, they attempt to transform a state of emergency into a state of emergence of new coalitions and cross-border solidarity. Since (and before) the stasis (still image) of Alan Kurdi in 2015 moved numerous solidarians to travel to Greece in order to participate in the grassroots efforts of welcoming refugees, many have stayed on, helping transform the emergency response into a self-reproducing movement infrastructure that can stay the course long after international NGOs have moved on to the next humanitarian crisis. As rising populist and fascist politics seek to hem us into homogeneous national communities comprised of static citizens, people are struggling to find ways to move from the categories of belonging that prevent them from standing together against this onslaught. The moment of arrival created the highly mediatized "refugees welcome" response; the management of crisis—including strategies of containment—calls for coalitions that burst open state categories, including those that we have internalized as the only ways to survive, care, and love. Here is, particularly, where the different etymological trajectories of stasis meet: in the moment in which people politicize the spectatorial border, becoming not only passive viewers of stills, not only by stepping into the frame but by changing the frame al(l)together.

90. Judith Butler and Athena Athanasiou, *Dispossession: The Performative in the Political* (Cambridge: Polity, 2013), 151.

91. Sandro Mezzadra, "Borders and Migration: Emerging Challenges for Migration Research and Politics in Europe" (lecture, Berlin, 2016, www.euronomade.info/?p=7535).

"We Are City Plaza"
Photograph by Xiaofu Wang and Claude Somot.

"We Are City Plaza"
Photograph by Xiaofu Wang and Claude Somot.

"We Are City Plaza"
Photograph by Xiaofu Wang and Claude Somot.

"We Are City Plaza"
Photograph by Xiaofu Wang and Claude Somot.

"We Are City Plaza"
Photograph by Xiaofu Wang and Claude Somot.

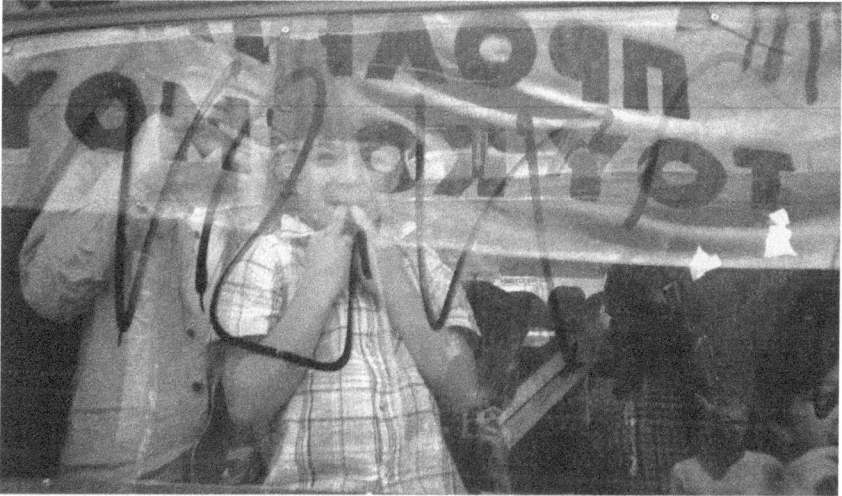

"We Are City Plaza"
Photograph by Xiaofu Wang and Claude Somot.

"We Are City Plaza"
Photograph by Xiaofu Wang and Claude Somot.

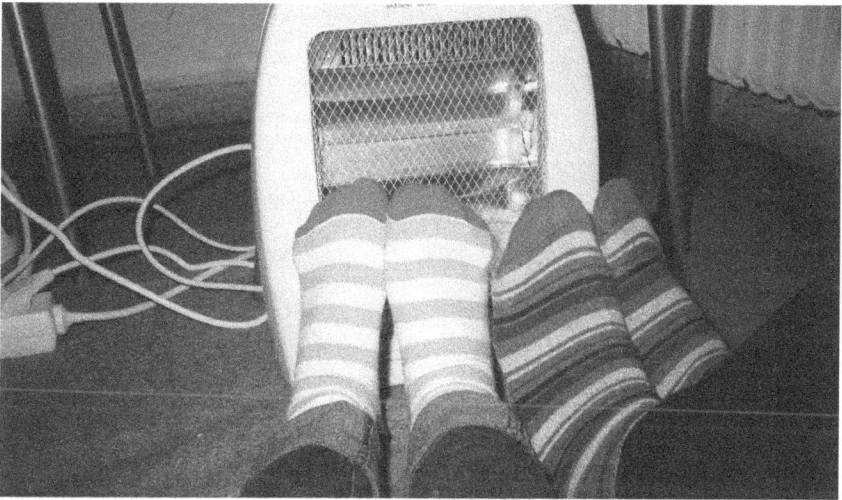

"We Are City Plaza"
Photograph by Xiaofu Wang and Claude Somot.

SNAPSHOTS FROM CITY PLAZA

In January 2017, Claude Somot brought me to City Plaza Hotel in Athens. This was the first time I had been in a squatted building, aside from the punk concerts I had attended as a teenager in Sydney. It looked nothing like I had imagined. Inside the café of the hotel there were people drinking tea and playing backgammon. Walking through the foyer I could hear at least four different languages. We went to the kitchen to help out with the lunch preparations of the day. Along with twenty other people, we chopped onions for an hour, for a lunch that would serve three to four hundred people.

What struck me from the moment I set foot in City Plaza was that there was a unique energy and atmosphere there. There was a feeling of ease and familiarity between those who lived there—people of all different ages and backgrounds. My first impression was that everyone seemed to be smiling! Refugees, smiling? This was definitely not an image that came to mind when one thought about the phrase "European migrant crisis."

Claude and I decided to try our best to capture City Plaza in photographic form. We felt that if we took the approach of regular photojournalists or documentarians, we would be ill-equipped to take on the task of representing City Plaza. Inspired by Zana Briski's project with children living in the Calcuttan Red Light district, Claude suggested that we give point-and-shoot cameras to the children of City Plaza, adding, "Children can go anywhere! And besides, they're short—the perspective will be amazing!" Along with giving out cameras, we planned to run workshops teaching basic photography skills, with the intention of giving something back to the community of City Plaza. The moment the first sessions started, however, many of our well-intentioned plans to teach photography fell apart. Before we could get a word out about anything, half the children simply grabbed the cameras and ran off. At best, a handful of them had the patience to stay with us while we ran a makeshift portrait studio in a hotel room turned language classroom on the seventh floor.

Eventually the pool of photographers grew to include not only children but adults too. In the space of a year, between February 2017 and February 2018, we collected over nine thousand photos, creating a huge archive of images that capture moments from day-to-day life at the hotel. Most of these photos have a "family album" feel, since they are taken on 35 mm point-and-shoot cameras and depict family or friends in City Plaza or around and about Athens. The normality—even mundanity—of these photos also serves as a sharp diversion from photojournalistic depictions of the "migrant crisis," since these depictions tend to center on a set of predetermined narratives. The snapshots from City Plaza capture everything from the joys and frustrations of communal living, to the boredom and inertia of being stuck in a place with no set timeframe, to carefree moments shared between friends. There are WhatsApp conversations on mobile phones, sunsets captured from the rooftop of the hotel, various meals, and personal items which bring homely qualities to impersonal spaces. There are even quaint moments of self-reflection, where the little analogue cameras are put on self-timer or turned around and used to take selfies.

Although we were driven by the idea of fostering self-representation, the project cannot be said to have achieved self-representation in the truest sense. In the end, Claude and I are the gatekeepers to the photos. We have the power to decide, through editing, what is shown and what is kept hidden, and we have the power to create narratives of our own. By showing City Plaza, we wanted to tell a story of harmony and of cooperation, an example of people getting along regardless of nationality, age, language, or other dividing factors. In hindsight, however, such a framework is also restrictive and falls into lockstep with the self-marketed image of City Plaza as a leftist political project. The photos don't address all of the problems that come with a self-organized space of four hundred people—either on a day-to-day or on an organizational level. The photos also don't address the disjunction between utopian ideas and everyday reality, or differences in privilege between those who lived at City Plaza as volunteers and those who were there as refugees. In the end, what they do capture is the sheer mass of experiences that are part of life in this unique place, with some intimate moments in between. They also provide another side to this multifaceted story, which offers a little bit of hope, laughter, and comic relief.

—Xiaofu Wang
Berlin, October 2018

Xiaofu Wang is a Chinese Australian photographer currently residing in Berlin.

Departures and Arrivals

"When photographs are being used to illustrate a type of situation, rather than to testify to a singular event, it is a sure sign that a disaster has become chronic, that the worst is still to come."[1] We echo these words in a time marked by broken promises and fading compassion.[2] In a time of Pacific Solutions, of hotspots technocratically transforming islands to closed doors,[3] taking us from refugee crisis to hostage crisis.[4] What might it mean to start listening to images, particularly those images speaking to us that, by frames seemingly as solid as walls and as deadly as electrified fences, have been muted: "We shout and shout but no one listens."[5] "How can I pass by all these cameras?" asks a person, captured and incarcerated, photographed "from the point of view of someone below the waist."[6] These are not lives lived in "shadows as distant 'negatives' of the original."[7] Rather, like long exposures in low light conditions, they slowly burn an irrepressible recognition—one we've been avoiding all along—into our retinas: in a war of images, "there is no nonviolent way to look at

---

1. Ariella Azoulay, *The Civil Contract of Photography* (London: Zone Press, 2008), 208.
2. Patrick Kingsley, "The Death of Alan Kurdi: One Year On, Compassion Towards Refugees Fades," *The Guardian*, September 2, 2016, www.theguardian.com/world/2016/sep/01/alan-kurdi-death-one-year-on-compassion-towards-refugees-fades.
3. Emi Mahmoud, "When an Island Becomes a Door, Who Will Answer?" 2016, spoken word performed at the Nansen Awards Ceremony. See twitter.com/Refugees/status/788504442945441793.
4. RISE, "'The "refugee crisis" in Australia is a Hostage Crisis where our members are being held captive by self serving politicians' —RISE member," Twitter post, October 25, 2016, twitter.com/riserefugee/status/790751000306921472.
5. Khaled Barakeh, Gohar Dashti, Nermine Hammam, Amel Ibrahimović, Alfredo Jaar, and Sandra Johnston, *We Shout and Shout, But No One Listens: Art from Conflict Zones*, ed. Frederikke Hansen and Tone Olaf Nielsen, trans. Rolf Mertz, Exhibition Catalogue, Center for Art on Migration Politics, 2017.
6. Behrouz Bouchani, *No Friend But the Mountains*, trans. Omid Tofighian. Epub version. (Sydney: Picador/Pan MacMillan, 2018), 196, 198.
7. Elena Fiddian-Qasmiyeh, "Shadows and Echoes in/of Displacement," *Refugee Hosts*, November 19, 2018, refugeehosts.org/2018/11/19/shadows-and-echoes-in-of-displacement.

someone."[8] Watching a glut of images, what have we learned? If nothing else, this: the eye is not only "the organ that sees, but the organ that weeps."[9]

* * *

Imagine you are standing on the shore of a sea staring across at a landmass opposite, which forms your horizon. You know, although they are not visible to you, that beneath the surface of this sea are the corpses of thousands of people who tried to cross it in order to arrive where you are now standing. Your horizon, then, is a border. This sea has long been viewed as a threshold, and yours is not the first epoch during which it has been crossed by masses of people in a rising tide of desperation, propelled by unspeakable violence. But crossing it has, in your epoch, become a crime. It is the liquid border between what is called "Greece" and what is called "Turkey"; and the solid ground on which you are standing is the "entrance gate to Europe." That you are standing here at all depends on prior crossings of people who, many years later, contributed to this threshold nation the semblance of solidity, even as they kept gazing across to a place they never ceased to remember as "home." Recently, this border has been multiplied; metaphorically and discursively, it travels; it exists in the imagination as far away as that "island nation" eager to "Brexit" from the continental project of Europe; it's being walled up and razor-wired shut, patrolled by border hunters chasing equally imaginary refugees. Your horizon has become a wall, a multilateral bargain, an aqueous cemetery. Staring at this horizon, things stop making sense. So you turn away. You stop imagining.[10]

* * *

Here I am, making another bound-to-fail attempt to position myself in a world characterized by mobility, liquidity, and speed, not the celebratory ones in which people, products, and ideas flow nicely as elaborated in the globalization studies mantra. The other one, in which you find yourself bumping awkwardly against walls, borders, fences, defenses, and hegemonic attitudes all the time. This is why I find it difficult to position myself, but for sure I know which side I am on. So, perhaps it is much more relevant to clarify this: I'm side by side with the ones who resist and revolt against dominant narratives, who fail and then join the collective depression, before they realize that they have to make room for queer failures and utopias, and, perhaps, then find the ways to resist again. At this very moment I'm struggling to make space again for hope and new utopias. Perhaps this is the most honest justification of this photographìa, accompanied by my belief that, sometimes, theory has the capacity to dismantle and provoke certain reactions. Photographs have the capacity to capture the untold, the unspeakable, the untranslatable, all those delicate perfor-

---

8. Boychild, Fred Moten, and Wu Tsang, "Sudden Rise at a Given Tune," performed by Wu Tsang and the Moved by the Motion ensemble as Sudden Rise, Onassis Stegi, Athens, May 5, 2019.
9. Veena Das, *Life and Words: Violence and the Descent into the Ordinary* (Berkeley: University of California Press, 2007), 62.
10. Extract from Research Diary (AC), Lesvos, July 2016.

mances that are not registered in speech. Photography adds an invaluable layer to our logocentric qualitative data collection mechanisms. Perhaps this is another reason to use the medium of photography in order to invoke the soft, daily, omnipresent affects of crisis and the things yet to come. To quote Ursula Le Guin, "You cannot take what you have not given, and you must give yourself. You cannot buy Utopia. You cannot make Utopia. You can only be the Utopia. Utopia is in the individual spirit, or it is nowhere. It is for all or it is nothing. If it is seen as having any end, it will never truly begin. We can't stop here. We must go on. We must take the risks."[11]

So, utopia is a transforming force that plays with the limits of the human. Yet, as Susan Sontag says, "humankind lingers unregenerately in Plato's cave, still revelling, its age-old habit, in mere images of the truth."[12] In this sense, most utopias are like photographs, offering glimpses at a moment or time that portrays the desirable outcomes of the utopian imagination. Utopia is a representation, evincing that which is not in itself present (this is the first meaning of the word "representation")—specifically, it puts on display and makes present the impossible itself. Yet, to return to Plato's cave, what limits and constitutes our understanding of utopian representations is the position of the guards.

I can't stop thinking of a graffiti slogan at the port of Lesvos underneath the stencil of faded, ghostlike figures of bodies arriving. *We are an image from the future.*[13]

---

11. Ursula K. Le Guin, *The Dispossessed (Hainish Cycle)* (New York: HarperCollins, 1974), 301.
12. Susan Sontag, *On Photography* (New York: Picador, 1973), 5. See chapter 2.
13. Extract from Research Diary (MT), Athens, July 2017.

Bibliography

Abounaddara Collectif. "En Syrie, refusons la fable d'un 'Orient compliqué': A l'heure où les dirigeants peinent à s'entendre sur le dossier syrien, un collectif de cinéastes du pays appelle à une intervention au nom de notre commune humanité." *Le Monde*, September 25, 2013. https://www.lemonde.fr/proche-orient/article/2013/09/25/en-syrie-refusons-la-fable-d-un-orient-complique_3483268_3218.html.

Abounaddara Collective, with Katarina Nitsch, eds. *The Question of the Right to the Image.* Damascus, 2019 [in Arabic]. http://kkh.diva-portal.org/smash/record.jsf?pid=diva2%3A1301510&dswid=5065.

Abounaddara Collective. "A Right to the Image for All: A Concept Paper for the Coming Revolution." n.d. http://www.veralistcenter.org/media/files/24f5ae024cdca7b1ca9c5c572cd14eb4.pdf.

Abounaddara Film Collective. www.abounaddara.com.

Abounaddara, collectif de cinéastes syriens. "Ne réduisons pas les Syriens aux images diffusées par la télé: Les médias européens travestissent la réalité syrienne en montrant trop peu les gens ordinaires, pour ne s'intéresser qu'au spectacle de la violence." *Le Monde*, October 21, 2014. https://www.lemonde.fr/idees/article/2014/10/21/au-dela-de-bachar-et-des-djihadistes-une-autre-syrie-existe_4509917_3232.html.

Abounaddara. "Regarding the Spectacle: What Happens When a Society No Longer Has the Ability to Defend Itself Against Post-Truth." *The Nation*, December 2, 2016. https://www.thenation.com/article/regarding-the-spectacle/.

Abounaddara. "The Syrian Who Wanted the Revolution." *documenta 14*, September 2, 2016. Originally published in *Al-Hayat Newspaper*, January 30, 2016. https://www.documenta14.de/en/notes-and-works/1524/the-syrian-who-wanted-the-revolution.

Abulafia, David. *The Great Sea: A Human History of the Mediterranean.* Oxford: Oxford University Press, 2011.

Adow, Mohammad. "Greeks Doing What They Can to Help Refugees." YouTube, March 5, 2016, 2:19. https://www.youtube.com/watch?v=rX-sXUb-A04.

AFP News Agency. "Ai Weiwei Life Jacket Installation Highlights Refugee Plight." YouTube, July 13, 2016, 1:13. https://www.youtube.com/watch?v=SEFQTsQ37hE.

Agamben, Giorgio. *Stasis: Civil War as a Political Paradigm.* Stanford, CA: Stanford University Press, 2015.

Agathangelou, Anna M., and Nevzat Soguk. "Rocking the Kasbah: Insurrectional Politics, the 'Arab Streets,' and Global Revolution in the 21st Century." *Globalizations* 8, no. 5 (2011): 551–58.

Agence France-Presse. "Refugee Boat Sinking: Dozens Including Children Drown off Greek Island." *The Guardian*, September 14, 2015. https://www.theguardian.com/world/2015/sep/14/babies-and-children-among-34-dead-in-aegean-migrant-boat-sinking.

Agence France-Presse. "Lafarge Charged with Complicity in Syria Crimes against Humanity." *The Guardian*, June 28, 2018. https://www.theguardian.com/world/2018/jun/28/lafarge -charged-with-complicity-in-syria-crimes-against-humanity.

Agustín, Óscar García, and Martin Bak Jørgensen. *Solidarity and the "Refugee Crisis" in Europe.* London: Palgrave Macmillan, 2019.

Ahmed, Sara. *Queer Phenomenology: Orientation, Objects, Others.* Durham, NC: Duke University Press, 2006.

Ahmed, Sara. *Strange Encounters: Embodied Others in Postcoloniality.* London: Routledge, 2000.

Ahmed, Sara. *The Cultural Politics of Emotion.* New York: Routledge, 2004.

Ai Weiwei at Cycladic, Museum of Cycladic Art, Athens, 2016. https://cycladic.gr/en/page/ai-weiwei-at-cycladic#.

Aiyar, Shekhar, Bergljot Barkbu, Nicoletta Batini, Helge Berger, Enrica Detragiache, Allan Dizioli, Christian Ebeke, Huidan Lin, Linda Kaltani, Sebastian Sosa, Antonio Spilimbergo, and Petia Topalova. *The Refugee Surge in Europe: Economic Challenges.* International Monetary Fund Staff Discussion Notes, January 2016, 4, 16. https://www.imf.org/external/pubs/ft/sdn/2016/sdn1602.pdf.

Akresh, Ilana Redstone. "Occupational Mobility among Legal Immigrants to the United States." *International Migration Review* 40, no. 4 (2006): 854–88.

Al Attar, Mohammad, Edward Blaise Ziter, and Lisa Wedeen. "Could You Please Look into the Camera?" *TDR/The Drama Review* 58, no. 3 (2014): 124–55. https://doi.org/10.1162/DRAM_a_00376.

Al Attar, Mohammed. Playwright's Note in "Could You Please Look into the Camera?" Translated by Lisa Wedeen, introduction by Edward Ziter. *TDR: The Drama Review* 58, no. 3 (2014): 124–55.

Al Jazeera. "Bags Made of Boats and Life Jackets." YouTube, March 8, 2016, 1:37. https://www.youtube.com/watch?v=tbIyB_SXtFY.

Alcoff, Linda Martín. "Habits of Hostility: On Seeing 'Race.'" *Philosophy Today* 44 (2000): 30–40.

Alcoff, Linda Martín. "The Problem of Speaking for Others." *Cultural Critique* 20 (Winter 1991–1992): 5–32.

Alexandropoulou, Electra, and Erifili Arapoglou, eds. *No Direction Home.* Athens: Rosa Luxemburg Stiftung, 2016.

"Algeria: Growing Number of Migrants Expelled into the Sahara Desert to Face Death by Exposure." European Council for Refugees and Exiles, June 29, 2018. https://www.ecre.org/algeria-growing-number-of-migrants-expelled-into-the-sahara-desert-to-face-death-by-exposure/.

Alimi, Eitan Y., and David S. Meyer. "When Repression Fails to Backfire: Movement's Powers, State Power, and Conditions Conducive to International Intervention." In *Popular Contention, Regime, and Transition: Arab Revolts in Comparative Global Perspective*, edited by Eitan Y. Alimi, Avraham Sela, and Mario Sznajder. Oxford: Oxford University Press, 2016.

Al-Othman, Hannah. "Tricked into Death: 150,000 Migrants' Life Jackets—Many of Which Are Useless Fakes—Lie Piled on the Coast of Lesbos in Grim Memorial to Those Who Die Crossing the Mediterranean." *Daily Mail*, February 6, 2017. https://www.dailymail.co.uk/news/article-4196010/150-000-migrants-life-jackets-lie-piled-Lesbos-coast.html.

Amnesty International. "Greece: Farmakonisi Migrant Tragedy—One Year on and Still No Justice for Victims." January 20, 2015. https://www.amnesty.org/en/latest/news/2015/01/greece-farmakonisi-migrant-tragedy-one-year-and-still-no-justice-victims/.

Anderson, Benedict. *Imagined Communities: Reflections on the Origin and Spread of Nationalism*. London: Verso, 1983.

Anderson, Bridget, Nandita Sharma, and Cynthia Wright. "Editorial: Why No Borders?" *Refuge* 26, no. 2 (2009): 5–18.

Anderson, Bridget. *Us and Them? The Dangerous Politics of Immigration Controls*. Oxford: Oxford University Press, 2013.

Anderson, Bridget. *Doing the Dirty Work? The Global Politics of Domestic Labor*. New York: Zed, 2000.

Andersson, Ruben. *Illegality Inc. Clandestine Migration and the Business of Bordering Europe*. Oakland: University of California Press, 2014.

Andrew, Lawrence. "Life Jackets in Parliament Square/International Rescue Committee." *Newsflare*. n.d. Accessed October 7, 2019. https://www.newsflare.com/video/86884/politics-business/life-jackets-in-parliament-square-international-rescue-committee#.

Anthias, Floya, and Nira Yuval-Davis, eds. *Women, Nation, State*. London: Palgrave Macmillan, 1989.

Antonopoulos, Thodoris. "Gay, Lesbian, Trans Refugees in Athens: One of the Most 'Invisible,' Dramatic but Also Heroic Sides of the Refugee Issue" [in Greek, our translation]. *Lifo*, November 8, 2016. http://www.lifo.gr/articles/lgbt_articles/120527.

Anzaldúa, Gloria. *Borderlands/La Frontera: The New Mestiza*. San Francisco: Aunt Lute, 1987.

AP Archive. "Ai Weiwei Turns Migrant Lifejackets into Art in Copenhagen." YouTube, June 30, 2017, 5:42. https://www.youtube.com/watch?v=T3u2zTWXi4s.

Apostolova, Raia. "Of Refugees and Migrants: Stigma, Politics, and Boundary Work at the Borders of Europe." *American Sociological Association Culture Section*, September 14, 2015. https://asaculturesection.org/2015/09/14/of-refugees-and-migrants-stigma-politics-and-boundary-work-at-the-borders-of-europe/.

Apostolova, Raia. "The Real Appearance of the Economic/Political Binary: Claiming Asylum in Bulgaria." *Intersections: East European Journal of Society and Politics* 2, no. 4 (2016): 33–50.

Appadurai, Arjun. *Modernity at Large: Cultural Dimensions of Globalization*. Minneapolis: University of Minnesota Press, 1996.

Arapoglou, Vassilis, and Kostas Gounis. "Poverty and Homelessness in Athens: Governance and the Rise of an Emergency Model of Social Crisis Management." Hellenic Observatory Papers on Greece and Southeast Europe, GreeSE Paper No. 90, 2015, 25–27. http://www.lse.ac.uk/europeanInstitute/research/hellenicObservatory/CMS%20pdf/Publications/GreeSE/GreeSE_No90.pdf.

Arapoglou, Vassilis, and Kostas Gounis. *Contested Landscapes of Poverty and Homelessness in Southern Europe: Reflections from Athens.* London: Palgrave Macmillan, 2017.

Are You Syrious. "EuroRelief: Evangelical Organization Providing More Harm Than Aid to Refugees." *Are You Syrious Daily Digest,* January 11, 2018. https://medium.com/@AreYou Syrious/ays-daily-digest-11-01-2018-eurorelief-u-s-807717ec51f8.

Arruzza, Cinzia. "Feminisms of the Left: On Gender, Marxism, Capitalism." The Editorial Board of Public Seminar, April 30, 2014. http://www.publicseminar.org/2014/04/feminisms-of-the-left-on-gender-marxism-capitalism/.

Arruzza, Cinzia. *Dangerous Liaisons: The Marriages and Divorces of Marxism and Feminism.* London: Merlin Press, 2013.

Arsenijevic, Jovana, Marcel Manzi, and Rony Zachariah. "Defending Humanity at Sea: Are Dedicated and Proactive Search and Rescue Operations at Sea a 'Pull Factor' for Migration and Do They Deteriorate Maritime Safety in the Central Mediterranean?" Report. Luxembourg: Médecins Sans Frontières, Operational Research Unit (LuxOR), 2017. http://searchandrescue.msf.org/assets/uploads/files/170831-%20Report_Analysis _SAR_Final.pdf.

Asediu, Michael. "The EU-Libya Migrant Deal: A Deal of Convenience." *E-International Relations,* April 11, 2017. https://www.e-ir.info/2017/04/11/the-eu-libya-migrant-deal-a -deal-of-convenience/.

Athanasiou, Athena. *Crisis as a "State of Emergency."* Athens: Savalas, 2012 [in Greek].

Athanasiou, Athena. *Crisis as a "State of Emergency": Critiques and Resistances.* Athens: Savvalas, 2012 [in Greek].

Azoulay, Ariella. *Once Upon a Time: Photography after Walter Benjamin.* Ramat Gan: Bar Ilan University Press, 2006 [in Hebrew].

Azoulay, Ariella. *The Civil Contract of Photography.* London: Zone Books, 2008.

Azzarello, Nina. "Ai Weiwei Wraps Berlin's Konzerthaus with 14,000 Refugee Life Jackets." *DesignBoom,* February 15, 2016. https://www.designboom.com/art/ai-weiwei-life-jackets -refugee-konzerthaus-berlin-02-15-2016/.

Back, Les, and Paul Halliday. "Inscriptions of Love." In *Cultural Bodies: Ethnography and Theory,* edited by H. Thomas and J. Ahmed, 27–55. Oxford: Blackwell, 2004.

Back, Les. "Portrayal and Betrayal: Bourdieu, Photography and the Sociological Life." *Sociological Review,* August 1, 2009. https://doi.org/10.1111/j.1467-954X.2009.01850.x.

Bakewell, Oliver. "Research Beyond the Categories: The Importance of Policy Irrelevant Research into Forced Migration." *Journal of Refugee Studies* 21, no. 4 (2008): 432–53.

Bakker, Isabella, and Stephen Gill, eds. *Power, Production, and Social Reproduction: Human In/ Security in the Global Political Economy.* London: Palgrave Macmillan, 2003.

Bakker, Isabella. "Social Reproduction and the Constitution of a Gendered Political Economy." *New Political Economy* 12, no. 4 (2007): 541–56.

Balan, Sarita S. "My Picture Led to the End of the Vietnam War: 'Napalm Girl' Photographer Tells TNM." *The News Minute,* March 9, 2018. https://www.thenewsminute.com/article/my-picture-led-end-vietnam-war-napalm-girl-photographer-nick-ut-tells-tnm-77703.

Balzan, Jurgen. "Made in China: 'Refugee Boats' Available on Alibaba.com. China Is the Main Source of Rubber Dinghy Imports to Malta: Between 2012 and 2016, €1.3 Million in Merchandise Was Imported." *Malta Today,* April 24, 2017. https://www.maltatoday .com.mt/news/national/76525/made_in_china_refugee_boats_available_on_alibabacom# .XMw_OC2B3OQ.

Barakeh, Khaled, Gohar Dashti, Nermine Hammam, Amel Ibrahimović, Alfredo Jaar, and Sandra Johnston. *We Shout and Shout, but No One Listens: Art from Conflict Zones*. Edited by Frederikke Hansen and Tone Olaf Nielsen. Translated by Rolf Mertz. Exhibition Catalogue. Center for Art on Migration Politics, 2017.

Barbelet, Veronique, Jessica Hagen-Zanker, and Dina Mansour-Ille. "The Jordan Compact: Lessons Learnt and Implications for Future Refugee Compacts." Overseas Development Institute, February 2018. https://www.odi.org/sites/odi.org.uk/files/resource-documents/12058.pdf.

Baron, Ellan. "Seven Sketches Inspired by Athens' Refugee Squats—in Pictures." *The Guardian*, September 8, 2016. https://www.theguardian.com/global-development-professionals-network/gallery/2016/sep/08/seven-sketches-inspired-by-athens-refugee-squats-in-pictures.

Barthes, Roland. *Camera Lucida: Reflections on Photography*. New York: Hill and Wang, 1980.

Baruah, Parasher. "Waste." YouTube, August 11, 2015, 37:53. https://youtu.be/bNpQ9W94LmI.

Baskakis, Yiannis. "All the Families Here Live Like One Family." *Efsyn*, April 22, 2017 [in Greek, our translation]. https://www.efsyn.gr/ellada/koinonia/107693_oles-oi-oikogeneies-edo-zoyn-san-mia-oikogeneia.

Bataille, Georges. *The Accursed Share: An Essay on General Economy*. London: Zone Books, 1988.

Bauman, Zygmunt. *Liquid Modernity*. Cambridge: Polity Press, 2000.

BBC. "The Worst Refugee Camp on Earth." YouTube, August 28, 2018, 13:51. https://www.youtube.com/watch?v=8v-OHi3iGQI.

BBC. "Hungary to Put Migrants in Converted Shipping Containers." *BBC News*, March 17, 2017. https://www.bbc.com/news/av/world-europe-39301003/hungary-to-put-migrants-in-converted-shipping-containers.

BBC. "Migrant Crisis: Turkey Police Seize Fake Life Jackets." *BBC News*, January 6, 2016. https://www.bbc.com/news/world-europe-35241813.

Beck, Ulrich. "Critical Theory of World Risk Society: A Cosmopolitan Vision." *Constellations* 16, no. 1 (2009): 3–22.

Bedard, Paul. "Refugee Costs: $8.8 Billion, $80,000 per Immigrant, Free Welfare, Medicaid." *Washington Examiner*, February 5, 2018. https://www.washingtonexaminer.com/refugee-costs-88-billion-80-000-per-immigrant-free-welfare-medicaid.

Belkin, Paul. "Crisis in Greece: Political Implications." CRS report IN10303, July 7, 2015. https://digital.library.unt.edu/ark:/67531/metadc743369/m1/1/high_res_d/IN10303_2015Jul07.pdf.

Benjamin, Walter. "Surrealism: The Last Snapshot of the European Intelligentsia." In *Walter Benjamin Selected Writings, Vol. 2, 1927–1934*. Cambridge: Harvard University Press, 2005/1929.

Benjamin, Walter. "The Work of Art in the Age of Mechanical Reproduction." In *Illuminations*, edited by Hannah Arendt. Translated by Harry Zohn. New York: Schocken Books, 1969.

Benjamin, Walter. *Selected Writings 1927–1934, Vol. 2 Part 2, 1931–1934*. Edited by Michael Jennings, Howard Eiland, and Gary Smith. Cambridge: Belknap Press, 1999.

Benjamin, Walter. *The Work of Art in the Age of Its Technological Reproducibility and Other Writings on Media, 2nd version*. Cambridge, MA: Harvard University Press, 2008.

Berger, John. *Ways of Seeing*. London: Penguin, 1977.

Betts, Alexander, and Paul Collier. *Refuge: Rethinking Refugee Policy in a Changing World.* Oxford: Oxford University Press, 2017.

Betts, Alexander, and Paul Collier. "Help Refugees Help Themselves: Let Displaced Syrians Join the Labor Market." *Foreign Affairs*, October 20, 2015. https://www.foreignaffairs.com/articles/levant/2015-10-20/help-refugees-help-themselves.

Betts, Alexander, and Paul Collier. "Jordan's Refugee Experiment." *Foreign Affairs*, April 28, 2016. https://www.foreignaffairs.com/articles/middle-east/2016-04-28/jordans-refugee-experiment.

Betts, Alexander, Louise Bloom, Josiah Kaplan, and Naohiko Omata. *Refugee Economies: Forced Displacement and Development.* Oxford: Oxford University Press, 2017.

Bhabha, Homi. "Foreword to the 1986 Edition: Remembering Fanon: Self, Psyche and the Colonial Condition." In *Black Skins, White Masks*, edited by Frantz Fanon. Translated by Charles Lam Markmann. London: Pluto, [1967] 1986.

Bhambra, Gurminder K. "Brexit, Trump, and 'Methodological Whiteness': On the Misrecognition of Race and Class." *British Journal of Sociology* 68, no. 1 (2017): 214–32.

Bhattacharya, Tithi. "Introduction: Mapping Social Reproduction Theory." In *Social Reproduction Theory*, edited by Tithi Bhattacharya. London: Pluto, 2017.

Bhattacharya, Tithi, ed. *Social Reproduction Theory: Remapping Class, Recentering Oppression.* London: Pluto, 2017.

Bindel, Julie. "Sun, Sea and Sappho: Should Only Those Born on the Greek Island of Lesbos Be Allowed to Call Themselves Lesbian?" *The Guardian*, May 8, 2008. https://www.theguardian.com/world/2008/may/08/gayrights.greece.

Birchnell, Thomas, Satya Savitzky, and John Urry. *Cargomobilites: Moving Materials in a Global Age.* London: Routledge, 2015.

Bleiker, Roland, David Campbell, Emma Hutchison, and Xzarina Nicholson. "The Visual Dehumanization of Refugees." *Australian Journal of Political Science* 48, no. 4 (2013): 399. http://dx.doi.org/10.1080/10361146.2013.840769.

Bleiker, Roland. *Visual Global Politics.* London: Routledge, 2018.

Bohrer, Ashley. "Intersectionality and Marxism: A Critical Historiography." *Historical Materialism* 26, no. 2 (2018): 46–74.

Bouchani, Behrouz. *No Friend but the Mountains.* Translated by Omid Tofighian. Sydney: Picador/Pan MacMillan, 2018, Epub version.

Bourdieu, Pierre, and Loïc Wacquant. *An Invitation to Reflexive Sociology.* Oxford: Blackwell, 1992.

boychild, Fred Moten, and Wu Tsang. "Sudden Rise at a Given Tune." Performed by Wu Tsang and the Moved by the Motion ensemble as Sudden Rise, Onassis Stegi, Athens, May 5, 2019.

Boyle, Shane. "Container Aesthetics: The Infrastructural Politics of Shunt's 'The Boy Who Climbed Out of His Face.'" *Theatre Journal* 68, no. 1 (2016): 57–77.

Bozdag, Cigdem, and Kevin Smets. "Understanding the Images of Alan Kurdi with 'Small Data': A Qualitative, Comparative Analysis of Tweets about Refugees in Turkey and Flanders (Belgium)." *International Journal of Communication* 11 (2017): 4064.

Brenner, Johanna. "Intersections, Locations, and Capitalist Class Relations: Intersectionality from a Marxist perspective." In *Women and the Politics of Class*, edited by Johanna Brenner, 293–324. New York: Monthly Review Press, 2000.

Broomfield, Matt. "Queer Refugees on Lesvos are Crying Out for Help." *New Arab*, November 10, 2017. https://www.alaraby.co.uk/english/indepth/2017/11/10/queer-refugees-on-lesvos-are-crying-out-for-help?utm_source=twitter&utm_medium=sf.

Broomsfield, Matt. "The Abusive American-Christian NGO with a Stranglehold over Refugees' Lives." *New Arab*, May 1, 2018. https://www.alaraby.co.uk/english/indepth/2018/5/1/the-abusive-ngo-with-a-stranglehold-on-refugees-lives.

Brown, Don. *The Unwanted: Stories of the Syrian Refugees*. Boston: Houghton Mifflin Harcourt, 2018.

Brunwasser, Matthew. "A 21st-Century Migrant's Essentials: Food, Shelter, Smartphone." *New York Times*, August 25, 2015. https://www.nytimes.com/2015/08/26/world/europe/a-21st-century-migrants-checklist-water-shelter-smartphone.html?_r=1.

Buck-Morss, Susan. "Anti-Stalinist Art: Benjamin, Shostakovich, and the End of the Story." Keynote lecture of the first Congress of the International Walter Benjamin Association, Amsterdam, July 1997. http://susanbuckmorss.info/text/antistalinist-art/.

Buss, Doris. "Rethinking 'Rape as a Weapon of War.'" *Feminist Legal Studies* 17 (2009): 148.

Butler, Judith, and Athena Athanasiou. *Dispossession: The Performative in the Political*. Cambridge: Polity, 2013.

Butler, Judith, Zeynep Gambetti, and Leticia Sabsay. *Vulnerability in Resistance*. Durham, NC: Duke University Press, 2016.

Butler, Judith. *Frames of War: When Is Life Grievable*. London: Verso, 2010.

Butler, Judith. "Is Kinship Always Already Heterosexual?" *Differences: A Journal of Feminist Cultural Studies* 13, no. 1 (2002): 14–44.

Butler, Judith. "Merely Cultural." *Social Text* no. 52/53 (1997): 265–77.

Butler, Judith. "Photography, War, Outrage." *Theories and Methodologies* 120, no. 3 (May 2005): 822–27.

Butler, Judith. "Torture and the Ethics of Photography." *Environment and Planning D: Society and Space* 25 (2007): 951–66.

Cabot, Heath. "Crisis, Hot Spots, and Paper Pushers: A Reflection on Asylum in Greece." *Cultural Anthropology*, June 28, 2016. https://culanth.org/fieldsights/898-crisis-hot-spots-and-paper-pushers-a-reflection-on-asylum-in-greece.

Cadava, Eduardo. *Words of Light: Theses on the Photography of History*. Princeton, NJ: Princeton University Press, 1997.

Caffentzis, George. "On the Notion of a Crisis of Social Reproduction: A Theoretical Review." *Commoner*, no. 5 (Autumn 2002): 1–2. http://www.commoner.org.uk/caffentzis05.pdf.

"Call Me by My Name: Stories from Calais and Beyond." Migration Museum Project, 2019. https://www.migrationmuseum.org/exhibition/calaisstories/.

Campbell, Zach. "Shoot First: Coast Guard Fired at Migrant Boats, European Border Agency Documents Show." *Intercept*, August 22, 2016. https://theintercept.com/2016/08/22/coast-guard-fired-at-migrant-boats-european-border-agency-documents-show/.

Canter, Alicia, Kate Lyons, and Matt Fidler. "'It's Like AirBnB for Refugees': UK Hosts and Their Guests: In Pictures." *The Guardian*, May 8, 2017. https://www.theguardian.com/world/2017/may/08/airbnb-for-refugees-uk-hosts-guests-in-pictures?CMP=Share_iOSApp_Other.

Capper, Beth, and Arlen Austin. "'Wages for Housework Means Wages *against* Heterosexuality': On the Archives of Black Women for Wages for Housework and Wages Due Lesbians." *GLQ* 24, no. 4 (2018): 445–66.

Carastathis, Anna, Aila Spathopoulou, and Myrto Tsilimpounidi. "Crisis, What Crisis? Immigrants, Refugees, and Invisible Struggles." *Refuge: Canada's Journal on Refugees/revue canadienne sur les réfugiés* 34, no. 1 (2018): 29–38.

Carastathis, Anna, and Myrto Tsilimpounidi. "Experts, Refugees, and Radicals: Borders and Orders in the Hotspot of Crisis." *Theory in Action* 11, no. 4 (2018): 1–21.

Carastathis, Anna. "Identity Categories as Potential Coalitions." *Signs: Journal of Women in Culture and Society* 3, no. 4 (2013): 941–96.

Carastathis, Anna. "Nesting Crises." *Women's Studies International Forum* 68 (December 2017): 142–48.

Carastathis, Anna. *Intersectionality: Origins, Contestations, Horizons.* Lincoln: University of Nebraska Press, 2016.

Casdorff, Stephan-Andreas, and Lorenz Maroldt. "'The List' of Banu Cennetoglu: Artist Documents the Dying of 33,293 Refugees." *Der Tagesspiegel*, November 9, 2017 [in German]. https://www.tagesspiegel.de/politik/die-liste-von-banu-cennetoglu-kuenstlerin -dokumentiert-das-sterben-von-33-293-gefluechteten/20558658.html.

Cassin, Barbara. *Dictionary of Untranslatables: A Philosophical Lexicon.* Edited by Emily Apter, Jacques Lezra, and Michael Wood. Translated by Steven Randall, Christian Hubert, Jeffrey Mehlman, Nathanael Stein, and Michael Syrotinski. Princeton, NJ: Princeton University Press, 2014.

Caters News Agency. "Thousands of Life Jackets that Saved Refugee Lives Are Converted into Laptop Cases and Bags." *Caters News Agency*, 2019. https://www.catersnews.com/stories/ latest-news/thousands-of-life-jackets-that-saved-refugee-lives-are-converted-into-laptop -cases-and-bags/.

Chakrabarty, Dipesh. *Provincializing Europe: Postcolonial Thought and Historical Difference.* Princeton, NJ: Princeton University Press, 2007.

Change. "Asylum for Amir Hampay Now! Waiting Two Years Is a Crime!" Petition, Asylum for Amir Hampay, Change.org. https://www.change.org/p/asylum-for-amir-hampay -now-two-years-waiting-is-a-crime?recruiter=2658267&utm_source=share_petition&utm _medium=facebook_link&utm_campaign=share_petition.

Charbau, Gaël. "Léa Belooussovitch, EIDÔLON: 'Before My Gaze Thy Soul's Eidolon Stands.'" Exhibition Statement, Galerie Paris-Beijing, April 2019. http://www.galerieparis beijing.com/exhibition/eidolon-gaze-thy-souls-eidolon-stands/.

Chouliaraki, Lilie. "Symbolic Bordering: The Self-Representation of Migrants and Refugees in Digital News." *Popular Communication* 15, no. 2 (2017): 78–94. https://doi.org/10.10 80/15405702.2017.1281415.

City Plaza. "Support the City Plaza Refugee Accommodation and Solidarity Center in Athens." June 13, 2016. http://solidarity2refugees.gr/support-city-plaza-refugee-accommodation -solidarity-center-athens-greece/.

City Plaza. "39 Months of City Plaza: The Completion of a Cycle, the Beginning of a New One." July 10, 2019. http://solidarity2refugees.gr/39-mines-city-plaza-oloklirosi-enos -kyklou-archi-enos-neou/ [in Greek].

Clarke, Kamari M., and Deborah A. Thomas. "Introduction: Globalization and the Transformations of Race." In *Globalization and Race: Transformations in the Cultural Production of Blackness*, edited by Kamari M. Clarke and Deborah A. Thomas. Durham, NC: Duke University Press, 2008.

Cohen, Cathy J. "Punks, Bulldaggers, and Welfare Queens: The Radical Potential of Queer Politics?" *GLQ* 3, no. 4 (1997): 437–65.

Cohen, Robin. "Refugia: The Limits and Possibilities of Buzi's Refugee Nation." *Postcards From*, July 30, 2015. https://nandosigona.wordpress.com/2015/07/30/refugia-the-limits -and-possibilities-of-buzis-refugee-nation/.

Cole, Elizabeth R. "Coalitions as a Model for Intersectionality: From Practice to Theory." *Sex Roles* 59, no. 5–6 (2008): 443–53.

Container City. "Designing and Building Shipping Container Architecture since 1998." Accessed October 7, 2019. http://www.containercity.com.

Cooper, Michael D. "Migration and Disaster-Induced Displacement: European Policy, Practice, and Perspective." Center for Global Development Working Paper No. 308, October 2012, 61–63. https://www.cgdev.org/sites/default/files/1426605_file_Cooper_disaster_displacement_FINAL.pdf.

Cooper, Vickie, and David White. *The Violence of Austerity*. London: Pluto, 2017.

Costa, Mariarosa Dalla, and Selma James. "The Power of Women and the Subversion of the Community." Libcom, November 23, 2005. https://libcom.org/library/power-women-subversion-community-della-costa-selma-james.

Council of Europe. "Realizing the Right to Family Reunification in Europe." Strasbourg: Council of Europe Commissioner for Human Rights, 2017. https://rm.coe.int/prems-052917-gbr-1700-realising-refugees-160x240-web/1680724ba0.

Council of the European Union. "Press Release: European Border and Coast Guard: Council Agrees Negotiating Position." February 20, 2019. https://www.consilium.europa.eu/en/press/press-releases/2019/02/20/european-border-and-coast-guard-council-agrees-negotiating-position/.

Cowen, Deborah. *The Deadly Life of Logistics: Mapping Violence in Global Trade*. Minneapolis: University of Minnesota Press, 2014.

Crawley, Heaven, and Dimitris Skleparis. "Refugees, Migrants, Neither, Both: Categorical Fetishism and the Politics of Bounding in Europe's 'Migration Crisis.'" *Journal of Ethnic and Migration Studies* 44, no. 1 (2018): 48–64. http://dx.doi.org/10.1080/1369183X.2017.1348224.

Crawley, Heaven. "Migration: Refugee Economics." *Nature: International Journal of Science* 544 (April 2017): 26–27. https://www.nature.com/articles/544026.

Creighton, Emily. "Environmental Impact of the Refugee Crisis." *Planet Forward*, March 2, 2017. https://www.planetforward.org/idea/environmental-impact-of-the-refugee-crisis.

Crenshaw, Kimberlé Williams. "Mapping the Margins: Intersectionality, Identity Politics, and Violence against Women of Color." *Stanford Law Review* 43, no. 6 (1991): 1241–99.

Cvetkovitch, Ann. *An Archive of Feelings*. Durham, NC: Duke University Press, 2003.

Daney, Serge. "Before and After the Image." Translated by Melissa McMahon. *Discourse* 21, no. 1 (1999): 181–90.

Das, Veena. *Life and Words: Violence and the Descent into the Ordinary*. Berkeley: University of California Press, 2007.

de Certeau, Michel. *The Practice of Everyday Life*. Berkeley: University of California Press, 1984.

De Genova, Nicholas. "The Border Spectacle of Migrant 'Victimization.'" *Open Democracy*, May 20, 2015. https://www.opendemocracy.net/en/beyond-trafficking-and-slavery/border-spectacle-of-migrant-victimisation/.

De Genova, Nicholas. "Spectacles of Migrant 'Illegality': The Scene of Exclusion, the Obscene of Inclusion." *Ethnic and Racial Studies*, May 24, 2013, 2. http://dx.doi.org/10.1080/01419870.2013.783710.

De Jong, Sara, and Jacquie Gabb, eds. "Focus: Families and Relationships across Crises." *Discover Society*, no. 44 (2017). https://discoversociety.org/2017/05/02/focus-families-and-relationships-across-crises/.

De'Ath, Amy. "Gender and Social Reproduction." In *SAGE Handbook of Frankfurt School Critical Theory*, edited by Beverley Best, Werner Bonefeld, and Chris O'Kane, 1534–50. Thousand Oaks, CA: Sage, 2018.

de-Andrés, Susana, Eloísa Nos-Aldas, and Agustín García-Matilla. "The Transformative Image. The Power of a Photograph for Social Change: The Death of Aylan." *Comunicar: Revista Científica de Educomunicación* 24, no. 47 (2016).

Deardon, Lizzie. "Refugee Crisis: European Leaders Blamed for Record High Deaths in the Mediterranean." *Independent*, November 2, 2016. https://www.independent.co.uk/news/uk/home-news/refugee-crisis-closing-borders-people-smugglers-human-trafficking-mediterranean-deaths-record-a7391736.html.

Debord, Guy. *The Society of Spectacle*. London: Rebel Press, 1967.

Dehghan, Saeed Kamali. "8,500 People Lost in Mediterranean since Death of Three-Year-Old Alan Kurdi." *The Guardian*, September 1, 2017. https://www.theguardian.com/world/2017/sep/01/alan-kurdi-khaled-hosseini-mediterranean-refugees-sea-prayer.

Demos, T. J. *The Migrant Image: The Art and Politics of Documentary during the Global Crisis*. Durham, NC: Duke University Press, 2013.

Department for International Development. "Prime Minister Pledges New UK Support to Help Tackle Migration Crisis." Press Release, September 21, 2016. https://www.gov.uk/government/news/prime-minister-pledges-new-uk-support-to-help-tackle-migration-crisis.

Derrida, Jacques. *Spectres of Marx: The State of the Debt, the Work of Mourning and the New International*. Translated by Peggy Kamuf. New York: Routledge, [1994] 2006.

Desmond, Michael. "Ben Quilty: Life Vests 2016–2017." Deathscapes: Mapping Race and Violence in Settler States, 2017. https://buff.ly/2LZtGxh.

Deutscher, Penelope. *Foucault's Futures: A Critique of Reproductive Reason*. New York: Columbia University Press, 2017.

Devichand, Mukul. "Alan Kurdi's Aunt: My Dead Nephew's Picture Saved Thousands of Lives." *BBC News*, January 2, 2016. https://www.bbc.com/news/blogs-trending-35116022.

Dickerman, Leah. "Camera Obscura: Socialist Realism in the Shadow of Photography." *October* 93 (Summer 2000): 138–53.

Dimitrakaki, Angela, and Kirsten Lloyd. "Social Reproduction Struggles and Art History." *Third Text* 31, no. 1 (2017): 1–14.

Douzinas, Costas. "Stasis Syntagma: The Names and Types of Resistance." In *New Critical Legal Thinking: Law and the Political*, edited by M. Stone, I. Rua Wall, and C. Douzinas, 32–45. London: Routledge, 2012.

Douzinas, Costas. *Philosophy and Resistance in the Crisis: Greece and the Future of the Eurozone*. Cambridge: Polity, 2013.

Drucker, Peter. *Innovation and Entrepreneurship*. London: Routledge, 2007.

Dussel, Enrique. "The Four Drafts of *Capital:* Towards a New Interpretation of the Dialectical Thought of Marx." *Rethinking Marxism* 13, no. 1 (2001).

Efsyn. "Ithaca Is Only the Beginning." Efsyn, August 21, 2018. http://www.efsyn.gr/arthro/i-ithaki-einai-mono-i-arhi.

Eisenstein, Hester, Martha E. Gimenez, Barbara Foley, Lise Vogel, and Shana A. Russell. "Intersectionality: A Symposium." *Science and Society* 82, no. 2 (2018): 248–91.

Elgot, Jessica. "Charity behind Migrant-Rescue Boats Sees 15-Fold Rise in Donations in 24 Hours." *The Guardian*, September 3, 2015. https://www.theguardian.com/world/2015/sep/03/charity-behind-migrant-rescue-boats-sees-15-fold-rise-in-donations-in-24-hours.

Elliot, Anthony, and Urry John. *Mobile Lives*. London: Routledge, 2010.

El-Tayeb, Fatima. *European Others: Queering Ethnicity in Postnational Europe*. Minneapolis: University of Minnesota Press, 2011.

Emejulu, Akwugo, and Leah Bassel. *Minority Women and Austerity: Survival and Resistance in France and Britain*. Bristol: Policy Press, 2017.

Euractiv and Reuters. "France's Le Pen Urges Show of Nationalist Force in European Elections." EURACTIV.com, September 17, 2018. https://www.euractiv.com/section/eu-elections-2019/news/frances-le-pen-urges-show-of-nationalist-force-in-european-elections/.

European Commission. "A European Agenda on Migration." Brussels, May 13, 2015. https://ec.europa.eu/anti-trafficking/sites/antitrafficking/files/communication_on_the_european_agenda_on_migration_en.pdf.

European Commission. "EU Action in Libya on Migration." European Commission, December 7, 2017. https://ec.europa.eu/home-affairs/sites/homeaffairs/files/what-we-do/policies/european-agenda-migration/20171207_eu_action_in_libya_on_migration_en.pdf.

European Commission. "Explanatory Note on the 'Hotspot' Approach." Statewatch.org, July 2015. http://www.statewatch.org/news/2015/jul/eu-com-hotsposts.pdf.

European Commission. "Hotspot Approach." Migration and Home Affairs, 2018. https://ec.europa.eu/home-affairs/content/hotspot-approach_en.

Evans, Natalle, and Richard Wheatstone. "Aylan Kurdi's Death Recreated by 30 People Dressed as Syrian Boy on Moroccan Beach." *Mirror Online*, September 10, 2015. https://www.mirror.co.uk/news/world-news/aylan-kurdis-death-recreated-30-6415214.

Federici, Silvia. "The Reproduction of Labor Power in the Global Economy." In *Revolution at Point Zero*. Oakland: PM Press, 2012.

Federici, Silvia. "Women, Reproduction and Globalization." In *Économie mondialisée et identités de genre*, edited by Fenneke Reysoo, 60. Geneva: Graduate Institute Publications, 2002. http://books.openedition.org/iheid/6171.

Federici, Silvia. *Caliban and the Witch, Women, the Body and Primitive Accumulation*. New York: Autonomedia, 2004.

Federici, Silvia. *Revolution at Point Zero: Housework, Reproduction, and Feminist Struggle*. Oakland: PM Press, 2012.

Fekete, Liz. "Introduction." *Humanitarianism: The Unacceptable Face of Solidarity*. London: Institute of Race Relations, 2017.

Ferguson, Sue. "Canadian Contributions to Social Reproduction Feminism, Race, and Embodied Labor." *Race, Gender, Class* 15, no. 1–2 (2008): 42–57.

Ferguson, Sue. "Intersectionality and Social Reproduction Feminism: Toward an Integrative Ontology." *Historical Materialism* 24, no. 2 (2016): 38–60.

Fiddian-Qasmiyeh, Elena. "Gender and Forced Migration." In *The Oxford Handbook of Refugee and Forced Migration Studies*, edited by Elena Fiddian-Qasmiyeh, Gil Loescher, Katy Long, and Nando Sigona. Oxford: Oxford University Press, 2014.

Fiddian-Qasmiyeh, Elena. "*Representations* of Displacement from the Middle East and North Africa." *Public Culture* 28, no. 3 (2016).

Fiddian-Qasmiyeh, Elena. "Shadows and Echoes in/of Displacement." *Refugee Hosts*, November 19, 2018. https://refugeehosts.org/2018/11/19/shadows-and-echoes-in-of-displacement/.

Fiddian-Qasmiyeh, Elena. *The Ideal Refugees: Gender, Islam, and the Sahrawi Politics of Survival*. Syracuse, NY: Syracuse University Press, 2014.

Flusser, Vilém. *Towards a Philosophy of Photography*. London: Reaktion Books, [1983] 2000.

Forrest, Adam. "UK's Biggest Shipping Container Village Opens up for Homeless People." *Big Issue*, December 7, 2017. https://www.bigissue.com/latest/uks-biggest-shipping-container-village-opens-homeless-people/.

Foucault, Michel. "Of Other Spaces: Utopias and Heterotopias." *Journal of Architecture / Mouvement/ Continuité*, October 1984. http://web.mit.edu/allanmc/www/foucault1.pdf.

Fox, Jason, and the Abounaddara Film Collective. "Representational Regimes: A Conversation with the Abounaddara Film Collective." *World Records Journal* 1, no. 10 (2018): 1–7, The Documentary Camera.

France 24. "France Opens Inquiry into Lafarge Deals with Syrian Armed Groups." *France 24*, June 13, 2017. https://www.france24.com/en/20170613-france-judicial-inquiry-lafarge holcim-syria-terrorism-jalabiya.

France 24. "France Warns Construction Firm Lafarge over Offer to Build Trump's Wall." *France 24*, March 10, 2017. https://www.france24.com/en/20170310-france-warns -construction-firm-lafarge-over-offer-build-trump-wall-ayrault-hollande.

Franck, Anja K. "The Lesvos Refugee Crisis as Disaster Capitalism." *Peace Review* 30, no. 2 (2018): 203.

Fraser, Nancy. "Crisis of Care? On the Social-Reproductive Contradictions of Contemporary Capitalism." In *Social Reproduction Theory*, edited by Tithi Bhattacharya. London: Pluto, 2017.

Fraser, Nancy. *Justice Interruptus: Critical Reflections on the "Postsocialist" Condition*. New York: Routledge, 1997.

Freedman, Jane. "Sexual and Gender-Based Violence against Refugee Women: A Hidden Aspect of the Refugee 'Crisis.'" *Reproductive Health Matters* 24, no. 47 (2016): 18–26.

Gans, Herbert J. "Acculturation, Assimilation, and Mobility." *Ethnic and Racial Studies* 30, no. 1 (2006): 152–64.

Gans, Herbert J. "First Generation Decline: Downward Mobility among Refugees and Immigrants." *Ethnic and Racial Studies* 32, no. 9 (2009): 1658–70.

General Assembly of the United Nations. "Agreement Concerning the Relationship between the United Nations and the International Organization for Migration." 70th Session of the General Assembly, July 8, 2016. http://www.un.org/ga/search/view_doc .asp?symbol=A/70/976.

General Assembly of the United Nations. "Convention and Protocol Relating to the Status of Refugees." United Nations High Commission on Refugees, 1951/1967. http://www.unhcr .org/3b66c2aa10.html.

Gereffi, Gaey, and Miguel Korzeniewicz. *Commodity Chains and Global Capitalism*. Westport, CT: Praeger, 1994.

Gharib, Malaka. "Photo of Omran Daqneesh, the Boy in Aleppo, Syria: Will It Help End the War?" *NPR*, August 19, 2016. https://www.npr.org/sections/goatsandsoda/ 2016/08/19/490679863/the-little-boy-in-aleppo-can-one-photo-end-a-war.

Gidley, Ben. "Who Is Allowed to Be Human? 'Bare Life' in Aleppo and on the Mediterranean." Wildcat Dispatches, December 22, 2016. http://wildcatdispatches.org/2016/12/22/ ben-gidley-who-is-allowed-to-be-human-bare-life-in-aleppo-and-on-the-mediterranean/.

Gillespie, Marie. "Refugee Waste: Death, Survival and Solidarity in Lesvos." In *A World Laid Waste? Responding to the Social, Cultural and Political Consequences of Globalization*, edited by Francis Dodsworth and Antonia Walford. New York: Routledge, 2018.

Gimenez, Martha E. "Marxism and Class, Gender, and Race: Rethinking the Trilogy." *Race, Gender, Class* 8, no. 2 (2000): 22–33.

Glick-Schiller, Nina, Linda Basch, Cristina Szanton Blanc. "From Immigrant to Transmigrant: Theorizing Transnational Migration." *Anthropological Quarterly* 68, no. 1 (1995).

Global Refugee Sponsorship Initiative. http://refugeesponsorship.org.

Gold, Scott. "The Artist behind the Iconic 'Running Immigrants' Image." *Los Angeles Times*, April 4, 2008. http://www.latimes.com/local/la-me-outthere4apr04-story.html.

Gómez-Cruz, Edgar, and Helen Thornham. "Selfies beyond the Self-Representation: The (Theoretical) F(r)ictions of a Practice." *Journal of Aesthetics and Culture* 7, no. 1 (2015). https://doi.org/10.3402/jac.v7.28073.

Gourgouris, Stathis. "Crisis and the Ill Logic of Fortress Europe." In *Can a Person Be Illegal? Refugees, Migrants, and Citizenship in Europe*, edited by Alexander Stagnell, Louise Schou Therkildsen, and Mats Rosengren. Uppsala: Uppsala Rhetorical Studies, 2017. http://www.engagingvulnerability.se/wp-content/uploads/2017/10/SRU_can_a_person_be_illegal_WEBPRINT_anthology_1002b.pdf.

Government of the United Kingdom. "The Jordan Compact: A New Holistic Approach between the Hashemite Kingdom of Jordan and the International Community to Deal with the Syrian Refugee Crisis." London, February 4, 2016. https://assets.publishing.service.gov.uk/government/uploads/system/uploads/attachment_data/file/498021/Supporting_Syria__the_Region_London_2016_-_Jordan_Statement.pdf.

Graham-Harrison, Emma, and Tim Finch. "Was It Wrong to Get Celebrities to Pose Wearing Emergency Blankets for Refugees?" *The Guardian*, February 20, 2016. https://www.theguardian.com/commentisfree/2016/feb/20/was-it-wrong-to-get-celebrities-to-pose-wearing-emergency-blankets-berlin-charlize-theron.

Grandi, Filippo. "Opening Statement at the 68th Session of the Executive Committee of the High Commissioner's Programme." United Nations High Commission on Refugees, October 2, 2017. http://www.unhcr.org/admin/hcspeeches/59d1f3b77/opening-statement-68th-session-executive-committee-high-commissioners-programme.html.

Greenslade, Roy. "Will the Image of a Lifeless Boy on a Beach Change the Refugee Debate?" *The Guardian*, September 3, 2015. https://www.theguardian.com/media/greenslade/2015/sep/03/will-the-image-of-a-lifeless-boy-on-a-beach-change-the-refugee-debate.

Greenwood, Phoebe, Noah Payne-Frank, and Apostolis Fotiadis. "The Greek Island Sinking under Europe's Refugee Crisis." *The Guardian*, August 20, 2015, 14:47. https://www.theguardian.com/world/video/2015/aug/18/greek-island-leros-europe-migrant-crisis-video.

Gunter, Joel. "Alan Kurdi: Why One Picture Cut Through." *BBC News*, September 4, 2015. https://www.bbc.com/news/world-europe-34150419.

Gutiérrez-Rodríguez, Encarnación. "Thinking the Crisis of Capitalism through Another Grammar: On 'The Refugee Crisis,' Coloniality, and Racism." Lecture delivered at Critical Feminist Research on Migration and Refugee Studies, Convened by the Critical Feminist Network on Migration and Refugees, University of Konstanz, June 22, 2017.

Gutiérrez-Rodríguez, Encarnación. *Migration, Domestic Work, and Affect: A Decolonial Approach on Value and the Feminization of Labor*. New York: Routledge, 2010.

Halasa, Malu, Zaher Omareen, and Nawara Mahfoud, eds. *Syria Speaks: Art and Culture from the Frontline*. London: Saqi Books, 2014.

Hall, Stuart. "The Spectacle of the 'Other.'" *Representation: Cultural Representations and Signifying Practices*. Edited by Stuart Hall. London/Thousand Oaks: Sage/The Open University, 1997.

Hall, Stuart. "A Conversation with Stuart Hall." *The Journal of the International Institute* 7, no. 1 (1999). https://quod.lib.umich.edu/j/jii/4750978.0007.107?view=text;rgn=main.

Hartmann, Heidi I. "The Unhappy Marriage of Marxism and Feminism: Toward a More Progressive Union." *Capital and Class* 3, no. 2 (1979): 1–33.

Harvey, David. *The New Imperialism*. Oxford: Oxford University Press, 2003.

Hedge, Radha S. *Mediating Migration*. Cambridge: Polity, 2016.

Heller, Charles, and Lorenzo Pezzani. "Liquid Traces: Investigating the Deaths of Migrants at the EU's Maritime Border." In *Drift*, edited by Caroline Bergvall, 658–59. New York: Nightboat, 2014.

Higgins, Charlotte. "Interview: Banu Cennetoğlu: 'As Long as I Have Resources, I Will Make the List More Visible.'" *The Guardian*, June 20, 2018. https://www.theguardian .com/world/2018/jun/20/banu-cennetoglu-interview-turkish-artist-the-list-europe-migrant -crisis.

Hochschild, Arlie. "Global Care Chains and Emotional Surplus Value." In *On the Edge: Globalization and the New Millennium*, edited by Tony Giddens and Will Hutton, 130–46. London: Sage, 2000.

Horner, Will. "'High-Quality Refugee Boats' for Sale on Chinese Website, Despite EU Criticism: The EU Has Taken Measures to Restrict the Sale of Boats in Libya, but Aid Groups Say the Sales Are Just a 'Symptom of a Wider Problem.'" *Middle East Eye*, August 8, 2017. https://www.middleeasteye.net/news/high-quality-refugee-boats-sale-chinese-website -despite-eu-criticism.

Houwen, Janna. "An Empty Table and an Empty Boat: Empathic Encounters with Refugee Experiences in Intermedial Installation Art." *American, British, and Canadian Studies* 27, no. 1 (2016): 49. https://www.degruyter.com/downloadpdf/j/abcsj.2016.27.issue-1/ abcsj-2016-0018/abcsj-2016-0018.pdf.

Howden, Daniel, and Apostolis Fotiadis. "The Refugee Archipelago: The Inside Story about What Went Wrong in Greece." *News Deeply*, March 6, 2017. https://www.newsdeeply .com/refugees/articles/2017/03/06/the-refugee-archipelago-the-inside-story-of-what-went -wrong-in-greece.

Huguenot Museum. "Exodus." https://huguenotmuseum.org/visiting/special-displays/.

Hull, Jonah. "Greece's Lesbos: 'Guantanamo Bay of Europe' for Refugees." *Al Jazeera English*, November 29, 2017. https://www.aljazeera.com/news/2017/11/greeces-lesbos-guantanamo -bay-europe-refugees-171129134253661.html.

Human Rights Watch. "Greece: Rescuers at Sea Face Baseless Accusations: Prosecution Seeks to Criminalize Saving Lives." *Human Rights Watch*, November 5, 2018. https://www.hrw .org/news/2018/11/05/greece-rescuers-sea-face-baseless-accusations.

Human Rights Watch. "Torture Archipelago: Arbitrary Arrests, Torture, and Enforced Disappearances in Syria's Underground Prisons since March 2011." *Human Rights Watch*, July 3, 2012. https://www.hrw.org/report/2012/07/03/torture-archipelago/arbitrary-arrests -torture-and-enforced-disappearances-syrias#_ftnref66.

Human Rights Watch. *We'll Show You You're a Woman: Violence and Discrimination against Black Lesbians and Transgender Men in South Africa*. Johannesburg: Human Rights Watch, 2011. https://www.hrw.org/sites/default/files/reports/southafrica1211.pdf.

Husserl, Edmund. *Analyses Concerning Passive and Active Synthesis: Lectures on Transcendental Logic*. Translated by Anthony Steinbock. Dordrecht: Kluwer, 2001.

Hyndman, Jennifer, William Payne, and Shauna Jimenez. *The State of Private Refugee Sponsorship in Canada: Trends, Issues, and Impacts*. Refugee Research Network/Center for Refugee Studies Policy Brief, December 2, 2016, Toronto: York University. https://refugeeresearch .net/wp-content/uploads/2017/02/hyndman_feb'17.pdf.

Hyndman, Jennifer. *Managing Displacement: Refugees and the Politics of Humanitarianism*. Minneapolis: University of Minnesota Press, 2000.

Icaza, Rosalba, and Rolando Vázquez. "The Coloniality of Gender as a Radical Critique of Developmentalism." In *The Palgrave Handbook on Gender and Development: Critical Engagements in Feminist Theory and Practice*, edited by Wendy Harcourt. London: Palgrave Macmillan, 2016.

Illich, Ivan. *Shadow Work*. London: Marion Boyars, 1981.

Imma, Z'étoile. "Zanele Muholi's Intimate Archive: Photography and Post-apartheid Lesbian Lives." *Journal of Lesbian Studies* 21, no. 2 (2017): 219–41.

Immigration and Citizenship Canada. "#WelcomeRefugees: Key Figures." Government of Canada, February 27, 2017. https://www.canada.ca/en/immigration-refugees-citizenship/services/refugees/welcome-syrian-refugees/key-figures.html.

Indymedia. "Enough Is Enough." de.indymedia.org, July 16, 2018. https://de.indymedia.org/node/22840.

InfoMigrants. "German Rescue Ship Named after Drowned Toddler Alan Kurdi." Info Migrants.net, February 11, 2019. https://www.infomigrants.net/en/post/15085/german-rescue-ship-named-after-drowned-toddler-alan-kurdi.

Institute of Race Relations. *Humanitarianism: The Unacceptable Face of Solidarity*. London: Institute of Race Relations, 2017.

International Law Commission. "'Force Majeure' and 'Fortuitous Event' as Circumstances Precluding Wrongfulness: Survey of State Practice, International Judicial Decisions and Doctrine." *Yearbook of the International Law Commission* 2, no. 1 (June 1977): 68, 66. http://legal.un.org/ilc/documentation/english/a_cn4_315.pdf.

International Organization for Migration. "Four Decades of Cross-Mediterranean Undocumented Migration to Europe: A Review of the Evidence." International Organization for Migration, 2017. https://publications.iom.int/books/four-decades-cross-mediterranean-undocumented-migration-europe-review-evidence.

Jayaraman, Gayatri. "Artist Ai Weiwei Poses as Aylan Kurdi for *India Today* Magazine." *India Today*, February 1, 2016. https://www.indiatoday.in/india/story/artist-ai-weiwei-poses-as-aylan-kurdi-for-india-today-magazine-306593-2016-02-01.

Jenks, Chris. *Visual Culture*. London: Routledge, 1995.

Jones, Jonathan. "Flight by Arabella Dorman Review: Relic of a Rough Crossing Illustrates Refugee Crisis." *The Guardian*, December 20, 2015. https://www.theguardian.com/artanddesign/2015/dec/20/flight-by-arabella-dorman-review-relic-of-a-rough-crossing-illustrates-refugee-crisis.

Jordan, Sharalyn. "Un/Convention(al) Refugees: Contextualizing the Accounts of Refugees Facing Homophobic or Transphobic Persecution." *Refuge* 26, no. 2 (2009): 165–82.

Karamesini, Maria, and Jill Rubery. *Women and Austerity*. Athens: Nisos, 2015 [in Greek].

Katsanevakis, Stelios. "Illegal Immigration in the Eastern Aegean Sea: A New Source of Marine Litter." *Mediterranean Marine Science* 16, no. 3 (2015): 605–8.

Kennedy, Liam, and Caitlin Patrick. *The Violence of the Image: Photography and International Conflict*. London: I. B. Tauris, 2014.

Kexri, Dimitri. "'Every Photograph Is a Kind of Refugee': Interview with Eduardo Cadava." *Efsyn*, May 27, 2018 [in Greek]. https://www.efsyn.gr/arthro/kathe-fotografia-einai-ena-eidos-prosfyga.

Kingsley, Patrick, and Safak Timur. "Stories of 2015: How Alan Kurdi's Death Changed the World." *The Guardian*, December 31, 2015. https://www.theguardian.com/world/2015/dec/31/alan-kurdi-death-canada-refugee-policy-syria-boy-beach-turkey-photo.

Kingsley, Patrick. "On the Road in Agadez: Desperation and Death along a Saharan Smuggling Route." *The Guardian*, November 9, 2015. https://www.theguardian.com/world/2015/nov/09/on-the-road-in-agadez-desperation-and-death-along-a-saharan-smuggling-route.

Kingsley, Patrick. "Aid Workers Accused of Trying to Convert Refugees." *The Guardian*, August 2, 2016. https://www.theguardian.com/world/2016/aug/02/aid-workers-accused-of-trying-to-convert-muslim-refugees-greek-camp-detention-centre-lesvos-christianity.

Kingsley, Patrick. "The Death of Alan Kurdi: One Year on, Compassion towards Refugees Fades." *The Guardian*, September 2, 2016. https://www.theguardian.com/world/2016/sep/01/alan-kurdi-death-one-year-on-compassion-towards-refugees-fades.

Klimaka. "The Configuration of Homelessness in Greece during the Financial Crisis." European Research Conference: Homelessness, Migration and Demographic Change in Europe, Pisa, September 16, 2011.

Knowles, Caroline. *Flip-Flop: A Journey through Globalization's Backroads*. London: Pluto, 2014.

Kofman, Eleonore, and Parvati Raghuram. *Gendered Migrations and Global Social Reproduction*. London: Palgrave Macmillan, 2015.

Koko, Guillain, Surya Monro, and Kate Smith. "Lesbian, Gay, Bisexual and Transgender Asylum Seekers: Multiple Discriminations." In *Queer in Africa: LGBTQI Identities, Citizenship, and Activism*, edited by Zethu Matebeni, Surya Monro, and Vasu Reddy. London: Routledge, 2018.

Kracauer, Siegfried. "Photography." Translated by Thomas Y. Levin. *Critical Inquiry* 19, no. 3 (1993): 432.

Krugman, Paul. *The Return of Depression Economics and the Crisis of 2008*. London: Penguin, 2008.

Kuo, Lily. "'Home': This Poem Is Now the Rallying Call for Refugees: 'No One Leaves Home Unless Home Is the Mouth of a Shark.'" *Quartz Africa*, January 30, 2017. https://qz.com/africa/897871/warsan-shires-poem-captures-the-reality-of-life-for-refugees-no-one-leaves-home-unless-home-is-the-mouth-of-a-shark/.

Latouche, Serge. *In the Wake of the Affluent Society: An Exploration of Post-Development*. London: Zed Books, 1993.

Lawson, Dominic. "Smartphones Are the Secret Weapon Fuelling the Migrant Invasion." *Daily Mail*, September 28, 2015. http://www.dailymail.co.uk/debate/article-3251475/DOMINIC-LAWSON-Smartphones-secret-weapon-fuelling-great-migrant-invasion.html.

Le Guin, Ursula K. *The Dispossessed (Hainish Cycle)*. New York: HarperCollins, 1974.

Lenette, Caroline. "Visual Depictions of Refugee Camps: (De)constructing Notions of Refugee-ness?" In *Handbook of Research Methods in Health Social Sciences*, edited by Pranee Liamputtong. New York: Springer, 2019.

Lenin, Vladimir Ilyich. *Imperialism, the Highest Stage of Capitalism*. Lenin Internet Archive. [1917] 2005. http://www.marxists.org/archive/lenin/works/1916/imp-hsc/.

Lesvos LGBTIQ+ Refugee Solidarity. "LGBTIQ+ Refugees at Grave Risk of Exposure, Violence, and Death as Conditions Worsen on Lesvos." Press Release, November 4, 2017. https://tinyurl.com/LesvosLGBTIQ. https://www.facebook.com/permalink.php?story_fbid=309129119494411&id=286931478380 842.

Lesvos Solidarity. "Safe Passage Bags Workshop." Lesvos Solidarity, 2018. https://www.lesvossolidarity.org/en/what-we-do/safe-passage-bags.

Levinson, Mark. *The Box: How the Shipping Container Made the World Smaller and the World Economy Bigger*. Princeton, NJ: Princeton University Press, 2006.

LGBTQI+ Refugees. "Our Own Home: Fighting for Safety, Stability, and Choice as LG-BTQI+ Refugees in Greece." Arts Everywhere, February 5, 2018, www.artseverywhere .ca/2018/02/05/lgbtqi-refugees/.

Linfield, Susie. *The Cruel Radiance: Photography and Political Violence*. Chicago: University of Chicago Press, 2010.

Litvin, Margaret. "Syrian Theatre in Berlin." *Theatre Journal* 70, no. 4 (2018).

Myriam Kellou, Dorothée. "Syrie: les troubles arrangements de Lafarge avec l'Etat islamique." *Le Monde*, June 9, 2016 [in French]. https://www.lemonde.fr/syrie/article/2016/06/21/ syrie-les-troubles-arrangements-de-lafarge-avec-l-etat-islamique_4955023_1618247.html.

Lonergan, Gwyneth. "Migrant Women and Social Reproduction under Austerity." *Feminist Review* 109 (2015): 124–45.

Lugones, María. "Heterosexualism and the Colonial/Modern Gender System." *Hypatia* 22, no. 1 (2007): 186–209.

Luibhéid, Eithne. *Entry Denied: Controlling Sexuality at the Border*. Minneapolis: University of Minnesota Press, 2002.

Luibhéid, Eithne. *Pregnant on Arrival: Making the Illegal Immigrant*. Minneapolis: University of Minnesota Press, 2013.

Lukács, György. *History and Class Consciousness: Studies in Marxist Dialectics*. Translated by Rodney Livingstone. Cambridge: MIT Press, [1920] 1971.

Lund, Aron. "The Factory: A Glimpse into Syria's War Economy." *Century Foundation*, February 28, 2018. https://tcf.org/content/report/factory-glimpse-syrias-war-economy/?agreed=1#easy -footnote-bottom-26.

Lutz, Helma. "Care as a Fictitious Commodity: Reflections on the Intersections of Migration, Gender, and Care Regimes." *Migration Studies* 5, no. 3 (2017): 356–68.

Mahmoud, Emi. "When an Island Becomes a Door, Who Will Answer?" Spoken word performed at the Nansen Awards Ceremony, 2016. https://twitter.com/Refugees/status/ 788504442945441793.

Mahrouse, Gada. *Conflicted Commitments: Race, Privilege, and Power in Transnational Solidarity Activism*. Montreal: McGill-Queen's University Press, 2014.

Maragkidou, Melpomeni. "Anarchists Have Taken Over a Building in Athens to House Refugees." *Vice News*, September 28, 2015. https://www.vice.com/en_uk/article/xd7vj4/ anarchists-have-taken-over-a-building-in-athens-to-house-refugees-876.

Martin, Craig. *Shipping Container*. London: Bloomsbury, 2016.

Marx, Karl. *Capital: A Critique of Political Economy Vol. I*. Translated by Ben Fowkes. London: Penguin and New Left Review, [1867] 1976.

Mavridis, Symeon, and Savvoula Mouratidou. "The Phenomenon of Homelessness during the Greek Economic Crisis 2009–2018." *Humanities and Social Science Research* 1, no. 2 (2018): 23–42.

Mbembe, Achille. "Necropolitics." Translated by Libby Meintjes. *Public Culture* 15, no. 1 (2003): 11–40.

McAlister, Edward. "Migrants Who Survive Sahara Face New Torture in Libyan Oasis Town." *Reuters*, May 4, 2017. https://www.reuters.com/article/us-europe-migrants-africa/migrants -who-survive-sahara-face-new-torture-in-libyan-oasis-town-idUSKBN18021C.

McCarthy, Joe, and Olivia Kestin. "Powerful Photos of Families Welcoming Refugees into Their Homes." *Global Citizen*, February 15, 2018. https://www.globalcitizen.org/en/ content/photos-families-hosting-refugees/.

Paolo Mancini, Donato. "The Italian Family Hosting Six Refugees in Their Home." *Al Jazeera*, February 25, 2017. https://www.aljazeera.com/indepth/features/2017/01/italian-family-hosting-refugees-home-170129120252941.html.

McClintock, Anne. *Imperial Leather: Race, Gender, and Sexuality in the Colonial Contest*. London: Routledge, 1995.

McNally, David, and Sue Ferguson. "Precarious Migrants: Gender, Race, and the Social Reproduction of a Global Working Class." *Socialist Register* 51 (2015): 1–23.

McNally, David. "Dialectics and Intersectionality: Critical Reconstructions in Social Reproduction Theory." In *Social Reproduction Theory*, edited by Tithi Bhattacharya, 94–111. London: Pluto, 2017.

Melichar, Julie. "The Political Legacy of the Refugee Crisis Volunteers." *Refugees Deeply*, May 1, 2018. https://www.newsdeeply.com/refugees/community/2018/05/01/the-political-legacy-of-the-refugee-crisis-volunteers?utm_campaign=coschedule&utm_source=facebook_page&utm_medium=Refugees+Deeply.

Merleau-Ponty, Maurice. *The Visible and the Invisible*. London: Routledge, [1968] 2004.

Mezzadra, Sandro. "Borders and Migration: Emerging Challenges for Migration Research and Politics in Europe." Berlin lecture, 2016. http://www.euronomade.info/?p=7535.

Mcmillan, Joyce. "Theatre Reviews: Could You Please Look into the Camera | Write Here." *Scotsman*, April 19, 2012. https://www.scotsman.com/arts-and-culture/theatre/theatre-reviews-could-you-please-look-into-the-camera-write-here-1-2241412.

Mies, Maria. *Patriarchy and Accumulation on a World Scale: Women in the International Division of Labor*. New York: Zed Books, 1986.

Miles, Tom, and Stephanie Nebehay. "Migrant Deaths in the Sahara Likely Twice Mediterranean Toll: UN." *Reuters*, October 12, 2017. https://www.reuters.com/article/us-europe-migrants-sahara/migrant-deaths-in-the-sahara-likely-twice-mediterranean-toll-u-n-idUSKBN1CH21Y.

Miller, Ruth. *The Limits of Bodily Integrity: Abortion, Adultery, and Rape Legislation in Comparative Perspective*. New York: Routledge, 2007.

Millner-Larsen, Nadja, and Gavin Butt. "Introduction: The Queer Commons." *GLQ: A Journal of Lesbian and Gay Studies* 24, no. 4 (2018): 399–419.

Mills, Charles. *The Racial Contract*. New York: Cornell University Press, 1997.

Mirzoeff, Nicholas. *How to See the World: An Introduction to Images, from Self-Portraits to Selfies, Maps to Movies, and More*. New York: Basic Books, 2016.

Mkhize, Nonhlanhla, Jane Bennett, Vasu Reddy, and Relebohile Moletsane. "The Country We Want to Live in: Hate Crimes and Homophobia in the Lives of Black Lesbian South Africans." Cape Town: Human Sciences Research Council, 2010. https://open.uct.ac.za/bitstream/handle/11427/7660/The_country_we_want_to_live_in_-_Entire_ebook.pdf?sequence=1.

Moffett, Helen. "'These Women, They Force Us to Rape Them': Rape as Narrative of Social Control in Post-Apartheid South Africa." *Journal of Southern African Studies* 32, no. 1 (2006): 129–44.

Mohanty, Chandra Talpade. "Women Workers and Capitalist Scripts: Ideologies of Domination, Common Interests, and the Politics of Solidarity." In *Feminist Genealogies, Colonial Legacies, Democratic Futures*, edited by C. T. Mohanty and M. J. Alexander. New York: Routledge, 1997.

Mohdin, Aamna. "Choose Love: The Shop Where Customers Buy Gifts for Refugees." *The Guardian*, November 23, 2018. https://www.theguardian.com/business/2018/nov/23/choose-love-pop-up-shop-london-customers-buy-gifts-refugees.

Mojab, Shahrzad. "De-Skilling Immigrant Women." *Canadian Woman Studies/les cahier de la femme* 19, no. 3 (1999): 110–14.

Mookherjee, Nayanika. "Reproductive Heteronormativity and Sexual Violence in the Bangladesh War of 1971: A Discussion with Gayatri Chakravorty Spivak." *Social Text* 30, no. 2 (2012).

Mookherjee, Nayanika. "Reproductive Heteronormativity and Sexual Violence in the Bangladesh War of 1971: A Discussion with Gayatri Chakravorty Spivak." *Social Text* 30, no. 2 (2012): 123–31. https://doi.org/10.1215/01642472-1541790.

Morales, Victor. "Iconic Sign Evokes Connection to Long Walk." *Indian Country Today*, October 12, 2008. https://indiancountrymedianetwork.com/news/iconic-sign-evokes -connection-to-long-walk/.

Mountz, Alison. "Where Asylum-Seekers Wait: Feminist Counter-Topographies of Sites between States." *Gender, Place, and Culture* 18, no. 3 (2011): 381–99.

Mudu, Pierpaolo, and Sutapa Chattopadhyay. *Migration, Squatting, and Radical Autonomy.* London: Routledge, 2017.

Muholi, Zanele. "Thinking through Lesbian Rape." *Agenda* 18, no. 61 (2004): 116–25.

Mumford, Andrew. *Proxy Warfare.* Cambridge: Polity, 2013.

Nabert, Alexander, Claudia Torrisi, Nandini Archer, Belen Lobos, and Claire Provost. "Hundreds of Europeans 'Criminalized' for Helping Migrants—as Far Right Aims to Win Big in European Elections." *Open Democracy*, May 18, 2019. https://www.opendemocracy .net/en/5050/hundreds-of-europeans-criminalised-for-helping-migrants-new-data-shows -as-far-right-aims-to-win-big-in-european-elections/.

Nail, Thomas. *The Figure of the Migrant.* Stanford, CA: Stanford University Press, 2015.

Nancy, Jean-Luc. *The Experience of Freedom.* Translated by Bridget McDonald. Stanford, CA: Stanford University Press, 1993.

Nayeri, Dina. "The Ungrateful Refugee: 'We Have No Debt to Repay.'" *The Guardian*, April 4, 2017. https://www.theguardian.com/world/2017/apr/04/dina-nayeri-ungrateful-refugee.

Nebehay, Stephanie. "UN Urges Greece to Take Charge of Refugee Crisis." *Reuters*, August 18, 2015. https://www.reuters.com/article/us-europe-migrants-greece-unhcr/u-n-urges-greece -to-take-charge-of-refugee-crisis-idUSKCN0QN14920150818.

Needham, Alex. "The List: The 34,361 Men, Women and Children Who Perished Trying to Reach Europe." *The Guardian*, June 20, 2018. https://www.theguardian.com/world/2018/ jun/20/the-list-34361-men-women-and-children-who-perished-trying-to-reach-europe -world-refugee-day.

Neocleous, Mark, and Maria Kastrinou. "The EU Hotspot: Police War against the Migrant." *Radical Philosophy* 200 (2016). https://www.radicalphilosophyarchive.com/commentary/ the-eu-hotspot.

Nguyen, Mimi Thi. *The Gift of Freedom: War, Debt, and Other Refugee Passages.* Durham, NC: Duke University Press, 2012.

Nyberg–Sørensen, Ninna, Nick Van Hear, and Poul Engberg–Pedersen. "The Migration-Development Nexus: Evidence and Policy Options." *International Migration* 40, no. 5 (2002). http://publications.iom.int/system/files/pdf/migration_dev_nexus.pdf.

O'Hagan, Sean. "The Photographs That Moved the World to Tears." *The Guardian*, September 6, 2015. https://www.theguardian.com/commentisfree/2015/sep/06/photograph -refugee-crisis-aylan-kurdi.

O'Kane, Chris. "Fetishism and Social Domination in Marx, Lukacs, Adorno and Lefebvre." PhD Dissertation, Center for Social and Political Thought, University of Sussex, 2013.

Observer, Libya. "Libya Rejects AU Free Movement Protocol." *Libya Observer*, March 24, 2018. https://www.libyaobserver.ly/news/libya-rejects-au-free-movement-protocol.

Occupy Directory, "1518 Occupations." Accessed October 7, 2019. http://directory.occupy.net.

Oikonomakis, Leonidas. "Solidarity in Transition: The Case of Greece." In *Solidarity Mobilizations in the "Refugee Crisis."* Edited by Donatella della Porta, 65–66. London: Palgrave Macmillan, 2019.

Oksala, Johanna. "Affective Labor and Feminist Politics." *Signs: Journal of Women in Culture and Society* 41, no. 2 (2015): 281–303.

Omareen, Zaher. "Malu Halasa on Art from within Syria's Prison Cells." Amnesty International UK Stories and Rights, June 16, 2014. https://www.amnesty.org.uk/blogs/stories-and-rights/art-within-syrias-prison-cells.

Onassis Stegi. "The Factory." November 8, 2018. https://www.onassis.org/whats-on/the-factory.

Ott, Stephanie. "How a Selfie with Merkel Changed Syrian Refugee's Life." *Al Jazeera*, February 21, 2017. https://www.aljazeera.com/indepth/features/2017/02/selfie-merkel-changed-syrian-refugee-life-170218115515785.html.

Oyewùmí, Oyéronké. *The Invention of Women: Making an African Sense of Western Gender Discourses.* Minneapolis: University of Minnesota Press, 1997.

Pallister-Wilkins, Polly. "There's a Focus on the Boats Because the Sea Is Sexier than the Land: A Reflection on the Centrality of the Boats in the Recent 'Migration Crisis.'" The Disorder of Things, December 9, 2015. https://thedisorderofthings.com/2015/12/09/theres-a-focus-on-the-boats-because-the-sea-is-sexier-than-the-land-a-reflection-on-the-centrality-of-the-boats-in-the-recent-migration-crisis/.

Papadopoulos, Yiannis. "Fake Life Vests Soak Up Chances of Survival for Shipwrecked Refugees." *EKathimerini*, February 2, 2016. http://www.ekathimerini.com/205666/gallery/ekathimerini/special-report/fake-life-vests-soak-up-chances-of-survival-for-shipwrecked-refugees.

Papataxiarchis, Evthymios. "Being 'There': At the Front Line of the 'European Refugee Crisis'—Part One." *Anthropology Today* 32, no. 2 (2016): 5–9.

Parrenas, Rhacel Salazar. "Migrant Filipina Domestic Workers and the International Division of Reproductive Labor." *Gender and Society* 14, no. 4 (2000): 560–80.

Pasion Y Presion. "Life Jackets Lying in Mute Witness to Tragic Inaction on Refugees. #WithRefugees #lifejacketlondon." Newsflare, n.d. https://www.newsflare.com/video/86839/other/newsflare-edit-lifejackets-lie-in-mute-witness-to-tragic-inaction-on-refugees-withrefugees-lifejacketlondon-httpstcogtcsn41rtl?a=on.

Pécoud, Antoine. "What Do We Know about the International Organization for Migration?" *Journal of Ethnic and Migration Studies* 44, no. 10 (2018): 1621–38. https://doi.org/10.1080/1369183X.2017.1354028.

Phelp, Jerome. "Why Is So Much Art about the 'Refugee Crisis' So Bad?" Open Democracy, May 11, 2017. https://www.opendemocracy.net/en/5050/refugee-crisis-art-weiwei/.

Pittaway, Eileen. *Only Rape: An Examination of the Power of Ideology and Discourse in the Policy Process with a Focus on Policy Pertaining to Refugee Women.* PhD Dissertation. Sydney: University of Technology, 2001.

Plato, "The Allegory of the Cave." *Republic* VII, 514a2–517a7, trans. Thomas Sheehan. Accessed 7 October 2019, https://web.stanford.edu/class/ihum40/cave.pdf.

Price, Jonathan. *Thucydides and Internal War.* Cambridge: Cambridge University Press, 2009.

Prime Minister of Greece. "Declarations of the Prime Minister A. Tsipras after the Conclusion of the Governmental Summit for the Management of Issues Related to Refugee Flows." Athens: Office of the Prime Minister, 2015 [in Greek, our translation; link is no longer functional]. http://www.primeminister.gov.gr/2015/08/07/13931.

Prime Minister Press Office. "Meeting with Dominique Strauss-Kahn, Statements." Athens: Office of the Prime Minister, December 7, 2010 [in Greek, our translation; link is no longer functional]. http://www.primeminister.gov.gr/english/2010/12/07/meeting-with -dominique-strauss-kahn-statements/.

Puar, Jasbir. *Terrorist Assemblages: Homonationalism in Queer Times*. Durham, NC: Duke University Press, 2007.

Raijman, Rebeca, and Moshe Semyonov. "Best of Times, Worst of Times, and Occupational Mobility: The Case of Soviet Immigrants in Israel." *International Migration* 36, no. 3 (1998): 291–312.

Ramírez Blanco, Julia. "Keynote Lecture, Rebel Streets: Urban Space, Art, and Social Movements." Université de Tours, May 28, 2019.

Rancière, Jacques. "Notes on the Photographic Image." *Radical Philosophy* 156 (July/August 2009). https://www.radicalphilosophy.com/article/notes-on-the-photographic-image.

Rancière, Jacques. *The Emancipated Spectator*. London: Verso, 2009.

Razack, Sherene. *Dark Threats and White Knights: The Somalia Affair, Peacekeeping and the New Imperialism*. Toronto: University of Toronto Press, 2004.

Redazione. "Appeal: Criminalization of Solidarity, Right to Escape, Solidarity Cities." EuroNomade, April 5, 2018. http://www.euronomade.info/?p=10517.

Refugee Support Aegean. "Reception Crisis in Greece: The Malignancy of Attica's Refugee Camps." Refugee Support Aegean, August 13, 2018. http://rsaegean.org/reception-crisis -in-greece/#_edn5.

Rettberg, Jill Walker, and Radhika Gajjala. "Terrorists or Cowards: Negative Portrayals of Male Syrian Refugees in Social Media." *Feminist Media Studies* 16, no. 1 (2016).

Rigaud, Kanta Kumari, Alex de Sherbinin, Bryan Jones, Jonas Bergmann, Viviane Clement, Kayly Ober, Jacob Schewe, Susana Adamo, Brent McCusker, Silke Heuser, and Amelia Midgley, eds. *Groundswell: Preparing for Internal Climate Migration*. Washington, DC: World Bank, 2018. https://openknowledge.worldbank.org/handle/10986/29461.

Risam, Roopika. "Now You See Them: Self-Representation and the Refugee Selfie." *Popular Communication* 16, no. 1 (2018): 59.

RISE. "'The 'Refugee Crisis' in Australia Is a Hostage Crisis Where Our Members Are Being Held Captive by Self Serving Politicians' —RISE Member." Twitter post, October 25, 2016. https://twitter.com/riserefugee/status/790751000306921472.

Rivas, Jorge. "Bansky Transforms Migrant Road Sign into DREAM Crossing." *Colorlines*, February 22, 2011. http://www.colorlines.com/articles/banksy-transforms-migrant-road -sign-dream-crossing.

Robinson, Cedric J. *Black Marxism: The Making of the Black Radical Tradition*. Chapel Hill: University of North Carolina Press, 1983.

Ross, Jerome. "Ten Years on, the Crisis of Global Capitalism Never Really Ended." *ROAR Magazine*, September 14, 2018. https://roarmag.org/essays/lehman-brothers-fallout-financial -crisis/.

Rozworski, Michal. "The Political Crisis in Greece." *Jacobin*, May, 7, 2015. https://www .jacobinmag.com/2015/07/oxi-tsipras-syriza-euro-default-referendum.

Ruhrtriennale Festival of the Arts. 2019. "The Factory: Mohammad Al Attar and Omar Abusaada." https://www.ruhrtriennale.de/en/agenda/30/Mohammad_Al_Attar_Omar _Abusaada/The_Factory/.

Saada, Emmanuelle. "Abdelmalek Sayad and the Double Absence: Toward a Total Sociology of Immigration." *French Politics, Culture and Society* 18, no. 1 (2000): 28–47.

Salami, Bukola, and Sioban Nelson. "The Downward Occupational Mobility of Internationally-Educated Nurses to Domestic Workers." *Nursing Inquiry* 21, no. 2 (2014): 153–61.

Sargent, Lydia, ed. *Women and Revolution: A Discussion of the Unhappy Marriage of Marxism and Feminism.* Boston: South End Press, 1981.

Satchell, Graham. "Impact of Greek Austerity Measures on Ordinary People." *BBC*, October 13, 2011. https://www.bbc.com/news/av/world-europe-15286028/impact-of-greek -austerity-measures-on-ordinary-people.

Sayad, Abdelmalek. *The Suffering of the Immigrant.* Edited by Pierre Bourdieu. Translated by David Macey. Cambridge: Polity, 2004.

Sayed, Hani. Untitled Lecture delivered at Abounaddara. "The Right to the Image." Vera List Center for Art and Politics, October 24, 2015. http://www.veralistcenter.org/engage/ events/1977/abounaddara-the-right-to-the-image/.

Sayed, Hani. Untitled Lecture, Panel V. "Abounaddara: The Right to the Image." Vera List Center for Art and Politics, New School for Social Research, October 25, 2015. https://livestream.com/TheNewSchool/abounaddara-the-right-to-the-image/videos/ 102806274.

Scott-Smith, Tom. "The Fetishism of Humanitarian Objects and the Management of Malnutrition in Emergencies." *Third World Quarterly* 34, no. 5 (2013): 913–28.

Sears, Alan. "Body Politics: The Social Reproduction of Sexualities." In *Social Reproduction Theory*, edited by Tithi Bhattacharya, 171–191. London: Pluto, 2017.

Sea-Watch. "Monitoring Moria." Sea-Watch.org, October 12, 2017. https://sea-watch.org/en/ monitoring-moria/.

Sekula, Allan, and Noel Burch. *The Forgotten Space.* Film essay, 2010. https://www.theforgotten space.net.

Sekula, Allan. *Fish Story.* Dusseldorf: Richter Verlag, 1995.

SelfieCity. "Investigating the Style of Self-Portraits (Selfies) in Five Cities across the World." SelfieCity.net. http://selfiecity.net.

Sharma, Gouri. "'The Factory': Play Exposes Murky Nexus of Western Business and Syrian War." *Middle East Eye*, November 6, 2018. https://www.middleeasteye.net/news/factory -play-explores-murky-nexus-western-business-and-syrian-war.

Sharma, Nandita. "From Crisis to Crisis: A History of Immigration Controls." Lecture delivered at the Feminist Researchers Against Borders Summer School Taster Workshop, National Technical University of Athens, July 21, 2018.

Sheth, Falguni. *Toward a Political Philosophy of Race.* Albany, NY: SUNY Press, 2009.

Shire, Warsan. "Home." In *Teaching My Mother How to Give Birth.* London: flipped eye, 2011.

Silverman, Kaja. *The Threshold of the Visible World.* New York: Routledge, 1996.

Simpson, Audra. "On Ethnographic Refusal: Indigeneity, 'Voice' and Colonial Citizenship." *Junctures* 9 (2007): 67–80.

Skanavis, Constantina, and Aristea Kounani. "The Environmental Impacts of the Refugees' Settlements at Lesvos Island." Conference Presentation at 13th International Conference on Protection and Restoration of the Environment, Mykonos, July 2016.

Slovic, Paul, Daniel Västfjäll, Arvid Erlandsson, and Robin Gregory. "Iconic Photographs and the Ebb and Flow of Empathic Response to Humanitarian Disasters." *PNAS* 114, no. 4 (2017): 640–44.

Smith, Helena. "Shocking Images of Drowned Syrian Boy Show Tragic Plight of Refugees." *The Guardian*, September 2, 2015. https://www.theguardian.com/world/2015/sep/02/shocking -image-of-drowned-syrian-boy-shows-tragic-plight-of-refugees?CMP=share_btn_tw.

Solomon-Godeau, Abigail. *Photography at the Dock: Essays on Photographic History, Institutions and Practices*. Minnesota: University of Minnesota Press, 1991.

Sontag, Susan. *On Photography*. New York: Picador, 1973.

Sontag, Susan. *On Photography*. New York: Picador, 1977.

Sontag, Susan. *Regarding the Pain of Others*. New York: Picador, 2003.

Spathopoulou, Aila. "Migrants' Uneven Geographies Within and Against the Hotspot Regime Governing Greece." PhD Dissertation, Department of Geography, King's College University of London, 2019.

Spathopoulou, Aila. "The Ferry as a Mobile Hotspot: Migrants at the Uneasy Borderlands of Greece." Forum: Governing Mobility through the European Union's "Hotspot" Centers. Edited by Lauren Martin and Martina Tazzioli. *Society and Space*, November 8, 2016. http://societyandspace.org/2016/12/15/the-ferry-as-a-mobile-hotspot-migrants-at-the -uneasy-borderlands-of-greece/.

Specia, Megan. "Refugees' Life Jackets Are Transformed into Message of Peace on Greek Island." *Mashable*, January 2, 2016. https://mashable.com/2016/01/02/refugee-life-jacket -greek-island/?europe=true.

Spivak, Gayatri Chakravorty. "Can the Subaltern Speak?" In *Marxism and the Interpretation of Culture*, edited by Cary Nelson and Lawrence Grossberg. Urbana: University of Illinois Press, 1988.

Spross, Jeff. "The Greek Crisis Is Dead. Long Live the Greek Crisis." *Week*, June 25, 2018. https://theweek.com/articles/780671/greek-crisis-dead-long-live-greek-crisis.

Staton, Bethan. "Jordan Experiment Spurs Jobs for Refugees." *Refugees Deeply* 25 (July 2016). https://www.newsdeeply.com/refugees/articles/2016/07/25/jordan-experiment-spurs-jobs -for-refugees.

Stuckler, David, and Sanjay Basu. *The Body Economic: Eight Experiments in Economic Recovery, from Iceland to Greece*. New York: Penguin Books, 2013.

Stuckler, David, and Sanjay Basu. *The Body Economic: Why Austerity Kills*. New York: Penguin Books, 2013.

Sukhdev, Sandhu. "Allan Sekula: Filming the Forgotten Resistance at Sea." *The Guardian*, April 20, 2012. https://www.theguardian.com/film/2012/apr/20/allan-sekula-resistance -at-sea.

Tagaris, Karolina. "Greece Pledges to Shut Immigrant Detention Centers." *Reuters*, February 14, 2015.

Taylor, Lin. "London Art Gallery Showcases Calais Migrant Stories." Thomson Reuters Foundation, June 7, 2016. http://news.trust.org/item/20160607115545-fxflr/.

Tazzioli, Martina. "The Politics of Counting and the Scene of Rescue." *Radical Philosophy* 192 (July/August): 2015.

The Guardian. "It's 34,361 and Rising: How the List Tallies Europe's Migrant Bodycount." *The Guardian*, June 20, 2018. https://www.theguardian.com/world/2018/jun/20/the-list -europe-migrant-bodycount.

The Guardian. "Margaret Thatcher: A Life in Quotes." *The Guardian*, April 8, 2013. https://
www.theguardian.com/politics/2013/apr/08/margaret-thatcher-quotes.

The Press Project. "UNHCR and NGO's [sic] Withdraw from Greek Islands, Tension Is Rising
in Idomeni." *Press Project*, March 23, 2016. https://www.thepressproject.gr/article/91468/
UNHCR-and-NGOs-withdraw-from-Greek-islands-tension-is-rising-in-Idomeni.

The World Bank Group. "Special Economic Zones: Performance, Lessons Learned, and
Implications for Zone Development." Washington, DC: The World Bank Group, 2008.
http://documents.worldbank.org/curated/en/343901468330977533/pdf/458690WP0Box
331s0April200801PUBLIC1.pdf.

Thomas, Kylie. "Zanele Muholi's Intimate Archive: Photography and Post-apartheid Lesbian Lives." *Safundi: The Journal of South African and American Studies* 11, no. 4 (2010):
421–36.

Thompson, Edward P. "The Moral Economy Reviewed." In *Customs in Common*, 259–351.
London: Merlin, 1991.

Timmons, Heather. "The Father of Syrian Toddler Aylan Kurdi on the Boat Ride That
Killed His Family." *Quartz*, September 4, 2015. https://qz.com/495211/the-life-jackets-we
-were-wearing-were-all-fake-the-father-of-syrian-toddler-aylan-kurdi-on-the-boat-ride
-that-killed-his-family/.

Tondo, Lorenzo. "Italy Orders Seizure of Migrant Rescue Ship over HIV-Contaminated
Clothes." *The Guardian*, November 20, 2018. https://www.theguardian.com/world/2018/
nov/20/italy-orders-seizure-aquarius-migrant-rescue-ship-hiv-clothes. See chapter 4 for a
discussion of rhetorics of contamination and containment of refugees.

Tonella, Yara Boff. "If You Want to Know the True Meaning of Fear, Hunger and Cold, Come
Here." *Amnesty International*, March 15, 2018. https://refugeeobservatory.aegean.gr/en/"if
-you-want-know-true-meaning-fear-hunger-and-cold-come-here"-amnesty-international.

Toscano, Alberto, and Jeff Kinkle. *Cartographies of the Absolute*. Winchester: Zero Books,
2015.

Townsend, Mark. "Police with Batons and Teargas Force Migrants to Flee Calais Camp." *The
Guardian*, December 1, 2018. https://www.theguardian.com/world/2018/dec/01/french
-police-step-up-calais-refugee-evictions.

Tronti, Mario. "The Social Factory." Libcom.org, June 22, 2007. https://libcom.org/library/
deleuze-marx-politics/4-social-factory.

Tsilimpounidi, Myrto. *Sociology of Crisis: Visualizing Urban Austerity*. London: Routledge, 2017.

Tuck, Eve, and K. Wayne Yang. "Unbecoming Claims: Pedagogies of Refusal in Qualitative
Research." *Qualitative Inquiry* 20, no. 6 (2014): 811–18.

Tucker, Emma. "16-Year-Old Artist Builds Igloos from Refugee Life Jackets for Moroso
Installation." *Dezeen*, April 6, 2017. https://www.dezeen.com/2017/04/06/achilleas-souras
-builds-igloos-refugees-life-jackets-morosos-sos-save-souls-installation-milan-design-week/.

Turak, Natasha. "The Future of Europe's Elections Will Be All about Immigration, Foreign
Minister Says." *CNBC*, June 1, 2018. https://www.cnbc.com/2018/06/01/the-future-of
-europes-elections-will-be-all-about-migration.html.

Turnbull, Samantha, and Joanne Shoebridge. "Syrian Refugees Being Sold Fake Life Jackets
with Absorbent Foam, Volunteer Says." *ABC News*, January 18, 2016. https://www.abc.net
.au/news/2016-01-18/volunteer-reveals-challenges-facing-syrian-refugees/7095006.

UN High Commissioner for Refugees (UNHCR). "Guidelines on International Protection
No. 9: Claims to Refugee Status Based on Sexual Orientation and/or Gender Identity

within the Context of Article 1A(2) of the 1951 Convention and/or Its 1967 Protocol Relating to the Status of Refugees." United Nations High Commission on Refugees, October 23, 2012. http://www.unhcr.org/50ae466f9.pdf.

UN High Commissioner for Refugees (UNHCR). *Refugee Family Reunification: UNHCR's Response to the European Commission Green Paper on the Right to Family Reunification of Third Country Nationals Living in the European Union (Directive 2003/86/EC)*. Geneva: United Nations, 2012, 3. http://www.refworld.org/docid/4f55e1cf2.html.

UN High Commissioner for Refugees (UNHCR). "'Refugees' and 'Migrants': Frequently Asked Questions (FAQs)." RefWorld.org, August 31, 2018. http://www.refworld.org/docid/56e81c0d4.html.

UNHCR. "Greece: The Refugees' Grandmother in Idomeni." YouTube, April 8, 2016, 3:06. https://www.youtube.com/watch?v=Hb_Hdjy4CVw.

Uniake, Hector. "You Can't Evict a Movement: A Story of Squatting and Migration in Athens." *Open Democracy*, March 21, 2017. https://www.opendemocracy.net/en/can-europe-make-it/you-cant-evict-movement-story-of-squatting-and-migration-in-athens/.

United for Intercultural Action. 2019. "The Fatal Policies of Fortress Europe." http://unitedagainstrefugeedeaths.eu.

United Nations System Organizations. "Directory of United Nations System Organizations." Accessed October 7, 2019. https://www.unsystem.org/members/related-organizations.

Urry, John. *Mobilities*. Cambridge: Polity Press, 2007.

Vaitsopoulou, Anastasia. "The Smallest Minority in Athens in Search of a Safe Haven." Medium.com, October 18, 2017. https://medium.com/athenslivegr/there-is-one-group-in-athens-1d2df920efdf.

Vaitsopoulou, Anastasia. "There Is a Group of People Who Are Not Safe in Greece, and Nobody Cares." *Popaganda*. October 8, 2017 [in Greek]. http://popaganda.gr/lgbtqi-prosfiges-athina/.

Vertov, Dziga. *Man with a Movie Camera* (1929), 1:07, https://vimeo.com/283595357.

Vogel, Lise. *Marxism and the Oppression of Women: Toward a Unitary Theory*. New Brunswick, NJ: Rutgers University Press, 1983.

Waddell, Lilly. "Penelope Cruz, 44, Cuts Ladylike Figure in Lovely Floral Dress and Heels at Glitzy Gala in Madrid." *Mail Online*, May 31, 2018. https://www.dailymail.co.uk/tvshowbiz/article-5792849/Penelope-Cruz-44-cuts-ladylike-figure-feminine-floral-dress-heels-glitzy-gala-Madrid.html.

Wagner-Lawlor, Jennifer. "Refugee Crisis Creates Ghostly Ocean Debris." Plastic Pollution Coalition, June 15, 2016. https://www.plasticpollutioncoalition.org/pft/2016/6/24/refugee-crisis-creates-ghostly-ocean-debris.

Wallerstein, Immanuel, and Terence Hopkins. "Commodity Chains in the World Economy. Prior to 1800." *Review (Fernand Braudel Center)* 10, no. 1 (1986): 157–70.

Walsh, Aylwyn, and Myrto Tsilimpounidi. "Virtues of Violence: A Testimonial Performance or an Affidavit of Lies, Excuses, Justifications." *Cultural Studies—Critical Methodologies* 15, no. 3 (2014): 1–10.

Watts, Jonathan. "A Crisis in the Natural World." *Guardian Weekly*, March 30, 2018. https://www.pressreader.com/uk/the-guardian-weekly/20180330/281505046767694.

Williams, Raymond. *Border Country: Raymond Williams in Adult Education*. Edited by John McIlroy and Sallie Westwood. Leicester: National Institute of Adult Continuing Education, 1993.

Wimmer, Andreas, and Nina Glick Schiller. "Methodological Nationalism and Beyond: Nation-State Building, Migration and the Social Sciences." *Global Networks* 2, no. 4 (2002): 301–34.

Wittig, Monique. *The Straight Mind and Other Essays*. Boston: Beacon, 1992.

Witty, Patrick. "See How Smartphones Have Become a Lifeline for Refugees." *Time*, October 8, 2015. http://time.com/4062120/see-how-smartphones-have-become-a-lifeline-for-refugees/.

Women Refugee Route. Facebook post, January 16, 2017. https://www.facebook.com/WRRoute/posts/370224510024648.

World Health Organization. "Fake Life Jackets Play a Role in the Drowning of Refugees." *Bulletin of the World Health Organization* 94 (2016): 411–12. http://dx.doi.org/10.2471/BLT.16.020616, https://www.who.int/bulletin/volumes/94/6/16-020616.pdf.

Zarzycka, Marta. "The World Press Photo Contest and Visual Tropes." *Photographies* 6, no. 1 (2013): 177–84.

Zetter, Roger. "Labelling Refugees: Forming and Transforming a Bureaucratic Identity." *Journal of Refugee Studies* 4, no. 1 (1991).

Zhang, Xu, and Lea Hellmueller. "Visual Framing of the European Refugee Crisis in *Der Spiegel* and *CNN International:* Global Journalism in News Photographs." *International Communication Gazette* 0, no. 0 (2017): 12. 10.1177/1748048516688134.

Zitter, Edward Blaise. *Political Performance in Syria: From the Six-Day War to the Syrian Uprising*. New York: Palgrave Macmillan, 2014.

Index